Fashion
in the
Western World
1500–1990

Doreen Yarwood

DRAMA BOOK PUBLISHERS   NEW YORK

Typeset by Best-set Typesetter Ltd
and printed in Great Britain
by Butler and Tanner, Frome, Somerset

Drama Book Publishers
260 Fifth Avenue
New York
New York 10001
ISBN 0-89676-118-5

Contents

Colour plates between pages 32–33, 80–81 and 128–129

The Renaissance and the Reformation; influence of Italy, Switzerland, Germany then Spain; men's dress; women's dress – farthingale and corset; swaddling of babies.

Exploration and Colonization of the East and the New World; development of the textile industries; Spanish dress – Moorish inheritance; men's dress – the ruff, the doublet and jerkin; trunk hose and stocks, capes and cloaks, coiffure and footwear; women's dress in Spain – the gown, corset and farthingale, coiffure and footwear; dress in France; dress in Italy; dress in northern Europe; dress in England; children's dress.

Influence of Holland; Spanish dress; textiles – silk and lace; costume plates; men's dress; jacket, falling band, cravat, boots; women's dress; regional and national variations; colonial north America; clothes for ordinary people.

Grand Règne of Louis XIV; fashion dolls; men's dress; French lace; Indian cottons; jacket and rhinegraves; the justaucorps; hair and wigs; hats and shoes; cosmetics; women's dress; the gown, échelle, paniers, capes; bonnet à la Fontanges; shoes; aprons; north America.

French dominance in fashion; beginnings of social change reflected in dress; textiles and inventions; the Huguenots and dissemination of silk weaving to northern Europe; men's dress; habit à la française; outdoor wear; garments for relaxation at home; linen and neckwear; wigs; footwear; women's dress; underwear and corsetry; paniers and hoops; contouche and sack gown; robe à la française; accessories and cosmetics; American colonial dress; the middle classes; the bedgown.

Trend towards egalitarianism; position of women in society; French modes; mode à l'anglaise; textiles and the industrial revolution; fashion journals; men's dress; the sans-culottes; dress of the Revolution and after; hedgehog wigs and the tricorne hat; boots; women's dress; robe à la polonaise and variations; robe à l'anglaise; chemise à la reine; Directoire gowns; the Greek influence; the pelisse; wigs, cloaks and calash; footwear; cosmetics, perfume and accessories; fashion designers; children's dress; American dress; clothes for the ordinary man and woman; ready-made clothes.

CONTENTS

Introduction

Fashion is one of the essential arts of civilization. No less than painting, sculpture or any of the applied arts does it reflect the great cultures of the past, illustrating the characteristics of individual societies over the centuries. It is, arguably, a more accurate barometer than the other visual arts since it affects everyone and not solely a specific section of the population: it represents a personal expression of life at a given point in time and place.

The factors which have influenced and generated artistic style, including that of fashion, are many and varied. The social and political background has always been influential, as has the national and regional character of the people in a given area. In dress, religion has played a particularly important role, regulating which parts of the body should be concealed with clothing and, in certain ages, has ruled more firmly and in greater detail, on specific colours, fabrics and forms of decoration which should or should not be worn.

One of the greatest influences has been that of climate. To the question 'Why do we wear clothes?' the obvious answer would be 'to keep warm' also perhaps, 'for reasons of modesty'. Most certainly climate has been of vital importance in forming a convenient dress style for a given region. The draped linen garments of the ancient Greeks and Romans were incongruously unsuited to the northern European winter as the Romans found when they came to rule in Britain and those posted for duty on Hadrian's Wall quickly took advantage of the trouser-styles of the Celts. However climate is clearly not the only arbiter of fashion or why would ancient Egyptians of rank clothe themselves in several layers of garments covering much of the body and adopt heavy wigs in a north African climate or French Directoire ladies brave a Parisian winter clad in a thin muslin dress worn over a minimum of underwear?

The state of technological development and the consequent availability of certain fabrics and finishes has always been of utmost importance in determining fashion. As long as animal furs, wool and coarse linen were the only clothing materials available, a figure-clinging elegance was impossible to achieve. The introduction of silks, satins and velvets greatly increased the range of possible designs. Equally important was the development of the art of tailoring to create clothes which closely fitted the human form, an ability quickly taken advantage of in the medieval hose which graphically displayed the masculine limbs. In modern times the introduction of artificial fibres has brought easy-care clothing and permanent pleating with little need for ironing so freeing the designer for a wider variety in line and shape.

In the western world, as elsewhere, fashion has always been set by countries which were, at the time, rich and powerful. Similarly, within such countries it has been the well-to-do who have led the field. The wearing of the latest mode in a rich and decorative form has always demonstrated the importance of leading members of a community. The resultant trend, which has not changed over the centuries, was for the wealthy and influential members of society to adopt a costume which would make them stand out from the common herd. At the same time everyone wishes to copy the fashion, whether in the sixteenth century or in the 1980s. In reaction the important classes have then had to adopt a new style to maintain the differential. It was such a pattern which led to the widescale imposition of sumptuary laws to define and regulate who could wear what. It goes without saying that this type of legislation was never very successful, such is the fundamental need of human beings to emulate their betters and to adorn themselves.

My purpose in this book is to present, as clearly as possible, the characteristics of (primarily) fashionable dress worn in the western world during the last five hundred years. There is no attempt, for space does not permit, to discuss regional or national costume or the specific dress worn by academic, military or ecclesiastical personnel.

The text is intended to present a broad outline of the trends and relate these to the historical, social and technological developments which were mirrored in the dress of the day and nation. The clothes of men, women and children are described and reference is made to those worn by ordinary people and their relationship to the fashionable style of the day. All garments, footwear, headcoverings, hairstyles, cosmetics, accessories and ornamentation are discussed as is the current figure silhouette (masculine and feminine) whether natural or distorted. The introduction and manufacture of textiles are included as well as the designing, making and caring for clothes. In later chapters the marketing and presentation of fashion is also described. Stress is upon the more modern scene with greater space being allocated to the costume of the last two hundred years.

The illustrations, which take up half of the available space in the book, are intended to give detailed information to complement this text. My own drawings have all been carefully made from original sources and captions to each illustration provide available data on fabrics, colours and garments as well as the source of each drawing. To gain such illustrative material I have travelled extensively in all the countries of western Europe and in north America. The illustrative material has been derived from a variety of sources in museums and galleries in these countries where I have made on-the-spot sketches and notes. I have used actual garments where possible and where these were not available have drawn from paintings, drawings, sculpture, stained glass, photographs, textiles and a diversity of artefacts. These sources are too numerous to list here but I would like to express my deep appreciation of the generous assistance which I received everywhere from the staffs concerned.

A proportion of the illustrations (twenty-five black and white and eight in colour) depict contemporary material. For these, the author and publishers would like to thank the following for permission to reproduce

Acknowledgments

My thanks to those who have very kindly given their permission to use the following illustrations reproduced in this book:

The Ashmolean Museum, Oxford, for figures 6 and 103;

Bath Museum Service, Fashion Research Centre, for figures 242, 251, 260, 262 and 432;

Batsford Collection for figures 76 and 77;

The British Library, London, for figures 54 and 55;

Costume Galleries, Castle Howard, for figures 290, 319 and 320;

Guildhall Art Gallery, London, for colour plates 32 and 36;

Hereford City Museum for colour plate 41;

Kunsthistorisches Museum, Vienna, for colour plate 4;

Louvre, Paris, for colour plate 22;

Lutterworth Press for colour plates 2, 6, 7, 11, 14, 16, 20, 31, 35, 37 and 38 from *Costume of the Western World*, Doreen Yarwood 1980;

Mansell Collection, London for figures 159, 203 and 204;

Musée Historique des Tissus, Lyons, for colour plate 26;

Museum of Costume, Bath for colour plates 18, 20 and 37;

National Gallery, London, for colour plate 33;

National Portrait Gallery, London, for colour plate 13;

Science Museum, London, for figures 162, 164, 165, 205 and 237;

Suffolk Collection, London, for colour plate 9;

Vatican Museum, Rome, for colour plate 1;

Victoria and Albert Museum, London, for figures 66, 67, 70

London 1992   *Doreen Yarwood*

All line drawings prepared by the author

CHAPTER ONE

1500–1540

The Renaissance extends Westwards

In western Europe the early decades of the sixteenth century saw the tentative, though definitive, emergence of mankind into a modern world, one in which the limitations bounding medieval society were gradually breached. This was a time for change, for expansion and for exciting new possibilities being presented in travel and communication, in greater wealth and higher standard of living, in intellectual and artistic achievement and in political adjustment. The design and ornamentation of costume, as always, reflected these happenings.

In Europe, powerful groupings of peoples and kingdoms were being established. A number of the small principalities of medieval times were merging, by intermarriage, political or military means into larger units and the dominant kingdoms now spreading over a greater area were influencing style in dress, according to the customs and concepts of their race. The Holy Roman Empire maintained its position in central Europe, the Ottoman Empire was extending its boundaries westwards while, in the west, England, France and Spain were moving towards nationhood.

As well as internal redevelopment, Europe was also looking outwards, beyond its borders. From Portugal, Spain and Italy especially, sailors were voyaging to explore the east and, across the Atlantic Ocean, towards the far west. Their journeys brought to Europe the acquisition of great wealth and the discovery of new materials, metals, jewels and, particularly, knowledge, all of which were incorporated into the dress of the leaders of European fashion.

In the first half of the sixteenth century, two significant movements of fundamental importance were greatly affecting the style of people's dress. Both intellectual and spiritual in origin and concept, the Renaissance and the Reformation influenced costume design through the ideals and morality of their creed but they differed markedly in both principle and effect.

The Renaissance, which had originated over a century earlier in Italy, found in costume an apt expression of its tenet of humanism and of the idealization of the human body. Elegant richness of dress was encouraged, natural in its shape but extravagant in the sumptuousness of the fabrics and decoration employed. Colours were vivid, the line was simple, figure-hugging (especially in men's attire) and clothes were worn with a gay, insouciant air. This type of wear was largely adopted by the Latin peoples of Europe living in southern areas round the Mediterranean. The Reformation, on the other hand, was dominant in northern Europe, in Germany, England, Holland, Switzerland, Scandinavia. Reformation leaders encouraged their peoples to eschew display and coquetry, richness of fabrics and gay colours. In countries where the movement was strongest people were exhorted to wear sombre hues, plain fabrics and enclose the body in multi-layered, bombasted, figure-concealing ensembles.

To assume though, that the peoples of northern Europe were attired stolidly in sombre tones and those of the south in exuberant gaiety would be too simplistic. Human nature does not differ as greatly as this on a

1 Three-quarter length gown of black silk with black velvet banding. Brown fur collar and lining. Inner sleeves red. White pleated shirt and wrist frills. Hose striped in white, grey and red. Upper part puffed and slashed. Black shoes. 1524–5, Austrian. Portrait of a gentleman by Amberger, Kunsthistorisches Museum, Vienna.

2 Pale blue dress with yellow bands at hem, neck and sleeves. Deep red lining. White pleated chemise. Pearl decorated headband. 1514, Swiss. Painting by Hans Fries, Kunstmuseum, Basle.

3 Doublet and skirt black with gold bands. Sleeves to match, puffed. Undersleeves pale grey with yellow material pulled through slashes. Black points. Dove-grey cloak. Grey hose. Black shoes. Black hat with ribbon threaded through. Gold brooch, white plume. 1525–30, Italian. Painting by Raphael, Vatican Rooms, Rome.

north/south divide. Peoples everywhere have a natural wish to wear clothes which are attractive and fashionable and it is primarily social status and financial means which determine their dress. Climate is also an important factor in the quantity of garments worn and in the fabrics from which they are made. It can be safely assumed, nevertheless, that the Reformation movement curbed some of the excesses of dress in the northern regions and that of the Renaissance encouraged the stylistic enhancement of the human figure in the south. In England the influence of Italy and France was strongest in the first two decades of the century, that of Germany, Switzerland and Holland in the succeeding two decades.

Dress was the outward, visible evidence of position and importance, one which compared with the twentieth century status symbol of the motor car. The leaders of fashion were the monarch and the royal court, then the aristocracy who dressed in a luxurious version of the current mode but, human nature being what it is, members of the lower strata of society attempted, in perhaps a less luxurious manner, to ape the attire of their betters. It then became necessary for the pace-setters to find a new mode. One method, which had been in use since the early fourteenth century to restrain and restrict this imitation of fashionable dress by those of lesser status, was the passing of sumptuary laws to forbid the wearing of certain materials (notably furs), colours, embroideries and jewels to people below a certain rank. The various attempts at sumptuary legislation were very detailed and most formidable but it has to be acknowledged that, by and large, they failed in their purpose; the desire for emulation was too strong.

Students of costume find their sources of knowledge greatly increased from 1500 onwards because of the burgeoning numbers of portraits. Many of these are painted in full colour and depict in infinite detail the appearance of the differing fabrics as well as their decorative patterning and applied ornamentation. In addition there are many drawings and engravings showing not only royalty and members of the aristocracy but also the bourgeois and poorer classes. As the Renaissance advanced westwards the influence of the superb quality of painting current in Italy was apparent in the proliferation of portraiture to be seen in all western European countries. Among such artists of high quality may be numbered Carpaccio, Raphael, Solario and Titian, Cranach, Clouet, Holbein, Eworth, Gärtner, Deutsch, Gossaert and Schöpfer.

Until about 1515–20 Italian modes, which had dominated the fashions of western Europe in the later fifteenth century, were still very influential. Italian cultural patterns had been a vigorous force for over two hundred years and, by 1500, the fashionable Italian was the most elegant, best-dressed and finely-mannered European, his and her dress a model of quality and cleanliness.

Italy had long been famous as a source of beautiful fabrics – damasks, velvets, brocades. Silkworm culture had become established in Tuscany, in Lucca and Florence, in the thirteenth century and, a hundred years later, superb brocades of silk, velvets and gold and silver cloth as well as ornately embroidered fabrics were being manufactured in Genoa, Milan, Bologna and Venice.

The sophistication of the Italian culture was apparent by 1500 in the accessories and adjuncts to dress as well as in the style itself. Jewellery in the form of belts and girdles, earrings and finger rings, buttons and brooches was ornate and of superb quality and design. Pearls, jewels and gold, used extravagantly in embroidery on garments and accessories, was richer than elsewhere. It decorated gloves, purses, hats, caps and shoes. Lace began to be made. Venetian ladies were noted for their elegant Oriental fans and tiny muffs of brocade or velvet. From Italy stemmed the manufacture of perfume, knowledge of which had come to the Veneto from the Orient. The handkerchief had also appeared here in the fifteenth century, then called a hand couvrechef or napkin. These early handkerchiefs were large, made of linen or cambric. They were richly embroidered and edged with lace or fringe: it goes without saying that they were costly!

The Italians loved clear, gay colours and display in their dress. Renaissance ideals demanded the glorification of the human figure and, in men's dress especially, this was revealed and accentuated. The Italians used fewer artificial aids than other nations, rarely employing padding or corsetry and relying for their beautification of the body upon designs which emphasized its natural line and which enabled them to move freely, with grace and elegance (3, 11, plate 1).

In the years 1520–40 the source of fashion moved north with a strong influence of the strange mode for padded puffs of material which were then decoratively slashed. This idea came from the Swiss and Bavarian mercenaries, the *lansquenets* or *landsknechten*. Several different explanations exist, offering reasons for the origins of this decorative form. One tells of how, after the battle of 1477, when the Swiss mercenaries had defeated the Burgundians, they mended their tattered uniforms with strips of banners and hangings from the tents of the vanquished enemy, so producing a multi-coloured attire slashed and showing different materials through the slits. Another states that the clothes of the *lansquenets* were too tight and that they slashed them to make them more comfortable, so displaying the undertunic or shirt beneath. Whatever the reasons for the beginnings of this custom, by 1520 the fashion had spread over Europe. All garments, for men, women and children, received this treatment, from tunics, hose and gowns to hats, boots and shoes. The undergarment or white shirt or chemise was pulled through the slits to form a puff of material. The edges of the slashes were embroidered or braided and the slash ends held by points or a jewelled clasp (4).

Clothes became more richly ornamented in the 1530s, slashes were extended into patterns of stars or diamonds and garments were padded on the shoulders and chest to give a squarer silhouette. This was especially

4 Richly-clad young man in full cloak with padded, puffed sleeves and slashed doublet and hose. Embroidered, finely patterned shirt. Velvet hat with ribbon tie and plumes. *c.* 1520, Swiss. Drawing by Niklaus Manuel Deutsch, Kunstmuseum, Basle.

5 Blue-green dress decorated in gold line. White chemise ruffle at neck and wrists. Gold girdle. Upper sleeves puffed, of purple and green-blue with gold decoration. Lower sleeves of purple with white puffs through slashes. Gold ornament. Chain necklace. Bead hair ornament. 1535–40, Italian. Portrait of a woman by Titian, Pitti Palace, Florence.

waist and sometimes hung down the centre front to a pendant jewel or pomander. In Spain the framework skirt, the *vertugado*, had been worn since 1470 but generally with the hoops set in the gown skirt and so visible. When adopted in other countries in the 1520s, the framework was made as an underskirt, then covered by further skirts, the bands not being shown on the outside. The name, taken from the Spanish, differed from country to country. It was a farthingale in England, a *vertugale* in France. It was accompanied by a stiffened bodice or corset to provide a slender waist to show off the skirt. Other characteristic features of this gown in the 1530s were the square neckline and full padded and slashed sleeves (5, 7, plate 4).

Men's Dress

In the later Middle Ages masculine hose had become fitting tights which covered the lower half of the body from waist to toe. Hose were made of material – wool, silk or linen – skilfully cut and shaped in vertical sections to fit the limbs closely. They were supported at waist level by being attached to the waist-length undertunic. Fastenings were by points, that is, laces with metal tag ends which were threaded through a row of holes in the lower edge of the undertunic and the upper edge of the hose. The metal tags, known as aglets or aiglets, were often of gold or silver, chased or jewelled and the laces were of coloured or gold silks. Once hose had become tights, the cod-piece became necessary. This was a bag covering the fork which was also fastened to the hose by points.

In order to display the masculine leg to advantage, younger men in particular wore hose which were patterned in stripes or ornamental designs or were particoloured, one leg coloured and patterned, one plain. In the early years of the century tunics were very short so displaying the hose. The Italians set the fashion in this. By the 1530s hose was often divided into two parts, the upper part slashed and banded, the lower fitting, gartered at the knee. At this time also the cod-

the mode for men who wore a knee-length gown, very full and with an enormous collar and padded sleeves. The chest was padded as was also the cod-piece which now protruded prominently between the open slit in the skirt which now usually covered the hose to the knees (1, 7, plates 2 & 3).

In women's dress, the Spanish style of framework skirt began to take over in Europe. The long, full skirt of the early sixteenth century now covered a frame of hoops which held it away from the body in a cone-shape from waist to ground and the fullness of the material was concentrated at the back in folds falling to a train. The gown skirts were often open in front, in an inverted V, to show the contrasting, but also rich material of the underskirt. An ornate girdle encircled the

piece was padded to make it protuberant. The word cod refers to a bag which, in later times, became a slang term for a purse. This was because in the years 1530–55 the codpiece was utilized to contain money and a handkerchief (plate 2).

In masculine underwear the shirt had become of greater importance as it was now often visible at the neck and wrists where the material was gathered into a narrow band. The full garment was of a white soft material – linen or silk – and might be embroidered where it showed at the neck or chest. In some tunic sleeve styles, particularly the Italian ones where the sleeve might be made in two sections laced together at shoulder and elbow, the full shirt sleeve was puffed out between the laces.

The outer tunic, now usually referred to as a doublet, might be waist-length or, as time passed, might have a matching hip- or knee-length skirt cut in gored panels, often of contrasting colours and materials (3).

The short fitting doublet and figure-revealing hose were less suited to the older or fatter figure. An alternative mode was available in a loose, full gown which could be worn on top. In length this varied from a hem-line six inches above the knee to ground level. Whatever the length, the style was similar. The garment had a wide collar and revers, turned back all the way down the front to display the lining of contrasting colour and fabric. Some gowns hung ungirded, some were cinched at the waist by sash or belt. This gown was known as a chamarre, a French term deriving from the verb *chamarrer*, meaning to bedeck or decorate gaudily. This referred to the rich fabrics from which it was made, also the ornamentation of braid, *passementerie* or fur. This garment, for the well-to-do, had stemmed from the sheepskin coat traditional to Spain, known there as a *chamarra* or *zamarra* (4).

With the German influence on masculine dress from the 1530s, the chamarre became wider at the shoulders and in length extended to the knees. It was heavily padded at the shoulder and had puffed and slashed and/or

6 Middle class lady in street wear. Dark cloth dress with velvet cuffs and stomacher panel. Thin linen partlet and headdress, the latter in gable shape but with a veil and no hood lappets or fall. Skirt held up by waist girdle displaying kirtle beneath. Dark hose and black leather shoes. *c.* 1540, English. Drawing by Hans Holbein, Ashmolean Museum, Oxford.

hanging sleeves. With its wide, full collar, this gave a square silhouette to the figure. In England, the Holbein portraits of King Henry VIII show this mode at its most characteristic (1, 7, plates 2 & 3).

In footwear, the slender shoe and boot styles of 1500 gave place by 1525–30 to a low-fronted broad-toed shape, the ubiquitous slashes extending to these articles. Shoes were made of leather, silk or velvet and sometimes were fastened on the instep by a strap (plate 2).

7   French Costume 1525–35 (background Château de Chaumont).

A   Doublet, skirt and gown of white silk striped vertically in black and gold embroidery. Slashed to show white chemise. Black edged neckline and wrist ruffles. Neck chain and pendant. Black jewelled hat with white plume. Black hose and shoes. *c.* 1525, Portrait of Francis I by Clouet, Louvre, Paris combined with portrait of Jean de Dinteville by Holbein, National Gallery, London.

B   Dark reddish-brown velvet gown with fur collar and edging and puffed, slashed fur-trimmed sleeves. Doublet of red silk, and locket. Black hat with jewel and white plume. *c.* 1538, Portrait of Francis I by Titian, Louvre, Paris.

C   Dark dress with fur cuffs and hanging sleeves, gold edging. Undergown of light-coloured fabric lined in black. Slashed sleeves. Jewelled girdle with pendant. Jewelled turban. 1540–7, Portrait of Eleanor of Austria, Francis I's second queen.

D   Doublet and hose all slashed and ruched. Sleeves padded and slashed. Short gown with wide collar and puffed upper sleeves. Jewelled hat and plume. *c.* 1530, Portrait of Duc de Guise.

Until about 1515–20 men were mostly cleanshaven and grew their hair shoulder-length at the sides and back. After this, short styles, together with small beards and/or moustaches, became fashionable. There was considerable variety in hats worn over the long hair. Many were large and wide-brimmed, made of beaver or felt and decorated lavishly with coloured plumes. The charac-teristic style after this was the dark or black velvet cap or bonnet with a flat crown and a turned-up brim. Often worn at a rakish angle, it was ornamented with brooches or jewels and a plume (**3**, **4**, **7**, plates 2 & 3).

Ladies' gowns of the early years of the century were usually characterized by a square neckline edged with embroidery or velvet banding, a closely-fitting bodice and a long, full skirt which was often held or fastened up at the sides or back to display the lining and the undergown, both of a different colour and fabric. Sleeves might be very full with turned-back cuffs edged with fur or showing the contrasting lining. The chemise, like the man's shirt, was gathered into a neck band or was also square cut; it was visible above the gown neckline. Some gowns were made in the Italian style with sleeves in two sections. In this case the long chemise sleeve could be seen, the material puffed out between the two sleeve parts. Over the chemise and under the undergown a fitted linen bodice was worn in order to preserve the slender body silhouette and to contrast with the full skirt (**2**).

From the years 1525–30, the feminine figure was dictated by the corset and far-thingale. The word corset, used in the sense of a garment which created some form of waist restriction is a more recent term. What was worn in the first half of the sixteenth century was a stiffened bodice, tightly-fitting in order to constrict the chest and waist and so provide a foil to the wide skirt. The gown bodice (basquine) closely followed the form of this stiffened supporting garment. It had a wide, square neckline, fairly low and arched upwards in the centre front. It was edged with jewelled embroidery and just displayed the edge of the frilled chemise above. Such a frill could also be discerned at the wrists. Beautiful pendants and necklace collars adorned the bare neck and bosom. Sleeves were full, padded and slashed and often had false or hanging cuffs in fur or a different material (**5, 7, 9, 10**, plate 4).

The Spanish farthingale (p. **20**) or *ver-dugado*, which produced a bell-shaped sil-houette, was introduced, via Italy, into France by 1530 and was there popularized by the Queen. By this time the framework skirt, called in France the *vertugade* or *vertugale* and, later, la mode *vertugadin*, was a canvas skirt inset at intervals with fabric-covered wicker hoops. It was tied on at the waist by tapes, the undergown and gown skirts being worn on top, so hiding the hoops. The French

8 Gold headdress. Gold neck chain and jewelled collar. Black neck cord. Bottle green gown. White chemise shows in front of bodice under lacing and in puffs on sleeves covered by bottle green straps. 1510–12, German. Painting of Salome by Lucas Cranach the Elder, Bayerische Nationalmuseum, Munich.

9 Gable headdress with striped silk underpad, gold, jewelled frontlet, gold lappets (one pinned up) and black velvet hood. English. Painting after Corvus of Catherine of Aragon, Henry VIII's first queen, National Portrait Gallery, London.

10 Velvet French hood with gold jewelled frontlet, pink satin band and white, gold-edged coif. Black gown with black velvet neck edging and white lawn partlet. *c.* 1530, Flemish. Painting by Van Orley, Musée d'Art Ancien, Brussels.

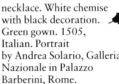

11 Brown turban. Bead necklace. White chemise with black decoration. Green gown. 1505, Italian. Portrait by Andrea Solario, Galleria Nazionale in Palazzo Barberini, Rome.

version was slightly less bell-shaped than the Spanish and, when soon adopted also in England, the sides were straight so giving a cone silhouette. Here the gown skirt was generally open in front in an inverted V to display the underskirt. The jewelled girdle hung nearly to the ground in the centre and usually terminated in a pendant or pomander. The skirt, held to the cone shape over the farthingale petticoat, was creaseless at front and sides, the folds being concentrated at the rear. This encouraged the development of the large motif floral patterns of the day which could then be displayed to advantage. In Spain the girdle usually encircled the waist only and had no pendant end, also the over-skirt was more generally closed in front, the edges held together by jewelled clasps set at intervals (**5, 7,** plate 4).

In the Mediterranean areas – Italy, Spain, southern France – the jewelled network cap or the turban with or without a veil, continued to be the fashionable headcovering but in northern Europe – Flanders, Germany, England, Scandinavia – a hood was worn for much of this period. The style varied in shape from area to area but most designs were made of black or dark velvet, lined with coloured silk, attached to a metal jewelled framework at the front edge. The sides fell in lappets on to the shoulders and the material hung down the back in folds or a tube. The hood was worn over a white cap or coif which was visible in front of the metal band. The hair was almost or entirely concealed. The typical English form, especially early in the century, had a gabled or pyramidal shape of frame, the French and Flemish a horseshoe form (**7, 8–11,** plate 4).

13 Boy aged about two years in a child's chair wearing a red velvet dress with darker red skirt banding and white pleated apron with gold embroidered bands. Gold embroidered neck edge and sleeve bands. White shirt in sleeve puffs and neck frill. Two necklaces. Hair in looped up plaits. Red velvet cap with white coif edged with gold. 1531, German. Painting of family of Duke Wilhelm of Bavaria by Peter Gärtner, Bayerische Nationalmuseum, Munich.

From the Middle Ages until the seventeenth century babies were swaddled; that is, wrapped in bandages from neck to toe, over a chemise, the arms and legs bound tightly to the body to protect the fragile limbs and make the baby easy to carry. It was felt that if this custom was not adhered to, the limbs would be damaged irretrievably. Also, for mothers working in the fields or in the home, it kept baby safe as it could be suspended or attached, like a parcel, to a hook or a piece of furniture.

The baby remained in swaddling bands, looking like an Egyptian mummy, until it was weaned though, at about four months, the arms were freed. The medieval method of swaddling was by criss-cross bands; by the end of the sixteenth century bands were wrapped horizontally round the baby. At this time also the baby was dressed in long clothes – a short-sleeved gown – over the swaddling bands. A cap covered the head (**53**).

When the baby was old enough to sit up and crawl, he or she (for both sexes were dressed alike until about five years of age) wore an ankle-length dress, an apron, a bib and a cap. After five years boys were dressed as a miniature version of their fathers and girls of their mothers, no matter how unsuitable such attire seems to have been to us (**13**).

12 Silver gilt pomander *c.* 1500. British Museum, London.

CHAPTER TWO

1540–1620

The Spanish Influence

These were the years when fashionable dress in western Europe reached its zenith of richness and luxury. There were several reasons for this. Quality of materials, cut of garments, enrichment, decoration and patterning of fabrics had been improving and evolving since the early Middle Ages. *Quattrocento* Renaissance Italy had introduced beautiful fabrics, jewelled embroideries, glorious colours and elegant modes to the rest of Europe. By the middle of the sixteenth century the multiplicity of small courts were amalgamating to become fewer, larger ones which were powerful and wealthy. A greater percentage of the population in western European countries was enjoying and expecting a higher standard of living and so was tempted to emulate the fashions of the truly wealthy patricians.

Of prime importance as a source of this increased wealth was the exploration and colonization of the East and of the New World. In north and south America, in particular, these vast resources in precious metals, primarily gold, and jewels were being exploited by the Spanish and the Portuguese who controlled the lucrative trade, reaping the reward for their initiative in discovery. When Charles I of Spain, later to be the Holy Roman Emperor Charles V, succeeded to the Spanish throne in 1516, he inherited the largest empire so far ruled by a European monarch. By the mid-century this encompassed (apart from Spain) peoples in Austria, Burgundy, Holland and Italy as well as the immense new lands in north and south America and in Africa. He set up a colonial administration in the New World and his son Philip II developed this into a comprehensive system. It was not until after the defeat of the Armada sent against England in 1588 and the break away of the Dutch provinces under William of Orange which declared their independence from Spain in 1581, that the Spanish empire and power began to decline. The dominant influence on the dress of the whole of Europe (not under Turkish subjugation) over much of the second half of the sixteenth century came, therefore, from the Iberian peninsula, an influence which extended into the early years of the seventeenth century until mitigated and finally replaced by fashions from the Low Countries.

By mid-century it was becoming clear that the potential of trade with these immense new areas of the world was too extensive for Spain and Portugal to handle in isolation. The commercial expertise of other countries, notably Germany, Flanders and France, was employed in building up countries in Europe to handle this trade and exploit the material wealth. In such western European countries cities were expanded and land developed. Plant was assembled for raising sheep for wool, for the culture of the silkworm, for the processes of spinning, dyeing, fulling and weaving of fabrics of all kinds from plain woollen cloth to the most exotic of patterned velvets and silks. Italy, which had long been the centre of production for such fabrics, joined in vigorously to protect her interests. Her cities of Venice, Florence, Milan and Genoa became richer than ever in competition with the newer centres of Lyons, Paris,

14 Black hat with coloured plumes and jewelled band. Lace-edged ruff. Dark velvet cape. White doublet and hose, silver decoration. White shoes. Portrait of Don Fernando d'Aragon by Pantoja de la Cruz, 1575–80. Nelahozeves Castle, Czechoslovakia.

15 Wired lace-edged collar and cuffs. Portrait of a Spanish princess by Coello, *c.* 1600. George Mercer College, New York.

16 Doublet, trunk hose, hose and shoes of yellow embroidered in silver. Gown of brown satin with sable fur. King Philip II of Spain. Portrait by Titian, Naples Museum.

luxury fabrics but never has the sixteenth century been surpassed for its glittering panoply of jewelled splendour.

At first there was strong resistance to Spanish domination in dress from the northern areas of Europe under the influence of the Reformation: Germany, Holland, Scandinavia in particular. It was Germany which resisted Spanish styles longest and finally capitulated only when the Roman Catholic south of the country had adopted these elegant modes. There were many in the Church there who railed against the 'wickedness' of wearing Spanish dress. Typical was the sermon preached at Frankfurt University in 1555 by the Professor of the Holy Scriptures in which he condemned trunk hose as being possessed of the Devil; he described them as *Hosenteufel*.

Roman Catholic countries such as Italy and France, whose garments had long displayed harmony and beauty, quickly followed the Spanish line, embracing these styles by adapting them to their own tastes and traditions, modifying the rigidity of the prototype to a softer line and introducing lighter colours into the predominance of black in the Spanish wardrobe.

Protestant England might have been expected to resist Spanish domination but the accession of the Roman Catholic Mary in 1553 and her subsequent marriage to Philip of Spain ensured the adoption of Spanish styles and, even when Elizabeth succeeded her sister in 1558 and engaged in the protracted struggle against the might of Spain, Spanish fashions remained paramount.

The influence of the military upon the civil dress, which had been clearly evidenced in the early sixteenth century styles of puffed, padded and slashed garments (p. 9), was much reduced by 1550 but a modified military influence reappeared later in the century. This is apparent in the padding of the masculine doublet at this time in the unusual form of the peasecod-belly protuberance and the shell contour of the still-projecting cod-piece; both features were derived from military attire in which vulnerable parts of

Rouen, London, Antwerp, Ypres, Munich and Augsburg. These luxurious fabrics were enriched by jewelled embroideries, fine lace and glittering jewellery of all kinds. In succeeding centuries costume of the upper classes has often been superb and elegant, displaying

the human body were protected by armour of this shape.

Spanish Dress

This was characterized by elegance and rigidity, by superb decoration yet a certain austerity and restraint. Black was normal wear for every day, dominating the majority of garments, brighter colours being reserved for festive and special occasions. The all-pervading power and control of the Roman Catholic Church and the formal ceremonial of the Spanish court were reflected in the constriction of the whaleboned costume. The ensembles were beautiful and elegant but markedly uncomfortable. Women, in particular, encased in farthingale and corset, were obliged to advance in a dignified, stately manner, their walk a gliding progression rather than a natural movement. This presented a marked contrast to the humanist fashions of Italy in the early sixteenth century which had preceded the Spanish modes. The Spanish introduced padding less than many other countries; their fashionable figure was elegantly slim, both men and women being strictly corseted as necessary in order to achieve this.

The Moorish inheritance was still apparent, especially in the textiles, the rich embroideries, the use of jewels and jewelled buttons, points and ornaments, the heavy girdles and collars. The Moorish type of coat dress clearly influenced the style of ladies' gowns. This could be seen in the jewelled buttons/brooches which clasped the whole length of the centre front of the garment – a characteristically

17 White gown and undergown with gold pattern. White satin lining. Gold, jewelled collar and girdle. Lace-edged ruff. Black hat with pearls, plumes and jewelled aigrette. Portrait of Infanta Isabella Clara by de Llano, 1584, Prado, Madrid.

18 Black figured silk gown. Silver brocade underskirt. Lace-edged cap with pearls. Pearl necklaces. Jewelled girdle and gold buttons. Sleeves white with gold bands. Portrait by Antonio Moro, Prado, Madrid, c. 1560–5.

19 White and gold embroidered doublet and trunk hose. Red velvet cape ornamented in gold. Red velvet lining. White hose and shoes. Black hat, white plume, gold decoration. King Sebastien of Portugal. Portrait by Cristoforo Morales. Monasterio de las Descalzas Reales, Madrid 1570–3.

20 Ruff hanging on wall peg.

21 Tally iron for setting (goffering) starched ruffs.

22 Spanish farthingale petticoat.

23 French or wheel farthingale.

24 Late sixteenth-century metal and whalebone corset.

Spanish fashion (**17**, plate 8) and one different from the long girdle chains terminating in pendant or pomander more usual in France and England. Moorish influence was also discernible in the leather shoes and chopines typically decorated in silver or gold and often displaying an oriental-type turned-up toe.

Spain contributed several innovations in sixteenth century costume – the ruff and high neckline, the farthingale and corset, the cape, the bombasted doublet and the trunk hose. Yet, paradoxically, it was not in Spain that any of these features were carried to excess to become over-elaborate and extravagant in size and decoration. Such extreme forms of these garments were to be found in the countries which adopted them from Spain, in England, Holland, France and Germany.

Men's Dress in Spain

The masculine shirt was now an elegant undergarment; it was made of white silk or cambric and, in Spain, usually decorated with black silk embroidery which became known as 'Spanish blackwork'. Such ornamentation was mainly confined to the neck and wrist ruffles. Spain led the way in adopting the high neckline to the shirt which replaced the square or boat shape of the 1540s and its finishing ruffle was just visible above the doublet high neckline (**14, 19**, plate 5).

By 1560 these neck ruffles gradually became ruffs which were known as bands. A ruff – made of fine linen, lawn or Holland cambric – was a separate article from the shirt. It consisted of a long strip of fabric,

pleated and set into a neckband and tied at the front with band strings. After 1565, with the introduction of starch, ruffs became larger. They required frequent washing and starching and needed to be goffered (gauffered) – a term derived from the French verb *gaufrer* meaning to crimp or flute. This process was carried out by means of heated goffering tongs which, resembling metal curling tongs, set the still damp ruff into the appropriate form. A tally iron (the word comes from a corruption of 'Italy' whence it originated) was then used to smooth the fabric. Often erroneously termed a goffering iron, this is a stand affixed to which are cigar-shaped barrels. Heated metal rods (poking sticks) were inserted into the barrels and the ruff material was drawn over them. When dry the ruff was placed into a low circular band box (**20, 21**).

The fashionable ruff became larger as time passed, reaching its maximum diameter about 1580–85 when it might extend some nine inches on either side of the neck and consist of 18 yards of material. Such large ruffs needed a form of support such as a wired edging or, more commonly, the use of a rebato (also called a supportasse or under-propper) beneath. Such support consisted of wires attached to a neckband at the back or a wire-edged pasteboard covered with white fabric. Lace-edging was common for costly ruffs or the ruff might even be made entirely of lace. Wrist ruffles were made in matching sets with the ruff and were termed a 'suit of ruffs' (**29**). The Spanish ruff tended to remain small and was discreetly but exquisitely decorated by silk embroidery sometimes set with tiny jewels.

The main body garment was the doublet which had changed its silhouette from the square chunky form of the 1530s into a slim waisted one. It was pointed at the waist in front and was finished there with narrow decorative tabs known as basques. The garment was buttoned centre front from its high neckline to waist. Decorative slashing was still in vogue but in Spain this was restrained, the undergarment barely visible through the slits which were still held together at intervals by points. The long sleeves were also decoratively slashed. Later, in the 1580s, the slim form was obscured by the characteristic padding applied to the front which produced an artificial paunch called a peasecod-belly. Whalebone was also inserted into the seams then to maintain the desired shape and, at the same time, sleeves were being padded on the upper arm. However, as with the ruffs, Spanish styles were restrained and such excess refrained from (**14, 19**).

A jerkin was often worn as an outer tunic. It took the same form as the doublet but was sleeveless, being finished at the shoulder in tabs or a slashed padded roll. In England these were later known as picadils, a term believed to have derived from the name of a house of Mr Higgins in the parish of St Martin-in-the-Fields called Pickadilly Hall. Mr Higgins, resident there in 1622, was a tailor who specialized in making garments decorated by 'pickadilles'. London's famous thoroughfare, Piccadilly, was named from the same source (plate 5).

The lower part of the body was covered by stocks. These, in the second half of the sixteenth century, were generally divided into two parts: the upper stocks (also known as canions) and the lower or netherstocks. The top part of the canions, which covered the buttocks, were full – loose or padded – and could be of varied length, extending from waist to mid-thigh or were more abbreviated. Called trunk hose they were fitted with a waistband and thigh bands, the full material blousing out between. Most designs were

25 Deep rose velvet gown with fur edging and cuffs. White satin undergown embroidered in colour. Jewelled girdle with pendant. Lace-edged handkerchief, *collet monté* and cap. Pearl ropes on bodice. French. Portrait of Henry III's queen, *c.* 1575.

26 Black velvet chamarre with white fur trimming and lining. Black velvet hat, white plume, jewelled band. Grey silk doublet and trunk hose, silver decoration. Grey hose and shoes. French. Portrait.

27 Black velvet gown with grey fur trimming. Gold embroidered partlet at neck and cap. Cut velvet underskirt. English.

28 and 29 Fig. 28 wears a white satin gown with gold hem over a red undergown. The ruff is supported at the back by an underpropper. Fig. 29 has a black doublet and upper stocks with dark red netherstocks and black

shoes. He wears a grey, gold-edged cape with crimson lining, a large ruff and a plumed black hat. Painting, *Ball for the Wedding of the Duc de Joyeuse* by unknown artist, Louvre, Paris *c*. 1580–1.

30 The queen wears a deep purple satin gown over a French farthingale. Pearl decoration. Lace-edged *collet*

monté. Painting of Marie de' Medici by Rubens, Louvre, Paris, 1610.

ornamented with added panes. These were strips of material, attached only at waist and thigh bands, which were decoratively embroidered in coloured, gold or silver thread and contrasted in colour and material with the trunk hose beneath. The exaggeratedly prominent cod-piece continued in fashion (*see* p. 11). Below the thigh bands the canions extended as a fitted stocking to below the knee where the netherstocks – of a different decoration and fabric – were pulled up and fastened over them by garter or sash. In Spain such stockings were increasingly, after 1560, of knitted silk. They were costly and of very fine quality, much prized and envied throughout Europe (**14, 16, 19**).

Capes and cloaks had long been traditional Spanish outer wear. In this period they came into their own and the fashion spread all over Europe. Spanish versions varied greatly in length, in fullness, in the use of a wide collar,

a small turned-back one or none at all; some designs boasted hanging or open sleeves. The methods of wearing were equally varied. The garment could be draped round both shoulders or only one. It might be draped over an arm or slung round the body by its fastening cords. Fabrics used in making these capes were rich and heavy, linings contrasted in colour and material, luxurious embroidered decoration was employed especially on collars. Earlier capes tended to be larger, later ones more abbreviated (**14, 19**). The German/English style of shaped outer gown was adopted in Spain after 1550 but never ousted the cape from favoured wear (**16**).

Masculine coiffure styles of this half century were carefully tended and curled but generally neatly trimmed and short. Men's faces were cleanshaven or sported dainty, pointed moustaches and/or beards. Hats were most often made from velvet or satin. Earlier styles had soft crowns and small brims; later in the century taller hats were fashionable with turned-up brims and were

33 Patterned velvet gown. Pale satin slashed sleeves. Cartwheel ruff with supportasse. Jewelled cap. Gold, jewelled girdle and pendant. Drawing by Hollar of a lady from Danzig, *c.* 1600.

31 White doublet with black embroidery, peasecod-belly shape. Trunk hose to match. Black cape. Cartwheel ruff. White hose and shoes. Miniature painting of a gentleman by Nicholas Hilliard. Victoria and Albert Museum, London. English, *c.* 1581.

32 Richly embroidered gown studded with pearls worn over a wheel farthingale. Lace-edged open ruff. Butterfly wings and veil. Decoration by pearl ropes and jewels. Engraving of Queen Elizabeth I by Crispin van der Passe the Elder from a drawing by Isaac Oliver of 1588, Victoria and Albert Museum, London.

of the ruff, was in black, though in various materials. The only relief to this was in silver or gold thread embroidery interspersed with tiny jewels. Colour, where introduced, was limited in quantity and muted. It might be discerned between the slashed openings or in a cape lining.

Ladies' Dress in Spain

This silhouette, as described on page 13, was created by the corset and the farthingale. Spain had been the instigator of these styles and maintained them, with variations, well into the seventeenth century, far longer than other countries which abandoned them for more natural forms after 1620. Upon this unnatural, though elegant, rigid form, there could be displayed the most beautiful fabrics, enriched and jewelled over almost the entire receptive surface. The women thus became display models, though in Spain less decoration and rich, black materials were more usual than elsewhere. The rigid figure, encased in this way, made any movement which was not stately, difficult. It expressed clearly the Spanish preoccupation with autocratic dignity and chastity; gaiety and frivolity were incongruous intrusions into such a costume

decorated by jewelled hat bands and ostrich tips or *aigrettes*. A jewelled brooch might be pinned at one side and the hat, especially when worn by a fashion-conscious young man, might be set at a rakish angle (**14, 19, 34**).

The broad-toed shoe styles of the 1530s had given way to a natural shape. They were still decoratively slashed and sometimes embroidered and jewelled. A variety of fabrics were used to make such shoes: velvet, satin, leather. For street wear they were covered by deep cork-soled chopines. Alternatively, boots might be worn.

In general, masculine dress in Spain in these years was elegant and restrained, costly yet dignified and essentially autocratic. Black was predominant, especially so for men and often the entire costume, with the exception

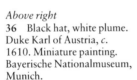

34   Jewelled black cap with white plumes. Dark cape. Light, striped doublet with jewelled buttons. Portrait of Infante Don Carlos by Coello, Spanish, Kunsthistorisches Museum, Vienna, c. 1565.

35   Black hat and plume with jewelled band. White ruff embroidered in black. Portrait of Sir Edward Hoby by unknown artist, Ipswich Museum, English, 1577.

Above right
36   Black hat, white plume. Duke Karl of Austria, c. 1610. Miniature painting. Bayerische Nationalmuseum, Munich.

37   Black velvet hat and doublet, both gold embroidered. Fur trimming. Ostrich plume. Charles IX of France, c. 1560. Portrait by François Clouet. Kunsthistorisches Museum, Vienna.

38   Black felt hat, jewel and aigrette. Cartwheel ruff. Portrait of Sir Henry Unton, c. 1580, English.

which even children in aristocratic families had to wear. Such constriction was no part of the average person's attire.

The fitting bodice and full skirt styles, based upon the early forms of corset and farthingale, were described on page 13. From mid-century the linen (sometimes leather) corset was shaped to maintain a slender waist, to flatten and raise the breasts to give a concave shape to the upper torso. This form was achieved by the insertion of strips of wood, horn or whalebone into the seams at front, sides and back. The garment was laced up centre back or front. As it was not shaped to cup the breasts, as in a modern corselette, shoulder straps were needed to hold it in place and to give an upwards thrust or lift, rather than the less flattering downward flattening to the breasts. In the final gown bodice form the outline of the breasts was not discernible as such but their forward prominence was not obliterated as in the flattening process of other periods, the 1920s for example (**24**).

The gown bodice worn over this underwear was, in Spain, almost always fastened up the centre to the high neckline above

which was displayed the circular, medium-sized ruff, beautifully decorated with embroidery and/or lace edging. In the earlier years, until the 1560s, the arch-fronted square neckline was retained, the part above this being covered by a transparent fabric jewelled and embroidered all over. Heavy jewelled pendants, brooches or necklaces decorated such bodices as well as jewelled buttons fastening the centre front. The bodice was generally pointed in front at the waist where it might be girdled but such girdles rarely had hanging pendants as in other countries (**15, 17, 18**, plate 8).

Sleeves were usually in two parts. The inner sleeve was long and fairly fitting, later styles being padded and slashed. They were made of contrasting fabric to the gown and were often banded horizontally in gold or silver. At the shoulder was a puff or padded roll sometimes cut into picadils like the men's doublets. From the shoulder hung a detachable outer sleeve which matched the gown fabric though this was lined with a differently coloured material. Sometimes this simply hung behind the arm; at others it was wide at the outer edge and was clasped at intervals by jewelled brooches. Wrist ruffles were made in matching sets as a suit of ruffs (**15, 17, 18,** plate 8).

While the upper torso was confined and its shape determined by the corset, the lower part of the body was encased in the far-thingale. In Spain this form continued (*see* p. 13) to be bell-shaped and of circular section though, as time passed, the sides became flatter and straighter making the bell nearer to a cone in form (**22**). Under the farthingale was worn a black petticoat and over it as many as three underskirts, the inner one ground length and the outer ones slightly shorter in front but long at the back. All skirts were cut to hang flat at front and sides, the fullness being concentrated at the rear. In Spain the two sides of the open front of the outer skirt were nearly always kept closed by jewelled clasps, buttons or points set at intervals from waist to hem. Where patterned it was these creaseless skirts which provided the backcloth to large motif designs, being uninterrupted by folds except at the back (**15, 17, 18,** plate 8).

Stockings and footwear resembled styles worn by the men. Chopines or pantoffles were often worn on top of the shoes. These gave extra height but, combined with the constriction engendered by the corset and farthingale resulted in an apparently mechanical form of motion which resembled a glide rather than a walk.

Spanish ladies, like the Italians, did not favour the wearing of hoods as in northern Europe. Their hair was dressed in curls or in loose pompadour style in front then braided at the back. It was then enclosed there in a gold, jewelled caul or pearl string net with a decorative little cap perched on the back of the head. Sometimes the hair was uncovered, decorated only by jewels or pearls. Hats, in styles like those of the men, provided alternative wear to the caps (**15, 17, 18,** plate 8).

Fabrics worn by ladies were rich and heavy. Black was general for everyday wear but less so than in masculine costume and the velvet or satin material was often enriched all over by silver or gold embroidered thread.

39 Red velvet dress with gold chain necklace and gold clasps. White puffs on sleeves. White open ruff. Jewelled cap with silver bows. Portrait by Alessandro Allori, Uffizi Gallery, Florence, Italian.

40 French hood with gold, jewelled biliments separated by white satin and black velvet fall. Dress of black velvet and black satin. Collar lined with white satin and edged with gold lace. Small ruff. Drawing of Princess Mary Tudor, *c.* 1549, English.

41 Underpropper of pasteboard covered in pleated white cotton. Italian, *c.* 1590.

42 Black velvet French hood, gold, jewelled biliment. Small lace-edged ruff. Drawing, English, *c.* 1562.

43 Black jewelled hat over jewelled cap. Black ropa decorated with jewelled buttons and gold bands. Red dress with horizontal gold lines. Jewelled necklace, girdle and bracelets. Small ruff. Painting by Lucas Cranach, Bayerische Nationalmuseum, Munich. German.

46 Black velvet hat and aigrette. Satin cloak with velvet lining. Slashed doublet and trunk hose. Black shoes with rosettes. Engraving by Giacomo France, Venetian, 1581.

44 White doublet and red loose breeches (slops, pluderhosen) tied with gold knee sashes. White stockings and shoes. Red rosettes. Gold cloak and hat. White plumes. Painting 'Banquet out of doors' by Van der Velde, Rijksmuseum, Amsterdam, Dutch, 1615–20.

45 Vlieger in figured black with black velvet edging. Pink taffeta skirt. Gold and black stomacher. Gold sleeves with black bands. Plain cartwheel ruff. White lawn cap with lace edging. Painting by Frans Hals, Mauritshuis, The Hague, Dutch 1590–1600.

Rich colours were also worn especially on festive occasions.

Important accessories included especially the fan. Feather fans with ivory handles were in general use but the folding fan, of Oriental origin, was first introduced into Europe in Spain, becoming popular during the sixteenth century. It was made of vellum or perfumed leather. Both sexes carried large lace-edged handkerchiefs, perfumed gloves of Spanish leather and sunshades.

Dress in France

The dress of both men and women was closely patterned upon the Spanish prototype in the years 1540–75 (14–16). Although black was not worn as widely as in Spain, clothes were made from darker coloured fabrics than previously and the materials and means of decoration were similar to the Spanish versions. The French home-produced much of this – silks, velvets and other rich fabrics – in the weaving centres, such as Lyons, Tours, Nîmes and Orleans. This also applied to the decorative materials, gold and silver thread and passementerie, for instance. It was in these years that France developed her system of state restrictions aimed against the competitive importation of such fabrics; this has been a bulwark of the French economy ever since.

It was after 1575 that the French produced a number of variations on the Spanish pattern of dress, both for men's and women's styles; these were all a form of exaggeration of the original mode. In men's attire of the years 1575–88, during the reign of Henry III, the chief characteristic was effeminacy and, to a certain extent, degeneracy. This tendency was also to be seen, though to a lesser extent, in other countries, England for example, but not in Spain. In France the trend was the most extreme. It took the form of excessive padding of the doublet in the peasecod-belly shape and of rigid whaleboning in the seams, in padded and abbreviated trunk hose, tightly fitting canions, slashed and puffed in rows, very short capes and very large cartwheel ruffs. Gentleman were particular about care of their skin, using cosmetics and perfume

47 Making music in Germany 1611. The lady playing the spinet (B) wears a patterned dress with hanging fur sleeves. Her large ruff has a framework support as does also that of the small boy (D). All wear cartwheel ruffs and the man (A) has pluderhosen with sash ties at the knee. The other gentleman (E), playing the lute, and the boy (D), have less full breeches. Note the wearing of hats indoors by men, a custom which survived well into the seventeenth century. Copper engraving by Von de Bry, Frankfurt-am-Main.

and wearing gloves and face masks out-of-doors for protection. Their hair was meticulously curled, their beards elegantly pointed, their moustaches plucked to give a fine precise line. They wore tall-crowned hats piled high with plumes and jewellery of all kinds, especially earrings. Shoes were slashed and jewelled, chopines or pantoffles being worn on top outdoors (**29**).

A more masculine line had returned by 1600. The number and type of garments had not changed but their cut and silhouette had. There was less padding. The peasecod-belly form had disappeared. Decoration was still by slashes. Trunk hose were longer and less bombasted. An alternative mode was called Venetians. These were a longer, looser form of knee-length breeches where they were tied with ribbon sashes. A smaller ruff or a small collar or, thirdly, a stand-up stiffened collar supported by a framework called a *col rotonde*, replaced the cartwheel ruff. Yet another form of neckwear, an unstarched ruff, called a falling ruff, presaged the elegant falling band of the next generation. After 1600 shoes began, for the first time, to have heels and instep decoration took the form of ribbon rosettes (**61**). Boots, made from soft leather from Spain or Russia, began to come into fashion.

By the 1570s feminine dress in France was also showing a divergence from the Spanish prototype. For some time ladies had worn a strict corset in the form of a stomacher. This was a bodice reinforced with metal strips and covered by rich fabric and was donned on top of the original linen bodice so producing a very slender waist, low and deeply pointed in front. Ladies had also begun to wear extra padding over the Spanish farthingale in the form of a circular roll tied round the waist which, when the very full gathered skirt was draped over it, gave a fuller bell shape to the silhouette.

Soon the Spanish farthingale was abandoned in favour of a fatter bolster roll tied round the waist which provided a yet fuller skirt line and, later in the century, this gave place to the last phase of this type of sixteenth century skirt framework, the wheel or drum farthingale which became widely known as the French farthingale. Like its Spanish predecessor, this was a canvas or linen petticoat reinforced with circular hoops of cane or whalebone set at intervals from waist to ground. However, the shape was quite different. As its name suggests, it resembled a drum, the hoops being of equal diameter so creating straight vertical sides to the underskirt. The top of the drum was also of canvas. It was pleated and was made with a hole for the waist, set nearer to the front of the circular rim and it could be drawn tightly here and affixed with tapes (23, 28, 30).

The corset, by this time, possessed a long central busk in front of metal or whalebone which extended almost to the pubic bone. The stiff picadil finish, at the now very slender waist of the corset bodice, extended to a low point in front. When worn with the wheel farthingale the busk point rested upon the front rim frame of the drum, so giving a fashionable tilt forwards of the whole dress. The gowns worn on top of such farthingales and corsets were extremely elaborate and artificially shaped. They contained an immense quantity and weight of material and were, without doubt, excessively uncomfortable. Sleeves were heavily padded, especially on the upper arm, finished at the shoulder in padded rolls (28, 30).

Feminine neckwear possessed even more variations than that of the men. The cartwheel ruff was largely replaced in France after 1575–80 by either a high standing ruff or collar or a falling ruff. If the collar were circular, extending all round the neck, it was called a *col rotonde*, if open in front with a décolleté neckline and standing up round the sides and back, it was called a *collet monté* (25, 30).

In the early years of this period the feminine coiffure was simply dressed, drawn back to a chignon; sometimes the hair was dressed over pads on the temples to add width to the style. The French hood was worn for some years, set far back on the head and, as the ruff grew larger, the fall was omitted. Later the coiffure was dressed higher and headdresses became rare. Pearl ropes and jewels decorated this style. Cosmetics and perfumes were used to excess (25, 28, 30).

Dress in Italy

The Italian peninsula continued to be divided into small states ruled by different factions so there was as yet no national style of dress. Spanish influence had been strong since the Pope and the head of the Hapsburg Empire, Charles V, came to terms in 1529. In that year Charles received the Imperial crown from Pope Clement VII at Bologna. It was agreed that the Papacy, therefore, held the largest state, around Rome, though much of the north was still controlled by Italian princes. Despite this, by 1559, Philip II, the new Spanish king, ruled over the larger part of Italy, the south and Sicily, including Naples and much of the north including Milan. Only Venice, under its old republican government, Genoa and Corsica under the Dorias and the small republics of Lucca and San Marino were free of Spain.

In the large area under Spanish domination styles were inherited from Spain. In the north these resembled those of Madrid. In the south the style of dress was characteristically more sumptuous, the fabrics richer, in glowing colours and elaborately decorated. This Neapolitan version was lighthearted and ebullient, a far cry from the serious austerity of Spain.

Outside the range of Spanish influence the

Italians followed their natural bent which, traditionally, was for a more comfortable natural line of dress: humanism survived. For both sexes this was reflected in little bombast or whalebone, a natural, less slender waistline, an elegant, less rigid form of costume and greater ease of movement. For women, corsets were softer, less severe and ladies preferred layers of petticoats to farthingales. They eschewed cartwheel ruffs, supportasses and décolleté necklines and preferred standing collars with dainty lace ruffs. Jewellery and decoration was more sparingly employed but was of superb quality. Ladies wore their hair loose or braided and bound in gold cauls decorated with pearl ropes, just as they had done for generations (39, 41, 46).

Travellers such as Fynes Moryson describe noticeable differences in a number of regions. He refers to the dress of Ferrara and Mantua as fashionable and elegant, to that in Genoa as being similar to that in France. Venice, traditionally individualist, showed greater variations from elsewhere. Venetians were noted for the extreme height of their chopines (called zoccolo), making walking outdoors difficult. Skirts had long trains and necklines were extremely décolleté. Cosmetics were heavily applied as was perfume.

Dress in Northern Europe

In this area, extending from England in the west to Poland in the east and Scandinavia further north, the chief influence in the 1540s and early 1550s continued to be the German pattern set in the late 1530s, of excessive padding and slashing of the dress and, for men, the square silhouette provided by the wide-shouldered, collared gown; women wore the Spanish farthingale and corset. After this the Spanish mode was the basis of dress but there were considerable variations from area to area due to climate and national character.

Garments were made from heavier materials, especially in the Baltic regions and Scandinavia and wool formed part of the staple wardrobe even in highly fashionable dress. Fynes Moryson commented, from his travels there in 1591, that 'the Germans spend least of all other nations on their clothes. They take care that the material is good and hard-wearing. Their linen is thick and coarse in Prussia and ruffs are very large and supported on wire frames. They carry large handkerchiefs'. Moryson also thought that the German styles were old-fashioned compared to those that he had left behind in England. There is no doubt, though, that the dress of the German nobility was lavish and luxurious (36, 47).

One of the richest cities in northern Germany in these years was Danzig (now Gdansk). It was a great merchant port acting as a link between east and west along the Baltic coastal area, handling trade from Russia to Holland. As befitted its wealth, fashions here were richer than elsewhere in northern Germany. Ruffs were immense. Velvet and silk was to be seen rather than broadcloth. Lace edging, pearl ropes, fur edging and satin linings were all to be widely seen. Stomachers were of brocade or fur. Jewellery was rarely worn in northern Germany but Danzig was different (33).

The very large cartwheel ruff was typical wear for both men and women in all these northern areas, particularly in the 1580s and 1590s. Such ruffs were, however, generally made of completely plain linen or cambric without lace edging or embroidered decoration; they required a supportasse collar at the rear to hold them up. Such plain, very large ruffs were especially characteristic of Germany and Holland where also a tremendous variety of designs of white linen or cambric starched caps were generally worn by ladies. Such caps were decorative headdresses and, for festive occasions, might be embroidered with gold thread and decorated with pearls (44, 45).

The Spanish style of dress was closely followed in the Low Countries from the 1550s until about 1580 though materials were heavier and designs never extreme.

48 Dark velvet gown with gold banding and fur lining. Black hat with plume and brooch. Light-coloured slashed doublet and upper stocks. Portrait of a boy by Francesco Salviati c. 1550, Italian. National Gallery, London.

49 Jerkin in two shades of pink over gold-decorated white doublet. Gold trunk hose. White hose and shoes. Ruff. Brown gloves. Portrait of Giulio Cesare Colonna by Scipione Pulzone, Galleria Colonna, Rome, Italian.

50 Embroidered silk cap. Brocade overdress with crimson lining. Silk underdress. Ruff. Baby boy c. 1570.

51 Brown jerkin with gold banding. Gold doublet sleeves, trunk hose and upper stocks. White stockings and shoes. Lace-edged ruff. Portrait of Infante Don Fernando by Coello, 1577. Monasterio de las Descalzas Reales, Madrid, Spanish.

52 Portrait of Infante Don Diego as a little boy by Coello. Private collection, London, Spanish.

53 White with gold embroidery. Baby in cap and swaddling clothes, c. 1605.

With the division of the country, however, when the southern part remained with the Hapsburg Empire, Holland became independent. From that time trade developed rapidly and the country became wealthier and began to lead fashion in its own styles. In the years 1600–20 the Spanish austere and rigid line was abandoned. For men the doublet became slim fitting but was neither padded nor corseted. Loose knee-length breeches replaced the trunk hose (in Germany called pluderhosen) (**48**). These were finished at the knee by silk fringed sashes. Low-heeled shoes had ribbon rosettes on the instep. Under the ostrich plume trimmed large-brimmed hats the hair was grown longer and allowed to hang loosely: the way was being set for the typical swashbuckling styles characteristic of European dress in the 1630s (**44**).

Women's costume passed through a similar metamorphosis. The skirt was wide and full, worn over a waist bolster roll and the bodice, less corseted than in Spain, was worn over a richly ornamented stomacher which was finished by basques at the waist. Padded sleeves ended at the shoulder with slashed rolls. In Holland, as in France and England, an overgown or surcote was often worn on top of the gown. This generally had no sleeves, was fastened at the throat, under the collar, by a brooch and hung open in front. In Holland called a vlieger, in France it was a marlotte and in England a ropa (**43, 45**).

After 1615 the feminine silhouette changed markedly, becoming much slimmer and more elegant. As with the men's styles, the Spanish form completely disappeared, particularly the stiffened skirt. The overskirt was then often pinned up all round to display the underskirt. Ruffs were still large. Tall hats might be perched on top of the cambric caps.

A characteristically Dutch garment, also to

Ye fhalbe led before Princes
and rulers for my names fake.
Math. 10.

54 The men wear skirted jerkins and shirts over plain hose. They have caps or hats and pouches depending from their waistbelts. The women wear kirtles, the skirts often pinned or held up, and kerchiefs and caps. Footwear is plain and heel-less. Woodcut from *Acts and Monuments of the Martyrs*, John Fox. British Museum, London. English.

be seen in Flanders and northern Germany, was the heuke (huik, hoyke). This was a voluminous veil or cape which was often fixed to a wire framework above the head, the material then falling down to ground level. Some designs were attached to the cap instead of to a frame. The designs varied considerably from region to region.

Dress styles in England followed a somewhat different path from those elsewhere in northern Europe. They began the same in the 1540s with the influence still from Germany but the marriage of Queen Mary in 1554 to Philip of Spain accelerated the trend towards the adoption of Spanish fashions (**27**). Men's costume became slenderer and less square in silhouette (plate 5). Women adopted the high neckline with ruff above

from 1550 and the wearing of the ropa was favoured (**35, 38, 40, 42**).

Though after Mary's death in 1558 England reverted to Protestantism under Elizabeth and increasingly followed a policy of resistance towards Spanish attempts at domination, there was no diminution in the popularity of Spanish dress. Indeed, in the 1580s, led by Elizabeth, English dress became extravagantly costly and exaggerated though less effeminate than contemporary French modes.

Men wore immense cartwheel ruffs, peasecod-bellied doublets, and abbreviated bombasted trunk hose (**31**). Ladies took to the long-busked corset, the waist bolster (called a bum roll) and, later, to the French farthingale, a style which persisted until

55   The falconer, 1575. A gentleman's dress but a simpler version than that worn by the aristocracy. Fitted jerkin in Spanish fashion with high neckline and small ruff. Padded rolls at shoulders. Doublet beneath. Full padded trunk hose over loose upper stocks and fitted netherstocks. Slashed shoes. Tall hat and plume. Engraving from *The Book of Falconrie* by George Turberville, British Museum, London. English.

almost 1620. Unlike the French, the English often wore a drum ruffle decorating the top of this type of farthingale. An especially English characteristic was the décolleté feminine neckline worn with *collet monté* and, behind the head, the two wings, wire and pearl-edged, with a long transparent veil which hung down to the ground at the back (**32**).

England imported her costly fabrics but was renowned for the quality of her own woollen cloth which was the staple material for the use of the bulk of the population. The country was self-sufficient in this from the flocks of sheep pastured and by means of the natural textile processes. Quantities of this cloth were exported all over Europe and amply paid for the importation of the luxury silks and velvets.

The clothes of children were still based upon those of their parents, boys being breeched at about five years and girls being put into restrictive corseting and farthingales at puberty (**48–52**). Clothes for most people changed little. Colours were subdued, wool was used for most garments with linen or cambric for aprons, shirts, collars and small ruffs and caps. The type of garments, though not their materials, complexity of cut or ornamentation, was fundamentally the same as those for the upper classes (**54–55**).

56   Velvet brocade chopine. Spanish. Barcelona Museum.

57   Ladies' figured velvet shoe, German, 1592. Bayerische Nationalmuseum, Munich.

58   White leather glove with green velvet cuff and silver fringe. German. Dresden State Museum, *c.* 1607.

59   Leather chopine decorated with lace and fringe. German. Dresden State Museum, *c.* 1610.

60   Man's shoe, Bally Shoe Museum, Switzerland.

61   Leather shoe with ribbon rosette, English, *c.* 1615.

CHAPTER THREE

1620–1660

Elegance and Naturalism

The dress of this period contrasted markedly with that of the sixteenth century. After 1620, as the power and influence of Spain waned, Spanish fashions disappeared from the European scene. With their passing vanished the rigid confinement of whalebone and bombast, the heavily be-jewelled embroideries and the starched, supported ruffs.

Under the new influence of Holland, a more comfortable relaxed style of clothing was adopted. Even the aristocracy rejoiced in this freedom, their status being marked by the beauty of the fabrics which they wore – silks, satins, velvets – the quality of these now more in evidence as the ornamentation became largely confined to sleeves and borders. Such fabrics were dyed in rich, bright colours, these not obscured but set off to advantage by the fashionable decorative medium which was lace. The characteristically Dutch line was closely adhered to in Protestant countries, notably northern Germany, Poland and Scandinavia. A slenderer, more elegant version was adopted in England and France while in the regions of southern Germany, Switzerland and Austria a fuller, more robust and baroque guise was preferred.

Only in Spain were the new forms not taken up. Here, the hierarchic dress of the court became still more extreme and this had a widespread influence upon Spanish fashionable dress. Women adopted even larger farthingales and the rigid corsetry dictated the entire silhouette. Men also retained their corseted, skirted doublets and bombasted trunk hose, preferring the ruff to the lace collar. Spanish fashions entered the doldrums, lagging far behind the new modes of western Europe.

The essence of the fashionable dress of these years was summed up aptly by Francis Kelly and Randolph Schwabe in their book *Historic Costume 1490–1790*, first published in 1925 by Batsford. They described this (particularly the male attire) as the time of 'Long locks, lace and leather'. This referred to the masculine coiffure of long, flowing hair, the exquisite lace collars covering the shoulders and the open-topped boots made from beautifully soft Spanish leather, displaying the lace-edged boot hose frothing over the edge of the bucket tops.

Textiles

Woollen cloth was the fabric worn by the mass of the population; this was made up for use either in the home or by the cottage industry. England and Holland produced immense quantities of such cloth and, due to maritime supremacy, exported it widely. Traditionally, since the Middle Ages, pure wool of high quality had been manufactured as broadcloth, so-called in order to distinguish it from single widths or 'streits' of one yard wide. Broadcloth was generally plain in colour and weave and used especially for men's clothing.

Silk remained the fabric of the wealthy, Italy and Spain being the main sources for this. By 1640 cotton was being imported into Europe from India by way of Asia Minor. These cottons were painted, not printed, and became very popular. Being an imported

62 Huygens wears a doublet, cloak and breeches of purplebrown broadcloth with gilt frogged decoration. His hat is black, he wears a white falling ruff. The costume is completed by light brown gloves, white hose and light fawn boots. The clerk's costume is in greyish purple with crimson sleeves, lining to cloak and shoe ties. He wears a lace-edged collar and cuffs, grey hat and black shoes. Painting by Thomas de Keyser of Constantijn Huygens and his clerk, National Gallery, London, 1627.

63 The woman wears a plain white ruff and lace-edged cuffs. Her cap is brown with white lace edge. Her dress is black with crimson sleeves, the skirt is brown and the apron white. The man wears a peacock blue doublet, slashed to show the white shirt. He wears a white scarf and cuffs. His breeches are grey, stockings white and shoes brown. His fawn hat has a dark green plume. Painting by Willem Duyster, National Gallery, London, 1625–30.

material, supplies were limited and the cost high so such cottons acquired a scarcity value and, in consequence, became an 'in' mode with the upper classes. An inverted snobbery made these cottons more prized than silk and elegant society used them especially to be made up into dressing gowns which became known as indiennes.

The most fashionable material of the time was lace. The industry flourished in Europe from the sixteenth century to about 1800, the best work being done in the seventeenth century. Lace-making developed in Italy rather earlier where both needle and bobbin lace were being made from the later fifteenth century, first as an edging for caps and collars, then as reticella to decorated suits of ruffs. By the later sixteenth century lace was being made here as a fabric, not just a trimming.

One of the most important lace-making centres was Venice, where the most beautiful laces ever made were produced – *gros point de Venise, point de Venise à brides picoteés* and *point de Venise à réseau.* Other centres in Italy making fine lace included Milan, Naples, Rome, Florence and Genoa (**67**).

The seventeenth century was the age of lace in costume. The falling bands (collars), sleeve cuffs, ruffles, lace overlay and decoration for gowns all displayed to perfection the baroque floral all-over designs with free-flowing arabesques and bold outlines so characteristic of Italian lace, especially in Venice. From Italy knowledge of the craft of lace-making spread westwards, notably to Flanders and to France. In England lace-making was established in the late sixteenth century by refugees from Flanders who set up their craft in Devonshire in the Honiton area.

RAPHAEL FRESCO, ROME, 1511-1514
1   Doublets with full sleeves and panelled skirts.
White shirts. Hose, leather shoes. The Swiss Guards.
Detail from 'Mass of Bolsena'. Vatican Stanza
dell'Eliodoro, Rome.

3   Cream satin chamarre, doublet and jerkin, embroidered in gold and with black and gold stripes. White shirt edged with black at neckline and wrist ruffles. Black velvet jewelled hat with white plume. After painting of King Francis I attributed to François Clouet, c.1525, Louvre, Paris.

2   Silk doublet, jerkin and skirt, jewelled and gold embroidered. Velvet, gold embroidered chamarre with fur collar and lining. Silk stockings, velvet shoes. Jewelled velvet hat with ostrich plume. After portrait of King Henry VIII by Hans Eworth (after Holbein), c.1539. Chatsworth Collection.

4   Red velvet gown with jewelled, embroidered neckline and skirt edge. Lining of gold and red seen in turned back sleeves. Undersleeves and underskirt of grey brocade. Gable hood of black velvet, one half pinned up. Gold lappets. After painting of Jane Seymour by Holbein, c.1536–7, Kunsthistorisches Museum, Vienna.

5   Embroidered silk jerkin, slashed and with shoulder picadils, worn over a velvet doublet visible on the sleeves. Suit of ruffs. Jewelled collar and pendant. Trunk hose with embroidered panes. Cloth cape, silk lining. Velvet hat with ostrich plumes and jewelled band. After a portrait in England dated *c.*1567.

6   Small boy aged about three years dressed in a full skirt with petticoats beneath. Apron. Suit of ruffs. Shoes, *c.*1605. After a painting in Czechoslavakia.

7   An embroidered and jewelled dress worn over an undergown and petticoats. Picadils at the shoulders. Suit of lace-edged ruffs. Jewelled cap. Little girl about six years old painted in a family group and wearing a dress almost identical to that of her mother. The portrait is of a Czech noble family c.1570.

8   Velvet gown lined with satin worn over a Spanish farthingale. Heavy jewelled girdle. Centre front of dress fastened, Moorish-style, by gold and pearl clasps. Undergown (seen on the sleeves) white satin with gold banding. Suit of ruffs. Gold, jewelled caul. After a portrait of Queen Isabella of Valois, Prado, Madrid, Spain.

9   Elegantly waisted patterned doublet with basques and picadils. Full embroidered slops. Silk hose with embroidered clocks and black knee sashes. Embroidered shoes with heels and instep rosettes. Lace-edged whisk style of collar and cuffs. Gloves with gauntlets to match. Portrait of Richard Sackville, 3rd Earl of Dorset by William Larkin. The Suffolk Collection, Ranger's House, Blackheath.

10   Doublet and breeches with braid and button trimming. Lace-edged falling band and cuffs. Braided cloak. Hat with ostrich plumes. Bucket top boots with lace-trimmed boot hose. Cavalier dress in France. Engraving by Abraham Bosse.

11   Gold braided jacket and breeches. Lace-edged falling band. Gloves. Boots and lace-trimmed boot hose. Portrait by Van Dyck, Koninkijk Museum, Amsterdam.

13 Doublet with slashed, braid and points decoration, with waist tassets. Breeches to match. Lace falling band. Leather gloves and boots. King Charles I from portrait by Daniel Mytens, 1631, National Portrait Gallery, London.

12 Queen Henrietta Maria. Satin gown, lace falling band and cuffs. Portrait after Van Dyck c.1632–5, National Portrait Gallery, London. Baby in swaddling clothes with long red gown on top and bib and cap. From painting of the family of Sir Richard Saltenstall by David des Granges c.1640, Tate Gallery, London.

14   The couple are wearing clothes made from
home-produced wool and linen in 'sadd' colours.
The man has chamoised leather doublet and breeches
and on top a wool mandilion. His Puritan-style hat is
of beaver with a metal buckle. Both have plain linen
falling bands with cuffs to match. Both wear leather
shoes. The lady wears a hood over a linen cap. From a
number of contemporary prints in America.

65 Of the four children, the child standing on the left is dressed entirely in white. The eldest daughter (standing at the rear) wears a dress of gold with white lace collar, white undersleeves and white apron. Ribbon bows are blue and she wears flowers in her hair. The baby, in a walking cage, is all in white. Her sister (on the right), aged about five years, wears a blue gown with white apron and sleeves and white lace collar. She has flowers and lace in her hair. A family portrait by Coques, National Gallery, London, c. 1655–60.

64 De Vos is dressed all in black except for a white lace-edged collar. His wife wears a gown of black with black and brown striped sleeves. Her ruff is plain white, her cuffs white lace and her stomacher ivory satin with a floral pattern in gold and red. Her underskirt is in brown and gold. The child standing wears a white cap and lace-edged collar and cuffs. The dress is of white self-coloured pattern and there is a grey-green apron and cross-over on the bodice. The underskirt is light brown and the shoes are brown. The child seated on the chair has a white cap, ruff and cuffs. The dress is black with gold stripes. A double bead necklace in red is fastened round the chest. The underskirt is gold and brown, the shoes fawn with red ties. A portrait by Cornelis de Vos of himself and his family, Musées Royaux des Beaux Arts, Brussels, 1621.

Costume Plates and Drawings

We are fortunate to possess, from these years, valuable documentation of the dress worn by all sections of society depicted in engravings made by a number of talented artists from several European countries. Earlier examples, showing especially regional and national dress, were drawn by such artists as Albrecht Dürer (as early as 1494) and, from about 1610, Giacomo Franco. The most important costume plate engravings of the years covered by this chapter are by the French etcher and engraver Abraham Bosse (1602–76) and the Bohemian artist Václav (Wenceslaus) Hollar (1607–77). Bosse taught at the Royal Academy of Painting and Sculpture in Paris. In his engravings his style was inspired by the work of his predecessor Jacques Callot. Some 1400 plates by Bosse provide a detailed record of French society of his day, with particular emphasis on the upper middle class, the plates depicting dress, furniture, domestic interiors and pastimes (plate 10, 70, 80).

Hollar was born in Prague. He fled from the city, where he was practising law, because of the Thirty Years' War and worked as an engraver in Frankfurt, Strasbourg and

Cologne before going to Antwerp, where he spent many years. He then came to England and, from 1640, made many plates illustrating individual costumes and details of accessories as well as figures set against a background of famous and typical London scenes of the time (**76, 77**).

Men's Dress

For some time the doublet continued to be the chief body garment. It was less tight-fitting than before and gradually became high-waisted. It was still buttoned down the centre front where it was pointed at the waist then was finished in very large tassets all round, forming a kind of skirt. Decoration at the waist seam was by ribbon points. Ornamental slashing continued to be fashionable on the torso and sleeves as did the wings at the shoulder. The Spanish-style trunk hose had been replaced by loose knee breeches which were fastened there by ribbon loops or a sash tie (plate 10, **62, 63, 68, 70, 72, 73,** plate 14, plate 16).

About 1635 the doublet slowly evolved into a hip-length jacket, still fastened centre front but generally worn open at the lower part, displaying the white shirt beneath. At this time also sleeves became very full, often one long vertical slash replacing the numerous ones. Such a slash might be repeated on the outer side seams of the breeches and, in both cases, buttons and buttonholes extended the full length of the slash; these might be partially or completely fastened (plate 11, **69, 70, 75**).

Linen and neckwear was of fine quality during the seventeenth century and was an important feature of the costume. The ruff and stiffened collar had been replaced first, in the 1620s, by a falling ruff – that is, one unstarched and so descending softly on to the shoulders (**62, 72**) – and secondly, in the 1630s, by the characteristic neckwear of the years until 1645–50, the falling band. This was an elegant white linen or lawn collar, lace-edged or made almost entirely of lace, fastened in front at the throat by tasselled

66 Portrait of a young man in a plumed hat and collared cloak. Pen and ink drawing by Rembrandt, Victoria and Albert Museum, London.

67 Panel of Milanese bobbin lace, seventeenth century. Victoria and Albert Museum, London.

band strings and covering the shoulders all round the body on top of the doublet or jacket. Long, elegant cuffs matched this collar (plate 10, plate 11, **68, 69, 70,** plate 13, plate 14, **74, 75, 79, 80**). Towards 1650 the falling band was gradually ousted from fashion by a cravat which, at this time, was simply a length of white linen or lawn, lace-trimmed, folded and tied loosely round the throat, the ends hanging down in front. The name comes from the Croatian word *crabate* and the fashion from Croat soldiers, who were serving at that time with the French army and who, for protection, wore scarves tied round their throats.

The Spanish cloak remained fashionable outer wear. It was now full and long and was very decorative, being lined with a different colour and material and ornamented with braid. It was draped round the body in a variety of ways (plate 10, **62**, **66**, **69**, **70**, **73**, **75**).

As the 1620s moved into the 1630s, men grew their hair longer and longer. It was generally natural hair, not a wig, and was curled softly to lie on the shoulders and fall down the back. Often one part was grown still longer, the end tied in a ribbon bow and dressed carefully to hang forward on to the chest: this was known as a love-lock. Upturned moustaches and small pointed beards were fashionable. These were widely known as Van Dyck beards after the painter who depicted so many of his sitters in this style. The fashionable hat had a round crown and a wide, curling brim and was decorated by sweeping ostrich plumes dyed in various colours (plate 10, **66**, **69**, **70**, plate 13, **79**, **80**).

This swashbuckling attire, characteristic in England of Cavalier dress and illustrated so graphically in Frans Hals' famous painting *The Laughing Cavalier*, was completed by the soft leather boots, the best leather coming from Russia, Hungary and Spain. These boots were neat and fitting over the foot and at the ankle but were high with a funnel top which covered the knee for riding. For town wear this funnel was turned down so giving the open bucket-top so typical of the time. The weight of this top caused the boot to sag in folds lower down. The boots had heels of medium height and, often, a platform sole connecting the heel and boot sole. On top of the boot was a leather flap called a *surpied* which was cut into four sections and was known as a butterfly flap. It and the spur were held in place by a leather strap fastened under the boot. Boots were especially fashionable between 1625 and 1650 (plate 10, **62**, **68**, **69**, **70**, **72**, plate 13, **83**, **87**). Shoes were generally of leather. They were of similar shape to

68 Pale blue doublet and breeches. Grey gloves. White leather boots and white lace boot hose. White lace-edged falling band. Portrait of the Duke of Lorraine, Museum Reims, France, *c.* 1630.

69 The man wears jacket and breeches with cloak over one arm. He has bucket-top leather boots and lace-edged boot hose. His long hair falls on to his lace-edged falling band. His hat is decorated by an ostrich plume. The lady wears a décolleté falling band and has pearls in her hair. Engraving, Gallery of the Palais Royale, Paris, by Abraham Bosse, 1637.

the boot, being narrow with tapering square-ended toes. Red heels were fashionable for important occasions. On the instep was a high tongue and a ribbon sash tie (**62**, **63**, **71**, **73**, plate 14, plate 15, **75**, **76**, **91**, **92**).

An important costume accessory was a pair of gloves. Often in gauntlet style, these were, like the boots, made from fine, soft leather. They were embroidered and fringed and, often, perfumed (plate 11, **68**, **72**, **73**, plate 13, **77**, **85**, **86**).

70 **French Elegance at the Ball, c. 1635.** Men in braided doublets and hose, long hair, large hats with sweeping plumes and cloaks. Ladies wear high-waisted gowns, open in front to show underskirts and with décolleté necklines and puffed and slashed sleeves. Engraving by Abraham Bosse, Victoria and Albert Museum.

Women's Dress

This underwent a similar transformation to men's fashions though feminine attire was more low key throughout the seventeenth century with man essentially the peacock of the sexes. The rigid corseted appearance of women's dress disappeared. The fabrics were plain or lightly figured. They were still heavy and rich but decoration was at a minimum. The silhouette which emerged by 1630 was more natural and comfortable. As with the masculine doublet, the waistline was high and often finished with tassels. The waist was almost unconstricted, only bones inserted into the bodice seams attempted to control this and to raise the breasts to a high level. This bodice was formed into a shaped plastron which dipped in front to a rounded end which extended down over the skirt. Sleeves were

full, padded and slashed and ended in lace-edged cuffs. The neckline was décolleté and, either finished with a lace-edged standing collar which framed the head, or a lace-trimmed falling band (**65, 69, 70, 71, plate 12, 82**).

The skirt was full and long but had no framework beneath. Generally three skirts were worn. The outer one, called in French *la modeste*, was either open in front from waist to hem or was held up to display the underskirt, termed in French *la friponne* or hussy, minx. The inner skirt, which was not displayed, was called *la secrète*. Underwear changed little over the centuries. It consisted of a full, long chemise tucked into drawers which were held up by a waist drawstring. Stockings were fastened to the lower edge of these (**69, 70, plate 12, 77**).

The feminine coiffure of this period was

71   The Capitol Rome, Italian Dress, 1625–70.
A   Dark doublet and breeches. Black hat and shoes. Portrait of a boy by Carlo Ceresa, 1633, Museo Civici, Milan.
B, C, D, E   The Duchess (B) wears an ornately jewelled embroidered gown over a farthingale. It is dark with light-coloured pattern. The undergown, visible at sleeves, stomacher and underskirt, is of a light-coloured material with a zig-zag design. She has a lace, wired collar, and cuffs, a pearl rope necklace and bracelets and pearls in her hair. She holds a fan. The little boy (C) wears a dark doublet and embroidered light trunk hose. He has a lace-edged collar and cuffs. The daughter (D) wears a gown over a farthingale. The gown has hanging sleeves and is decorated in a sprig design. She has a lace falling band. The Duke (E) is dressed in black apart from a white lace collar, cuffs and knee sashes. Gold decorates the sleeves which are slashed to show the white shirt. The Duke and Duchess of Forano with their two children, 1626, Florentine School of Painting, Strozzi Palace, Florence.
F   Dark coloured gown with all sprig floral pattern. White lace collar and wrist ruffles. Gold necklace, jewelled brooch and hair band. Portrait of Lucia Valcarenghi by an unknown artist, 1670, Palazzo Marino, Milan.
G   Gown decorated in gold with white lace collar. White sleeves. Pearl necklace. Hair ribbon. Portrait of the young daughter of Vittorio Amedeo by an unknown artist, 1640–50, Galleria Sabauda, Turin.
H   Chocolate brown satin gown with gold edging. White collar and sleeves. Underskirt of pale blue satin with black lace appliqué decoration. Gold embroidered shoes. Portrait by Giovanni Bernardo Carbone, 1660, Palazzo Bianco, Genoa.

distinctive. In the 1620s and 1630s the hair was dressed flat on top with a short curly fringe on the forehead. The sides were then fluffed and crimped out in puffs over the ears. The long back hair was twisted into a knot worn high on the crown. By about 1637–8 the side hair was dressed in ringlets and, as time passed, these became longer and were eventually wired to stand out from the cheeks.

Decoration of the coiffure was simple, usually limited to large pearls, pearl ropes and ribbon bows. Out-of-doors scarves or hoods were worn as were, often, face masks to protect the complexion from the cold or rain. Sometimes the hood was attached to a cloak which was the usual exterior outer wear (**65, 69, 70, 71, plate 12, 81, 82**).

Ladies wore elbow-length gloves of kid or

72 Silver-grey doublet and breeches. Slashed on chest and upper sleeve to show white shirt. Tassets. Points at waist. Soft buff leather boots with lace-edged boot hose. Falling ruff. Hat with feather. Based on portrait of the Duke of Hamilton by Daniel Mytens, 1629.

73 He wears a brown doublet and breeches ornamented all over in silver. His cloak is darker, also silver embroidered. The sleeves are white and silver. At the neck he wears a valona over a golilla. His stockings are white, shoes plain black, gloves brown. Portrait of King Philip IV by Diego Velasquez, 1626–30, National Gallery, London.

until about 1645, then influenced by England and France. Some specific differences were evinced in certain countries within these mainstream fashions.

The Dutch, for instance, clung to the type of neckwear which had characterized their dress since the 1580s and continued to wear the enormously wide white ruffs. These were plain, quite undecorated, and were goffered in narrow gauge but were of such a large diameter that they swayed and dipped over the shoulders (63, 64). Such ruffs were more typical of feminine dress than masculine and women were also noted for the infinite variety of caps – plain or ornamented – which they wore. Sometimes more than one was worn, one on top of the others, each set further back on the head than the others. After 1630 both men and women wore falling ruffs for some time before they adopted the generally fashionable falling band. In men's dress, a military-style deep sash was often bound round the waist on top of the hip-length jacket; it was then tied in a bunch at the side or back and the fringed ends hung down to knee or ankle level. Paintings by Frans Hals or Rembrandt, in particular, show this style. In ladies' gowns the classic mode had a jacket form of bodice which was open in front, displaying the decorative stomacher which had been in fashion since 1600 (64, 65, 70).

English dress also followed mainstream fashions but the struggle between monarchy and parliament, which culminated in the Civil War and the execution of Charles I, created two modes of attire. Both were based upon the current trends but one was plainer than the other. Sometimes this difference is defined in too simplistic a manner, indicating that royalists wore a richly elegant form of dress with a wealth of lace and ribbons, enormous bucket-top boots and long, curling locks, whilst Puritans eschewed all decoration and cut their hair as if in the penitentiary. Human beings do not act as predictably as that. Many parliamentarians dressed elegantly also, a number of royalists wore plainer clothes, at least, for much of the time. In general, the 'Cavalier' style, as depicted by the court

silk. They carried be-ribboned long canes and/or parasols and lace-edged handkerchiefs. Ladies liked to have a posy of flowers on them. To keep these fresh they were inserted in a tiny bottle filled with water. This was secreted away into a tiny pocket sewn into the front of the gown neckline. Jewellery of many types was worn but its use was restrained in these years in great contrast to those of the later sixteenth century.

Regional and National Variations

The descriptions given for men's and women's dress of the years 1620–60 represent the mainstream pattern, set largely by Holland

painter Sir Anthony Van Dyck, was paramount in the years up to 1645. During the Protectorate (1649–60), the Puritan influence on dress became more extensive and the clothes of many Englishmen in these years were less ornamented than those worn in France, for example, but the excessively plain attire, which was inspired by the normal middle class version of the fashions of the day, was only adopted by Puritans of extreme views. In this men wore their hair short and uncurled, a tall black hard hat on top, collars and cuffs of plain untrimmed white linen; there was no lace or ribbon in the costume. Fabrics were of linen and wool. Colours were sombre: black, mauve, grey, brown. Ladies wore the Puritan hat also, in this case over a white cap which matched their long, white aprons (plate 11, 72, plate 14, 74, 75).

In the 1620s and early 1630s fashions were slower to change in Germany, Austria, Switzerland and Scandinavia and there was a tendency to retain the doublet, with deep tassets and the fuller knee breeches (*pluderhosen*). Men kept to tall-crowned, narrow-brimmed hats and to shoes with ribbon rosettes on the insteps longer than elsewhere while women retained the farthingale, hip bolster and deep corset well into the 1630s, these accompanied by a wired, lace-edged collar with cap to match.

In the Iberian peninsula time seemed to stand still until nearly 1650. Men continued to wear trunk hose, corseted, bombasted doublets, short capes and ruffs though, in 1623, Philip IV ordered the ruffs to be abandoned in favour of the simple white starched collar called a *valona*. This was open in front but at the sides and back was supported upon a card or stiffened material under-collar which was faced with silk; this was the *golilla* (73). The Spanish version was small and quite plain. When other nations had worn such an upstanding collar, it had been fashionable earlier, was larger and had been decoratively embroidered and trimmed with lace. Such a collar, worn chiefly *c.* 1600–20, was known in England as a whisk and in France as a *col rotonde* (71). In Spain

74 Based on plainer version of painting by John Tradescant of his wife, 1645, Ashmolean Museum, Oxford, together with several contemporary engravings.

75 Based on a number of engravings of the period.

the valona style lasted until *c.* 1650 and the falling band was rarely to be seen. Trunk hose were replaced by knee breeches in the 1630s. Women retained their farthingales and stiff corsetry (71) though they replaced the ruff with a collar and lower neckline later. They continued to adopt a costume richly decorated all over with jewelled embroideries. The last phase of the farthingale evolved in the 1640s. This was very wide at the sides and flatter at front and back but farthingales of immense size continued to be *de rigueur* for court dress, even for children, until nearly 1660.

Colonial North America

During the seventeenth century north America was colonized from northern and western Europe. The dress worn by the people of each area reflected that of their country of origin but it was also influenced by the climate of that part of the New World to which they had come. For instance, the Spaniards, who were the earliest settlers, came to Florida in 1565.

76 Warm gown worn over petticoat and hip pads. Plain square folded neckwear and lace-edged cap under hood. Wooden soled pattens attached to an iron ring worn on top of shoes and attached by a leather strap. These were worn to keep the shoes out of the filth of the streets. Servant's dress, 1640. Engraving by Wenceslans Hollar. Batsford Collection.

77 A more up-to-date fashionable attire evidenced in the lace-collared décolleté neckline, the three-quarter sleeves, gloves, feather fan and skirt drawn back to show the underskirt but a large lace-edged ruff shows, at this date, a deep-rooted conservatism. The hat is worn over a simple, unfashionable coiffure. Mayor of London's wife 1649. Engraving by Wenceslans Hollar. Batsford Collection.

From the beginning English settlers set great store by preserving existing class distinctions. To maintain such differentials, numerous sumptuary laws were passed in many areas, displaying dependence upon this type of restriction which, in Europe, had largely been abandoned by this time because the method had so signally failed to achieve the desired ends. In America the men and women of wealth whose breeding and education had marked them in Europe for positions of importance, expected to maintain this status even more carefully in order to set a standard for future generations to follow. It was firmly believed that everyone should dress according to his station and that to be attired correctly in the latest fashion was setting an example which would uphold the standards of the community. Protocol in dress was a visible expression of the determination of these early communities to maintain the highest standards of behaviour and culture.

The early years were hard. Apart from the minority of colonists who were well-to-do, people made their own clothes. They cultivated flax and cotton and, in a few selected regions, silk. They raised sheep for wool and learned, mainly from the Indians, how to dress and tan skins; because of this, they often adopted the chamoising method, using oil, as the Indians did, to produce the characteristically soft leather suited for garments. Everyday clothes were plain simple versions of the fashions back home. Best clothes were kept for Sundays and holidays. They lasted, so styles changed only slowly.

Virginia, named for Queen Elizabeth I after its discovery in the sixteenth century, was the first English settlement in north America; Jamestown was built as a fortified village in 1607 by the first colonists. By the 1620s women and children joined their menfolk and communities were established. The cultivation of tobacco had been introduced in 1612 and a flourishing industry was built up here, in Delaware and the Carolinas, by means of the labour of thousands of negro slaves. Many of the early English planters were Cavaliers of substance, their numbers reinforced after the

Here, as in their later settlements in Texas and California, the climate was not dissimilar to that of Spain so they were able to continue to wear the same type of clothing. Spanish sixteenth century policy did not intend to make their colonies self-supporting and it was envisaged that the needs of the colonists should be met from the mother country so not encouraging integration. Further north, in New England, it was quite different. Here, the winters were harsh so that, while styles of clothes worn were similar to those of northern Europe, a far greater use was made of furs, hides and skins.

execution of Charles I. These men and their families sent to England for their fashionable clothes and, in years of good crop yield, would spend lavishly on their London charge accounts. Tobacco was of such vital importance to the community that it became a currency and prices for garments and fabrics were quoted in pounds of tobacco. Clothes for children and servants were made in America from imported materials but the planter and his wife wore English manufactured garments.

Soon after the building of Jamestown, the English were settling in New England where they went on to found colonies in Massachusetts, Connecticut, Rhode Island, New Hampshire and Maine. The first settlement was just south of Boston, landfall of the small ship *Mayflower* which carried the first separatists, the Pilgrim Fathers, who nostalgically named their settlement Plymouth after their Devon port of embarkation. These pilgrims suffered great hardship in a rigorous climate very different from that of Virginia where they had expected to land. Also they were chiefly artisans, ordinary men and women who had few possessions or substance and the land too was poor.

The next wave of settlers, the Puritans of the Massachusetts Bay Company, derived from people of higher social class. Many were wealthy professional men and women and landed gentry. They settled in Salem and, later, in Boston and others followed to move further afield so that, by the 1630s, settlements were well established. Most were of Puritan faith and believed in dressing in a sober, dignified manner but those of greater wealth tended to follow more closely the fashions of the English royalists, wearing rich fabrics, only limiting excessive ornamentation and maintaining a restrained colour scheme. The Plymouth settlers abstained from the use of richer fabrics and could not afford to import clothes from England.

In the early years people needed warm, durable clothing; most garments were made from leather, linen and wool, suited to an open air life of hard labour. Styles were simplified versions of those worn at home (plate 14). As time passed and industries were established and harvests were good, a higher standard of comfort and prosperity was enjoyed by most settlers. By the 1650s more people were sending to England for their clothes or for rich fabrics from which to make them. A greater differential then became apparent as those less successful continued to make their own garments from home-produced furs and skins, wools and linen.

A different type of sumptuary law then began to be passed. These were not so much

78 Quaker style black hat, 1650. From engravings of Quaker dress.

79 Natural hair with love-lock. Lace-edged falling band. Portrait of King Wladyslawa IV, Polish, Narodowe Museum, Cracow, *c.* 1640.

80 Large, wide-brimmed beaver hat trimmed with ostrich plumes of different colours. Lace-edged falling band. Engraving of French dress by Abraham Bosse, 1637, Bibliothèque Nationale, Paris.

81 Dark green silk hood, black silk mask. From portrait *c.* 1644.

82 Black gown embroidered in red and silver. White lace-edged collar. Pearl decorated cap. Portrait of an unknown lady, 1630. Bayerische Nationalmuseum, Munich.

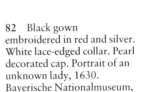

83 Brown leather boots with gold edging and lace-edged boot hose. From painting by Bartholomeus van der Helst, 1649–50, Rijksmuseum, Amsterdam.

86 Yellow leather glove with red and silver ribbons. Cuff of blue and silver brocade. Dresden State Museum.

90 Enamelled silver perfume case. Victoria and Albert Museum, London.

84 Gold enamelled in green and white set with diamonds and pearl. Miniature inside. Pendant, seventeenth century, English.

88 Gold locket with portrait inside. Enamelled and jewelled decoration. British Museum, London.

91 English embroidered silk shoe with rosette, 1624.

85 Leather gauntlet with scaled cuffs, seventeenth century, German.

87 Buff leather boot c. 1655. From Danish portrait.

89 White leather chopine. Victoria and Albert Museum, London.

92 Spanish shoe with ribbon tie. Rocamora Costume Museum, Barcelona.

laws to maintain the social differential as to restrain excessive richness in dress for both economic and spiritual reasons. It was an attempt to curb extravagance and limit spending on foreign imports to a certain proportion of income. But the result was very much a case of one law for the rich and one for the poor; the wealthier classes found little difficulty in obtaining velvet and lace, silk, ribbons and embroidered fabrics.

Many Puritans believed sincerely in the rightness of adopting a plainer mode of dress and Church ministers encouraged their flocks to eschew lace and embroideries, long hair and ribbons. The so-called 'sadd' colours were recommended. These were of quieter, softer shades such as greys, greens and browns. Brighter touches were reserved for linings or hoods. A characteristic masculine garment, which had been adopted by the Puritans in England, and was brought to the New World, was the mandilion. This was derived originally from a tabard-like loose overgarment worn by the ordinary man of the later Middle Ages. It became a fashionable garment in the later sixteenth century. The colonists' mandilion was a hip-length loose overgarment, its sleeves hanging loose. It was generally lined with cotton (plate 14).

Clothes for Ordinary People

Fabrics plus all the trimmings and fastenings had long been purchased at fairs and markets or from travelling pedlars and salesmen. As population centres in towns became larger, shops began to appear, most of them displaying their wares in the shop front open to the street. Considerable variety was available in home manufactured cloth. In England, not only the fine broadcloth was being made but cheaper, coarser wools such as baize and frieze or kersey, which was made in ribbed narrow widths suitable for stockings. Mixtures too could be purchased, for example, linsey-woolsey made from wool and linen; this was later made in the American colonies of wool weft on a cotton warp. Garments could be made up at home or the local tailor could be employed. His charges were not too high and he was certainly used by the middle classes (76).

CHAPTER FOUR

1660–1715

Baroque Richness

The *Grand Règne* of Louis XIV of France lasted from 1643 to 1715. During this time the king established France as a great European power and, from about 1660, France became the arbiter of European fashion, a position which remained un-challenged – apart from the last 30 years of the eighteenth century – for nearly three hundred years. The mode was set in Paris and the rest of Europe followed suit, basing its designs upon fashion dolls sent out each month from the French capital. These life-size mannequin dolls were despatched to the capitals of Europe as well as to America. They acted as ambassadors of French fashion, replaced only by the later establishment of the fashion journal.

In addition to the dolls, information about Parisian modes was further disseminated by the work of artists – chiefly French – who followed Hollar's tradition of engraving costume plates. These plates, unlike the later fashion plates which illustrated a design for a new fashion, depicted styles which were actually being worn by those who were lead-ing the mode of the time. Hollar himself had returned to England at the Restoration and was working excessively long hours in London. He produced 2740 plates over a period of time, timing his work by an hour glass on his desk and charging 4d per hour: he died in poverty there in 1677. Artists of note working in this field from about 1678 included Jean Dieu de Saint Jean, N. Bonnart, Antoine Trouvain and Nicholas Arnoult. In some plates, actual pieces of fabric were glued to the engraving as a type of collage.

Men's Dress

There were two distinct styles in these years. The first was a continuation and elaboration of those current in 1660 then, from 1665–70 onwards, this was superseded by a completely new mode, that of coat, breeches and waist-coat which, later in the eighteenth century, became established as a man's three-piece suit, the basic attire until modern times.

The years from the start of Louis XIV's reign in 1643 until the changes of *c.* 1670, were those of transition, representing the final phase of the type of garments worn since the 1530s. They comprised a doublet or jacket, trunk hose or knee breeches and a cloak. The mid-seventeenth century version of these was, however, so blurred by the excessive decorative use of ribbon and lace as to be barely recognizable as the last phase of the styling of these garments. It was, essentially, a period of elaboration and apparent effemi-nacy. Ribbon, as we now know it, with a selvedge edge on each side, was, in the 1640s, a novelty. Soon it was being used all over the costume, in bows, rosettes, loops and streamers. The attire of the 1660s had become a riot of ribbon decoration.

This type of costume ornamentation had come about despite and, to a certain extent, in response to, the flood of sumptuary decrees which had been promulgated by succeeding administrations in an attempt to curtail the extravagant use of foreign imported fabrics and decoration. It was a basic tradition in France, in all fields of production, to ensure that the indigenous products did not suffer from competition from abroad. A country which possessed most of the necessary raw materials, an equable climate, a fertile soil, a talented people and a population of a size suited to the available land had always succeeded in this object and there was no shortage of home-produced goods of high quality.

In the mid-seventeenth century Louis XIV looked with interest and with some envy at the flourishing textile industries of England and Holland. Decrees against the purchase of foreign materials had been stepped up in the 1630s. In the 1650s Cardinal Mazarin had promulgated further edicts banning the import of Venetian and Flemish lace and Italian gold and silver fabrics. It was after Mazarin's death in 1661, however, that Louis' chief minister Jean-Baptiste Colbert advised the king to adopt the classic French solution of establishing France as an equally great or greater textile source. The more widescale prohibition of importation of foreign fabrics such as lace, silks and cottons was initiated and the few materials which were permitted entry carried a heavy duty. Manufactories were set up in France based upon numbers of foreign craftsmen and these were given all the financial assistance necessary to establish them. In particular, Colbert brought in Venetian lace-makers to teach French craftsmen and so set up manufacture. The king helped to popularize the new lace made in France at his court. At first these Venetian workers set up near Alençon and there continued to make their famous *point de Venise* but, gradually, French lace was adapted to French design and influence and the name was changed to *point de France* (114).

With foreign competition stifled France quickly became a major producer, in quality and quantity, of lace, silks and other fabrics. One famous manufactory which was set up at this time was that of the Gobelins, making tapestry. From the 1660s onwards French fabrics were generally worn and the main possibilities for decoration were by yards of silk and velvet ribbon and by lace so these finally replaced the imported jewelled embroideries so fashionable in the later sixteenth century. The lace-making industry grew apace and later in the seventeenth century many centres were developed: chief of these were Le Puy, Argentan, Lille, Chantilly, Bayeux, Caen and Valenciennes.

Colbert also encouraged the textile trade with India, exporting France's goods in exchange for Indian cottons. Soon these became so popular that French weavers begged for protection and imports from India were stopped. In the 1680s, for the same reason, sales of Indian cottons made in France were also forbidden. This, together with the revocation of the Edict of Nantes, caused a flood of Huguenot French textile workers to emigrate to largely Protestant countries such as England, Holland, north Germany, Scandinavia and America. The French Protestants, known as Huguenots, had been gradually losing their religious rights over a long period during the seventeenth century but it was Louis XIV who, in 1685, revoked the Edict of Nantes which had been promulgated by Henry VI at the turn of the century to give them protection. Louis XIV's action destroyed the Huguenots as a political faction but at the cost to France of the loss of a whole generation of its best textile craftsmen and seriously set back the French industry in many textile fields.

Due to this and to the French prohibition of the making of Indian cottons, a smuggling trade arose to supply from Europe the French aristocracy with the now unobtainable, and so more desirable, cottons. For many years cotton was the chief luxury black market commodity in France, just as cognac and silks later became in England during the Napoleonic wars. The imported Indian cottons had been painted in floral designs based upon Indian and Chinese motifs. The European versions were printed cottons. Their quality was excellent and they wore well.

Typical of the transitional period of masculine attire in the years 1660–70 is the abbreviated jacket worn open and reaching barely to the waist. The full white shirt was

93 French Costume 1660–1678 (background: Château Veux-Le-Vicomte)
A Blue silk jacket and petticoat breeches decorated by gold embroidered bands. White lace cravat. Black hat with coloured plumes.
Blue stockings, light fawn shoes with red heels and white ribbon bows. White shirt. Painting by Le Brun *c.* 1660, Louvre, Paris.
B and D B is wearing a red coat with silver embroidered decoration. He has a powdered wig, white breeches with gold ribbon
sashes, white stockings and shoes with gold ribbon bows. D wears a dark cloak with gold decoration and be-ribboned petticoat
breeches. Tapestry, Versailles Palace, 1660s.
C The lady wears a red dress with gold embroidered banding. She has a gold embroidered stomacher, a white lace collar, white
sleeves and a white patterned underskirt. Painting, artist unknown, *c.* 1675. Museum, Versailles.

displayed beneath and on the sleeves which
ended in lace and silk flounces falling over the
hand. The linen, made of lawn or silk, was
finished at the neck by an elegant lace ruffle,
replacing the falling band of the 1640s' dress.
On top of the jacket either a cloak was slung
round the body or a longer short-sleeved coat
was worn (**93, 99**, plate 15).

The style of breeches, usually made of
matching colour and fabric to the jacket, was

also changing at this time. These either took
the form of full knee-length designs, fastened
there by a tie or sash, or, more often as
time passed, more fashionably what are aptly
described as 'petticoat breeches'. These were
full knee-length shorts, so full that they
resembled a kilt or full skirt reaching to the
knees. The shape was obscured to a great
extent because the garment was decorated
all over by ribbon loops and bows and lace

94 French Costume 1680–1700 (Background: The Grand Trianon, Versailles)
A Brocade justaucorps with gold frogging. White lace cravat, white shirt sleeves. Gold, decorative baldric. Black tricorne hat with gold braid. Periwig. White breeches and stockings. Black shoes. Tapestry, Palace of Versailles, late seventeenth century.
B and E B is wearing a red dress with gold all-over pattern. White lace collar and white lace sleeve ruffles. E is Louis XIV in a brown justaucorps with gold decoration and buttons. He wears a brown periwig, a white cravat with fringed ends, white shirt and gold embroidered wrist ruffles, brown stockings and black shoes with a red lining. He carries a black tricorne hat with gold braid and white ostrich frond trimming, also brown gloves. Painting, Museum, Versailles.
C Blue justaucorps with silver brocade decoration. Red hat with white plumes over periwig. White shirt sleeves and cravat. Red breeches and stockings. Black shoes. Tapestry, Palace of Versailles, 1680s.
D Fontange headdress with lace and jewels. Pearl necklace. Jewelled, brocaded stomacher. Gown with ruched, flounced and fringed decoration. Elbow-length gloves. Engraving. The Court of Louis XIV, 1690s.

ruffles. A small apron of ribbon loops covered the front closure. The Rhineland of Germany seems to have been the source of this style of breeches where they were worn and made fashionable by Rhinegrafen Karl, a count who gave his name to the style – rhinegraves or rhinegrave breeches. The mode was then taken up with enthusiasm by Louis XIV and his court. The fashion was popular there between 1652 and 1665 (**93, 99**, plate 15).

95 Dark coloured justaucorps with light satin lining. Brocade waistcoat. White shirt, wrist ruffles and lace trimmed cravat. Embroidered sword belt. Black felt, ribbon trimmed hat. Silk breeches with ribbon sashes. Silk stockings. Black leather shoes with red heels, ribbon ties. Cane. Cloak. Portrait, English, *c.* 1670.

96 Dress with ribbon bows. Embroidered white apron. White ruff. Banded cap. Portrait of Joseph von Orelli as a very young child by Conrad Meyer of Zurich. Landesmuseum Zürich. Swiss, 1657–60.

97 Dark blue dress with red cuffs. White apron, sleeve ruffles, neck frill and fontange headdress. Black fur muff. A lady from Zürich, *c.* 1700, Swiss. Engraving.

Reference was made in Chapter Three (p. 31) to the fact that Spanish fashions for the aristocracy in the seventeenth century seemed to be frozen in late sixteenth century modes and lagged far behind the rest of Europe. This phase of short jacket, petticoat breeches and beribboned costume had no counterpart in Spain. This marked difference in fashionable dress is vividly depicted for us in the Gobelins tapestry designed by Charles Le Brun and now in the National Museum of Versailles. This shows a scene in 1660 on the occasion of the marriage of Princess Maria Theresa, daughter of Philip IV of Spain, to Louis XIV of France, when the two courts met. The contrast between the beribboned, bewigged, petticoat breeched French and the corseted, sombre, farthingaled Spanish is extreme. It was after this meeting that Spanish dress gradually came into line and followed French fashions like the rest of western Europe.

Between 1665 and 1670 the coat began to be accepted as the current mode for fashion-

98 and 99 98 wears a dress with white collar and sleeve puffs. Jewelled necklace on top of collar. Jewelled cap. 99 wears a black jacket and rhinegrave breeches with ribbon decoration. White collar, shirt and stockings. Black shoes with red heels. Black hat over natural hair. Attire for both figures old-fashioned due to great distance from fashionable centres. Painting, Swedish, Nordiska Museet, Stockholm, *c.* 1665.

able dress, replacing the short jacket completely. The wearing of this coat, of eastern, notably Persian origin, was initiated in France where it was called the *justaucorps*. It was fairly long, at first reaching to hip or knee level and it was worn open, flared and loose, its front edges turned back showing the contrasting lining. Sleeves were short, ending in deep decorative cuffs. Under the *justaucorps* was worn the *veste*, a waistcoat. Similar to the coat in style, the *veste* was slightly shorter and had long narrow sleeves. Indoors it might be worn without a coat on top (**93, 95**).

As time passed the *justaucorps* settled in to become the characteristic coat of the early eighteenth century. It was knee-length, buttoned at the waist, where a sash might be worn on top. The waist was narrow and fitting and, in contrast, the skirts were full and flared out. Sleeves were long and had large,

buttoned-back cuffs. Pockets were set low on the hips on each side near to the front. The coat was generally made of a plain coloured material, decoration being confined to the length of the front edges, the cuffs and pocket flaps. This was by passementerie and/or embroidery. There was still no collar due to the heavy periwig covering the neck and shoulders. The waistcoat, in contrast, was often made from material, probably brocade, which was decorated all over, embroidered or printed. About six inches shorter than the coat, it was visible in front. Breeches were often made to match the coat. They were plain and fitting, ending at the knee with a tie or garter. The white shirt had full sleeves, gathered at the wrist and ending in ruffles which draped over the hand. The neck cravat was fringed or lace-trimmed. It had now become more sophisticated in design, being tied round the throat with a bow, its ends hanging in formal folds over the chest (**94, 100, 103, 104, 105**).

Men continued to wear their hair very long as in the first half of the century but after 1660–70 this was more often a wig rather than natural hair. In 1633 King Louis XIII had lost much of his hair due to illness and his wearing of a wig helped to popularize the fashion. Louis XIV, on the other hand, had a

100 Scarlet coat with silver braid and frogging. Brown periwig. White silk and lace cravat. White lace sleeve ruffles. Black stockings and shoes, red heels. Cane with ribbon. Spanish dress 1690–5. Painting, Prado, Madrid.

101 Bright blue gown with floral pattern in orange, red brown and black. Apron of white embroidered transparent gauze. Lace neck frill and sleeve ruffles. Hair powdered white, flower decoration. Fan. Children's dress in France, 1714–15. Portrait of Mlle de Béthisy by Alexis Belle, Palace of Versailles.

102 Gold and brown embroidered gown still worn over a farthingale. Sleeves white with red ribbons. Red and gold striped underskirt. Red ribbon and jewel in her hair, gold earrings and jewel-edged white neck band. White silk handkerchief. Spanish dress *c.* 1665. Portrait of the Duchess del Infantado by unknown artist. Hispanic Society of America, New York.

103 A couple in typical, though informal, French attire. No framework worn under the lady's skirt. A large linen and lace bonnet. Drawing by Bernard Picard, 1708. Ashmolean Museum, Oxford.

fine head of curly hair so, like other men of note in a similar position, was reluctant to take to a hat and uncomfortable wig. However, by the early 1670s, the fashion was paramount so he capitulated. From then until about 1710, the full-bottomed periwig was ubiquitous. The fine quality wig, made from human hair, was the status symbol of the well-to-do. Men who could not afford these very costly items wore wigs made from horse or goat hair or wool. In the 1670s the periwig was dressed in a similar manner to natural coiffure styles, curled and flowing on to the shoulders and down the back. By 1680 it had become very large. It was then arranged in a mass of formal curls and ringlets which rose to a peak in front on either side of a centre parting. These then cascaded down over the shoulders and, at the back, nearly reached the waist. The wig was made in natural hair colours, blond to black, according to preference. With these wig styles men were generally

cleanshaven. The French were the chief European wig makers. They imported the hair and made up the wigs in France, then exported them to other countries (**93, 94, 95, 99, 100, 103, 104, 105, 109, 111, 113**).

The style of hat in the 1660s and 1670s was round and either ostrich plume or ribbon trimmed. The crown was lower than previously. Towards the end of the century the vast periwigs made it impracticable for men to wear hats on top of them unless bad weather made it absolutely necessary. Custom, however, dictated that a hat must accompany the costume so, since the article had often to be carried under the arm, the design slowly changed. The round crown became lower still and the brim was turned back. This evolved into the tricorne or three-cornered hat which became the chief design of the eighteenth century. In English the turned-up brim was called a cock so these tricornes were referred to as cocked hats. There were many variations on the style during this long period, each being named as, for example, the Monmouth Cock of the 1680s named after the Duke of Monmouth. The tricorne was generally made of black felt, the edges decorated with gold braid or white ostrich tips. In general, the fashionable design in the years 1680–1720 was for a large hat suited to accompany the large wig (**93, 94, 95, 99, 104, 105**).

After about 1650, with the introduction of petticoat breeches, shoes returned to fashion to replace boots which would have appeared incongruous with such breeches. The ribbon rosette on the instep then became a ribbon bow and, later, a metal buckle. Styles from 1685–90 were cut high, often up to or above the ankle and toes were more pointed (**120, 121**).

Men, like women, used cosmetics heavily. Beauty spots (termed *mouches* by the French) were made of black silk. They were adhesive on one side and were cut into a variety of shapes – stars, moons, hearts etc. – and were carried on the person in tiny patch boxes, each with a tiny mirror in the lid. The spots drew attention away from the smallpox scars which marred the faces of the majority of people. Beautiful snuff boxes were also carried. These were jewelled or enamelled. Some were painted with miniature pictures. Both sexes in France took snuff and both also carried fans. Some of these were now painted with figure compositions or landscapes. Alternatively they might be made of beautiful lace. Combs were carried and spectacles were worn. The wearing of jewellery was restrained, unlike the custom of the previous century; a variety of types were worn with the costume. Men and women possessed beautiful, lace-edged handkerchiefs. Men arranged them to dangle from the coat pocket. Very fashionable was the large, be-ribboned muff, carried out-doors in winter by both sexes (**104**).

Women's Dress

In these years fashions for women took a back seat in comparison with those of their menfolk. Ladies were dressed attractively and in a feminine manner; fabrics were beautiful, heavy, yet restrained in their ornamentation. There was little of the masculine version of over be-ribboned appearance and less of ostentation. As with the masculine mode, though, the Court of Versailles was the arbiter of the European fashionable world and fundamental to this dominance was the characteristically French attitude to the relative status of women in court life. It was not the queen and the wives of court gentlemen who led the vogue but the mistresses of the king and his courtiers. The French aristocracy's view of marital fidelity was that this was in order for the bourgeoisie but not

104 Depicts a fashionable gentleman wearing a full coat with large cuffs, a waist sash and fur muff, also powdered wig and cocked hat trimmed with ostrich tips. Costume plate by J. Mariette, 1698. Private Collection.

105   English Dress 1690–1710. (Background: Library, Trinity College, Cambridge).
Men wearing coats with large, buttoned cuffs and frogged front fastenings over embroidered waistcoats and fitted breeches. Full-bottomed periwigs, tricorne hats, canes and gloves. Ladies wearing full-skirted gowns, the skirts looped back with ribbon bows displaying flounced underskirts. Low, square necklines, brocaded stomachers, elbow-length sleeves. Fontange headdresses. Dress taken from portraits of this date in the National Portrait Gallery, London.

for them. The undisputed leader of feminine fashion was the current mistress of the king and every nuance of her toilette was carefully studied and copied.

Unlike masculine fashions, changes to the feminine form came slowly, almost imperceptibly, but the trend, over decades, may be discerned. This was towards a tighter, corseted bodice, a lower waistline, décolleté neckline and a fuller, longer skirt worn over many petticoats and, eventually, some form of framework to support the weight of the fabric.

In the 1670s the gown neckline was low and cut almost straight across, slightly off the shoulder; it was generally finished by a deep band of lace. The bodice became slenderer, its form maintained by stiffening and boning in the seams. At the waist it was rounded at the back but came to a point in the centre front. It was laced up the back and, in front, opened over a central panel or stomacher of richly ornamented material. By the later seventeenth century this centre panel was fashionably ornamented by a row of ribbon bows diminishing in size from bosom towards the waist: the French aptly entitled this an *échelle*. Under the bodice it had become customary once more to wear a corset. This was cut high in front, supporting and restricting the breasts. Sleeves were at first three-quarter length but gradually shortened to finish above the elbow where they terminated in a deep cuff, decorated by a large ribbon bow. Below this fell rows of lace, lawn or silk ruffles known as *engageantes*. The long full overskirt was looped up and back on each side and fell to a train at the rear; the higher the rank of the wearer, the longer the train. The increasingly important underskirt was fashioned from a rich, heavy fabric and decorated by flouncing and ruching (**93, 94, 98**).

From about 1690 the neckline, still décolleté, changed its shape, no longer off the shoulders but round or square edged with a low frill. The corset had become tighter and longer, descending to a lower, more pointed waistline at the centre front (**116, 117**). Below

106 A gold brocade dress with sprig all-over pattern. Deep red overgown with gold braid edging. White lace sleeve ruffles, neck bows and fontange headdress with scarf. Beauty spots. Engraving 1695–1700. Princess of Bavaria.

107 Pink taffeta gown with gold stripes, red lining. White undergown, silver edging. White lace neck-edging, sleeve ruffles and fontange headdress. White lace-edged apron. White kid gloves, ivory fan, pearl necklace. English c. 1690, portrait.

this the waistline ended in a row of tabs which were covered by the underskirt waistband. The boned centre front of the bodice extended over this waistband, often reinforced there by a metal strip. The overskirt was now bunched further back almost in a bustle shape. The skirt silhouette had returned to a bell shape and petticoats above were no longer able to maintain the fashionable form so, once again, as in the sixteenth century, a framework was needed to support the weight of the material. This time it took the form of *paniers* (the French term) or basket frames worn at each side and tied on at the waist. The fashion did not become established in France until the early eighteenth century but was common in England from a few years earlier (**94, 97, 103, 105, 106, 107**).

At this time, while masculine dress was becoming plainer and less effeminate, feminine attire attracted a more excessive form of decoration. The complete ensemble was ornamented by ribbon bows and loops, lace ruffles and flounces as men's dress had been in the 1660s. The *échelle* became more prominent, the underskirt more lavishly enriched by lace, gold embroidery, fringing and tassels.

Out-of-doors women wore capes or hooded, long cloaks which, in winter, were warmly lined, often with fur.

Unlike the men, women did not adopt wigs at this time but dressed their natural hair. Towards the end of the seventeenth century the tall coiffure and headdress was adopted, one which provided a parallel to the lofty, peaked masculine periwig. By the 1680s ladies were curling their hair high on top and tying it there with a ribbon bow. Long ringlets were still customary at the sides. By 1690 the *bonnet à la Fontanges* was fashionable, this named after the French Duchess of Fontanges. In this style the coiffure was piled very high with curls in front and this was then surmounted by a lace cap made in rows of fluted and pleated ruffles, each row behind and above the previous one and resembling organ piping. The whole headdress was decorated by ribbons – hanging and in bows – and a lace scarf which depended in lappets on

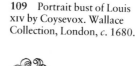

108 Curled coiffure with headdress of striped ribbons. Black lappets. Lace collar. Black gown. Italian 1690–5. Portrait of the Marchesa Ardizzone, unknown artist, Palazzo d'Arco, Mantua.

109 Portrait bust of Louis XIV by Coysevox. Wallace Collection, London, c. 1680.

110 Lace and ribbon fontange headdress and scarf. Portrait of Mary II c. 1694.

111 Full-bottomed periwig and lace-edged cravat. Portrait of William III

112 Coiffure decorated by flowers and ribbon loops. Lace-edged gown, brocade bows. Gold ruching on stomacher. Portrait of an Italian lady, Galleria Doria, Rome, c. 1680.

113 Black periwig. Lace-edged cravat. Portrait bust of Charles II, 1684.

each side of the neck in front. Long ringlets were also carefully arranged on the shoulders. Especially tall creations were supported with the aid of wire frames or pads. This fashion was short-lived; its zenith was reached about 1695 and by 1705 it was over. It is noteable that this headdress and coiffure mode, as well as the tall masculine periwig were accompanied, for precisely the identical period, by unusually tall chair and settee backs and bedsteads (94, 105, 106, 107, 110).

Ladies' shoes resembled those of the men in style but heels were higher, especially towards the end of the century, and most styles were made in brocade or embroidered silk or velvet rather than leather. Pantoffles or slippers were worn indoors; these had heels but no backs (118, 119).

Towards the end of the century fashionable ladies adopted the wearing of elegant aprons. Traditionally a utilitarian garment for the bourgeoisie, the aristocratic version was totally impracticable, being made from beautiful fabrics, embroidered and trimmed with lace. It might be large or very tiny. Like the men, ladies carried fans and combs and,

114 Point de France lace, late seventeenth century.

115 Dress and apron in silver grey with orange bands and sprig pattern. White lace sleeve ruffles, neck frill and fontange headdress. Gold embroidered shoes. Pearl rope bracelets. Painting of a little girl 1700–5. Galleria Nazionale, Parma, Italy.

116 Boned bodice, c. 1660. Actual garment.

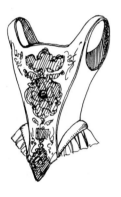

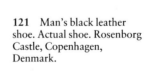

117 Soft leather corset, embroidered and jewelled. Actual garment c. 1700.

118 Red velvet lady's shoe embroidered in gold. Silver buckle. Actual shoe. Rocamora Costume Museum, Barcelona.

119 Lady's slipper. Red velvet with gold bands. Actual item. Dresden State Museum, Germany.

121 Man's black leather shoe. Actual shoe. Rosenborg Castle, Copenhagen, Denmark.

120 Brown suede man's shoe with red bow. Actual shoe. Rocamora Costume Museum, Barcelona.

outdoors and according to season, fur muffs or parasols (**97, 107**).

In north America, French colonists, assisted by their government with clothing, provisions and equipment, were founding a settlement on the lower reaches of the Mississippi river. They named the area Louisiana after Louis XIV. The chief city, New Orleans, was founded in 1717. Early French settlers here wore a mixture of garments; those brought from France, others made and woven by themselves together with skins and moccasins acquired by bartering with the Indians.

CHAPTER FIVE

1715–1760

Rococo Delicacy

In these years France was the undisputed arbiter of fashion. In all the trades and skills – basic and peripheral – essential to *la mode*, she had built up complete pre-eminence: dressmaking and tailoring, millinery, wig-making, textile design, ornamentation and haberdashery, cosmetics and corsetry. The quality of design and craftsmanship in the work of the leaders of these trades was superb and imitated everywhere.

The French language was that of Europe's ruling class. French customs and dress were those of its cultured leaders. There were apparent variations upon the basic theme, evidenced in certain areas of Europe, which derived from regional and national character and preference but these were minimal, much less than had been the norm in earlier ages. For example, in German-speaking regions costume was often made from richer, heavier fabrics, was more elaborately ornamented and the rigidity provided by whaleboned coat seams, corsetry and paniers was noticeably greater. Spanish influence in the Iberian peninsula, in southern Italy and in Vienna, led to a greater retention of baroque characteristics and a more belated adoption of the paler shades and dainty textile patterns evident in France. But, in general, the French mode was paramount until much later in the century.

However, during the eighteenth century, the balance of political and economic power was shifting. Gradually England became the supreme power at sea with consequent growth in her influence on trade and colonization. France gradually ceded first place in this field, losing her previously-held position at the head of international affairs. She continued to hold though, her overall cultural, and thus fashion, supremacy. These two countries – England and France – constituted the major European powers; the influence of other nations, such as Holland and Spain, which had previously held a more important position, became less strong and the countries less wealthy.

These years saw the beginnings of a freer and more liberal society, an assault upon the established order which had pertained for years but which was to crumble in the French Revolution later in the century. The middle classes were establishing themselves and increasing their numbers and influence. The arbiters of dress were less the individual members of the royal courts than a broader unit of society; this was still aristocratically led but was more widely based.

A reflection of this gradual evolution could be seen in the early signs of egalitarianism in dress. It was a very slow change and, for decades, barely perceptible but it was from these years that the concept of high quality and privilege, for so long maintained only for the benefit of the few, the ruling class, came under attack. This concept was eroded and the quality was, bit by bit, slowly diluted to become an acceptance of quantity. This was reflected in dress in a closer adherence to prevailing fashion by most classes of the community, not only the aristocracy, as previously. The richness of fabrics used and the quantity and quality of the decorative medium varied according to the wealth of the wearer but the styles were similar.

Under French leadership eighteenth century dress was characterized by the use of exquisite fabrics in silks, taffetas, satins and velvets in delicate colours, painted, embroidered or printed in dainty floral patterns and enriched by gold and silver thread, lace, plumes, ribbons, ruching, ruffles and fur. As in painting and interior decoration the bolder designs and stronger colours of the baroque movement had given place to French rococo forms, the colours light, bright and clear with a restrained use of decoration in white and gold. Motifs were dainty, the stress upon S-shaped scrolls, shells, flowers in small scale designs. Naturalistic forms predominated. There was a tendency towards asymmetry and detail inspired by exotic and Oriental themes. For men the delicate fabrics were elegantly embroidered round the edges of garments, for women there were quantities of ribbon and flouncing. The silhouette was an artificial one, distorted by corseting, paniers and wigs.

Textiles

This industry developed rapidly during the eighteenth century. This was the case in many countries but Britain led the world in the production of fabrics. This was partially due to her establishment of supremacy at sea, which increased possibilities for overseas trade, and in part because of the influx of Huguenot textile workers at the end of the seventeenth century. All Protestant countries had benefited from this influx but Britain, as undisputed leader of the Industrial Revolution, was able to offer greater advancement to such workers because of the technological advances being made, so speeding up production of fabrics. The date of the onset of the Industrial Revolution is debatable – somewhere between 1740 and 1755 is generally put forward – but there is no doubt that Britain was far ahead in its development, the vast majority of inventions in the textile industry stemming from England and Scotland.

Most of these inventions were initiated and developed in the second half of the century

but the years 1715–60 saw the introduction of the weaving flying shuttle, also the establishment of the triangular trade in cotton. It was the Kays, father and son, who found an ingenious answer to the problem of the slow, awkward method, used traditionally for centuries, of throwing the shuttle across the

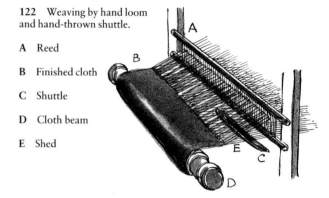

122 Weaving by hand loom and hand-thrown shuttle.

A Reed

B Finished cloth

C Shuttle

D Cloth beam

E Shed

123 Flying shuttle

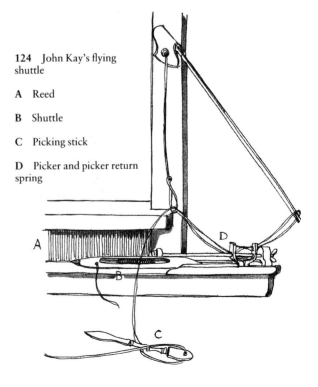

124 John Kay's flying shuttle

A Reed

B Shuttle

C Picking stick

D Picker and picker return spring

width of a loom. Where a wide piece of fabric was being woven, two operators were needed, one standing on each side of a loom to throw the shuttle containing the weft thread across from one side and back to the other through the shed, that gap created in the warp threads by raising and lowering the heddles. This was a painfully slow and boring action. Faster weaving and wider pieces of finished cloth became possible with the invention by John Kay in 1733 of the flying shuttle. Kay made reeds for looms in Lancashire; he later replaced the reeds by wires which caused less wear to the warp threads. His flying shuttle consisted of a shuttle box which he constructed on either side of the loom, the two being connected by a board called a shuttle race to which the reed was attached. Each box was fitted with a metal spindle with a picker which could slide along it. The weaver held a picking stick which was attached by cords to the pickers. He jerked the stick from side to side making each picker in turn slide along the spindle, taking the shuttle with it, so that it was thrown across the loom and back again from one shuttle box to the other. This invention not only speeded up the action of the shuttle but made it run a true and correct course from one side to the other so reducing the friction on the warp threads (**122–4**).

John Kay's shuttle only permitted one colour thread to be used at a time. His son Robert Kay invented a multiple shuttle box in 1760. This introduced a so-called drop box which could be raised and lowered to enable the weaver to use more than one colour thread at a time.

Silk fabric was beginning to be produced in quantity in England, given an important impetus by the establishment of Huguenot silk weavers in Spitalfields in east London. In the early years the raw silk was imported from Italy and Persia. The throwing process was carried out in various centres in England: Derby, Macclesfield, Leek, Sherborne. These centres supplied Spitalfields and Bethnal Green where the weavers lived. Their workshops occupied the top floors of buildings where the best daylight was to be found. By

125 Blue satin coat, gold frog and button fastenings. Dark blue velvet breeches. Silk stockings. Black leather shoes with jewelled buckles. Powdered bag wig. Tricorne hat. Portrait. English 1735–45.

126 Dark coat decorated with gold braid and buttons, breeches to match. Brocade waistcoat. White stockings. Black shoes. Powdered periwig. Wig and garments old-fashioned because of great distance from France. Actual costume, Hermitage Museum, Leningrad. 1716. Russian.

127 Brown coat with gold buttons. Fawn stockings. Black shoes. Grey powdered wig. Painting by Pietro Longhi, Galleria Accademia, Venice, 1745–50.

128 Contouche in lavender silk with dark green velvet échelle. Cream satin petticoat. Lace sleeve ruffles. Portrait *c.* 1720–4, English.

129 Navy blue coat. Black breeches. White stockings. Black shoes. Grey tie wig. Red velvet waistcoat. Black tricorne hat with silver braid. Actual costume, Schweizerisches Landesmuseum, Zürich, Switzerland, 1745.

130 Patterned velvet coat. White stockings. Black shoes. White powdered bag wig. Actual costume, Museum of Costume, Bath, England, *c.* 1755.

the 1740s English silk weavers were coming from other centres such as Canterbury to join the Huguenots at Spitalfields. The mercers' shops for marketing the fabric were nearby in London, in Ludgate, for instance.

Woollen broadcloth remained a staple English textile, made in quantity for the home market as well as for the rapidly-expanding colonial trade. Traditional cloth-making areas, Norwich and the west country, continued till after mid-century when new ones in Yorkshire, notably Leeds and Bradford began development.

Cotton was being worn more and more as the century progressed; by 1800 the industry had surpassed the woollen trade. The chief expansion took place in the second half of the century but, by 1700, the infamous, so-called 'triangular trade' was well established. Trading of negroes to the New World had been in operation since the mid-sixteenth century and the British had gradually acquired a larger share of this. Cotton was grown in the southern states of North America and this accelerated the flourishing slave trade. In this 'triangular trade' the English merchants

(from Bristol) sailed to Africa to exchange their manufactured goods – arms, hardware, jewellery, spirits and tobacco – with the African chiefs for slave labour. The second leg of the journey took the Africans to America where they were sold as slaves, at great profit, to work in the cotton plantations. The ships then returned to England laden with raw cotton to be cleaned, processed, spun and woven into cotton fabric.

Apart from a set-back caused by the British blockade during the War of the Spanish Succession early in the century, the French textile industry also grew apace, particularly during the years 1730–50 when manufacture of silk expanded greatly. The French produced quality fabrics which were sold all over Europe to be made into characteristically French-styled garments for both sexes.

In other European countries the Swiss were noted for their quality cottons and silks and, especially, for their ribbons. The Germans, Belgians and Spanish also produced and exported, in particular, woollens and silks. This was in contrast to Italy, Austria and Holland where textile industries declined.

131 Silk banyan and cap. Portrait, English, 1720.

132 Riding habit. Masculine style of dress worn with a skirt. Pink silk coat, waistcoat and skirt ornamented in gold. Leather gloves. Black tricorne hat. Portrait of the Countess of Mar, Scottish National Portrait Gallery, Edinburgh, 1715.

133 Striped flannel bedgown worn with checked petticoat. White cap and chemise. Actual costume, Welsh Folk Museum, St. Fagan's, Cardiff.

Men's Dress

The three-piece suit, comprising coat, waistcoat and breeches – known by the French name of *habit à la française* – was the accepted attire for gentlemen all over Europe. These three garments were worn until the end of the eighteenth century though the silhouette, materials and decoration changed slowly during this time, the changes before 1760

being almost imperceptible. The trend was towards a slenderer, plainer, more stream-lined effect. Fabrics became darker in colour, heavier and were less richly ornamented. There was a tendency, especially after 1760, to make the coat and breeches of one fabric but, before this date, this was unusual.

The coat – the *justaucorps* of the previous century – kept its flared skirts until about 1725. After this the fullness was arranged in a fan of pleats radiating on each side from a button set at the hip seam. This fan-like spreading at the hip was the masculine counterpart of the feminine panier skirt and was particularly in evidence in England and Italy. To maintain the desired shape whale-bone was inserted into the coat seams and buckram into the lining for stiffening (**125, 127**).

As long as wigs with tails were worn (into the late 1770s), for comfort the coat remained collarless. Sleeves were fairly full and ended in large cuffs which were particularly so up to 1745–50. These buttoned cuffs, the pocket flaps and the front buttoned edges were beautifully and elaborately embroidered in coloured silks. The coat itself was made in bright colours from velvet, silk or satin. Gold frogging and passementerie were fashionable forms of decoration. The garment was knee-length and was open or buttoned only at the waist. The centre back of the skirt was slit, originally for ease in riding (plates 19, 20).

The most decorative garment of the suit was the waistcoat (vest in America, *gilet* in France). It was made of brocade or other rich fabric, patterned all over in front with coloured silk embroidery or gold or silver thread, the unseen back being of plain, cheaper material. The waistcoat was designed like the coat in style but was about six inches shorter and had long fitted sleeves; after mid-century most waistcoats were sleeveless (**126**).

Breeches changed little in style. They were fitting, fastened at the knee with buckle or buttons. Early designs were closed in front with vertical buttoning. After about 1730 the closure was a panel with horizontal buttoning (**129, 130**).

134 The Card Game, German dress, 1730 engraving, Nüremburg City Library. For all figures except boy on right: he is illustrated wearing actual costume from Bayerische Nationalmuseum, Munich. Brown wool coat with navy braid. Waistcoat of navy silk with gold braid. Silver buttons. Powdered bag wig.

Out-of-doors various capes, cloaks and coats were worn in bad weather. Cloaks were more usual early in the century; typical was the roquelaure cloak, called after the Duke of that name. Most voluminous, it was suited for travelling and riding; it was knee-length and had a back vent. It was made from woollen cloth, had a large collar and often a hood as well. The cloak was worn all over Europe but, its name often abbreviated to roquelo, it was especially adopted in the north American colonies.

After mid-century long coats were in more general use, when the redingote was the most usual style. It had been worn since about 1725 for travelling and riding and, until about 1780, was a heavy, long double-breasted coat with large collar and revers, also a shoulder cape. Redingote was the French name, derived from the English term riding coat. In France, a similar type of heavy coat had been worn in the seventeenth century by coachmen exposed to bad weather.

In ages when, for both sexes, corseting and rigid clothing were the fashion, the luxury of being able to shed, in the privacy of one's home, a hat and irritating wig and a *habit à la française* or paniered gown, was fully appreciated. This custom was taken advantage of from the sixteenth to the nineteenth centuries but especially so during the eighteenth. Men, in particular, so favoured themselves in their nightgowns or banyans with negligé cap that they sat so attired for their portraits to be painted, leaving to posterity a clear record of what such garments were like. There were many names for these gowns, most of them interchangeable; in the eighteenth century the most usual were nightgown, Indian gown, banyan, morning gown (**131**).

A nightgown was, therefore, not in the least what is understood by this term today. It was a full, almost ground-length coat worn from the sixteenth century onwards. Made from velvet, silk, brocade or wool, it was intended for warmth and could be lined and trimmed with fur then tied by a sash at the waist. Both sexes wore these garments at home. Indian gown was a more usual seventeenth century term. A more fitting garment, this was often made from Indian patterned silk or cotton and, again, was worn by men and women. A banyan – the term derived from that for an Indian trader in the west of the country, particularly those from the province of Gujarat (now in Pakistan) – was, by the eighteenth century, made from a very rich material. Also known as a morning gown, it was elegantly cut, on kimono lines, flaring out in the skirt. It could be worn loose, tied with a waist sash or buttoned. Most banyans were ground length. It was particularly fashionable for European gentlemen of the eighteenth century to wear at home, for comfort and relaxation, over a waistcoat and breeches. It was worn extensively in the southern states of north America, where in a warm climate and more

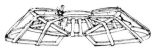

136 Whalebone and tape folding panier

135 Side paniers

138 Holland, non-folding panier

137 Cotton and cane pocket paniers

139 Panier skirt

informal plantation life, it was regularly adopted as an outdoor garment.

In men's linen, the seventeenth century cravat was replaced about 1720 by the folded stock. Made of white silk or muslin, this was a pleated band of material worn round the neck and fastened at the back. A finely-pleated

140 Maroon velvet, ermine-trimmed jacket. Pale blue taffeta gown. White fichu. Straw hat, blue ribbons. Fan. Portrait, English, *c.* 1740–50.

141 Sacque gown of ivory satin embroidered in cream silk. White lace collarette and sleeve ruffles. Lace-edged cap decorated with flowers and ribbon. Folding fan. Painting by de Troy *The Declaration of Love*. Staatliche Schlösser und Garten, Berlin. French dress 1728–30.

142   English Dress 1735–50 Palladian Bridge, Wilton House
A   Dark red silk coat with brocade cuffs. White tie wig.
Gloves. White stockings, black shoes. 1732. Portrait.
B   Pale blue silk gown, English style. Satin bows. White fichu
and sleeve ruffles. Straw hat with striped ribbon. Painting,
1745–50.
C   Pink gown with embroidered silk pattern in colours. White
cap. Actual Costume. Victoria and Albert Museum, London,
1750.
D   Red velvet coat, waistcoat and breeches. Gold decoration

and buttons. White pig-tail wig. Black tricorne hat with white
ostrich tips. Portrait of Frederick, Prince of Wales. National
Gallery, London, 1745–50.
E, F   Children dressed like A and B.
G   Brocade gown in green, crimson and white on a gold
ground. White cap, sleeve ruffles and neck frill. Actual
costume. Museum of Costume, Bath, 1735–40.
H   Cream silk gown with embroidery in coloured silks.
Échelle bodice. White cap with lappets and ribbons. Reticule.
Painting, 1750.

or lace-edged jabot frothed on the chest on
the opening of the waistcoat. The solitaire, a
black ribbon attached to the wig bow at the
nape, was often brought round to the front of
the neck on top of the stock and tied there in a
bow (**150–155**).

Wigs were worn by men of nearly all classes
of the community in these years and, for
gentlemen, they were *de rigueur*. The great
full-bottomed periwig of the late seventeenth
century had given way to smaller, simpler
styles which were powdered white or grey.
Pomatum was used for this to which the rice
or wheat powder would adhere. A variety of
styles of wig succeeded one another between
1715 and 1760 and, in fashionable dress, it is
one of the features which make it possible
to date the costume accurately. Until about
1740–5 the wig was dressed softly in waves

back from the forehead (no parting now) and
in soft curls on the temples, a style known as
pigeons' wings. The wig was then tied back at
the nape with a black ribbon bow and the
curls hung loosely down the back: this was a
tie wig (plate 20, **150, 151**).

Towards mid-century the pigeons' wings
were replaced by more formal horizontal
curls at the sides, one above the other. This
style, known as a buckled* wig, began with
three curls which, over a period of time, were
reduced to one. At the back, below the nape
bow, a variety of styles evolved. The queue
could be plaited in one, two or three tails and
tied at the ends with another bow(s). This or
these might be encased in black silk or left

---

* Derived from the French *bouclé* meaning curled

uncovered. The former style was called a pig-tail wig, the latter a ramillie (after the battle in which the Duke of Marlborough was engaged). Fashionable alternatives were the bag-wig in which the tail was encased in a black silk bag drawn up with cords at the nape and finished with a black bow or the cadogan wig (said to be named after the Earl of Cadogan) in which the queue was looped under then over and up then tied in place with a black ribbon. Many other styles were available such as the short-tailed bushy campaigne wig worn for travelling and the tailless bob wig or even shorter scratch wig, both more typical wear for less the fashionable classes.

The wearing of wigs, continuous since the 1660s, had permanently changed the custom of wearing hats. Before *c.* 1660 men had worn hats all the time indoors and even at table. The fashion for large periwigs had rendered the wearing of a hat superfluous and men usually carried their hat under one arm, wearing it only in bad weather. With the smaller wigs of this period the custom continued because of the powdering of wigs and because the wearing of a hat would disarrange the side curls. The hat style remained the tricorne, made of black felt and trimmed with gold braid or ostrich tips. As wigs became smaller so did the tricorne (**152–155**).

Men wore shoes rather than boots. These were generally of black leather with low heels. The toes were now rounded and up-standing tongues were smaller. The metal shoe buckle (preferably in silver) was generally square, curved to fit the instep and superbly made and ornamented (**146**).

Men carried canes and still wore swords. Fur muffs and gloves were still worn and handkerchiefs carried. The snuff box continued to be a prized article, often beautifully fashioned in gold, enamel-work or ceramic.

Women's Dress

The feminine silhouette was dominated in these years, as it had been in the sixteenth century, by the restriction of the corseted bodice and framework under the skirt. As

143 and 144 163, the little boy, wears a pale blue coat with silver embroidery and buttons, darker blue breeches and light brown boots. His hair is powdered white. 164, the little girl, wears a pale pink dress with white apron and ruffles. Her hair is powdered white and she wears a pink bow. Painting by Pietro Longhi, Ca' Rezzonico, Venice, 1752.

always with such framework skirts, seen equally with the sixteenth century farthingale and the nineteenth century crinoline, a small waist and rigid bodice were adopted in order to set off the fullness of the skirt and, at the same time, in order not to detract from the domination of these two features, the coiffure and headcoverings were small, dainty and simple; large hats and bouffant hairstyles belonged to periods when the silhouette was slim and svelte as in the 1820s and 1890s.

The type of underwear and corset, therefore, was similar to that worn in the first decade of the century (p. 52). The framework under the skirt, however, passed through several phases between 1700 and the 1770s. Until about 1730 the shape was circular in section and in the form of a dome. In England this was called a hoop petticoat, in France a panier. Several hoops of whalebone were inserted into a petticoat made from a rich, heavy, fabric and whalebone strips were added across these to maintain the shape. These hoops, unlike the farthingale petticoat, only extended partway to the knee. These wide, circular hoops lent a lilting, gentle motion to the skirt as the lady walked;

145 Pink silk with silver lace lady's shoe. Actual shoe, German, *c.* 1750.

146 Man's buff leather shoe, jewelled metal buckle. English, 1720.

147 White kid mule embroidered in coloured silk and silver. French, 1750.

148 Lady's mule in striped silk. Spanish actual mule, Barcelona.

149 Man's slipper of white silk embroidered in silver. Spanish, Barcelona.

it was a flowing movement, feminine and provocative (**135–139**).

After about 1725–30 the shape, in France, gradually changed to an oval with the greater width at the sides. By 1750 the sides were excessively wide and the front and rear considerably flattened. It was then necessary to turn sideways to pass through a doorway, enter a sedan chair or be seated on a chair, despite the furniture being designed with extra width to accommodate both these gowns and the men's coat skirts. A new type of panier evolved which consisted of several cane or whalebone hoops, not inserted into a petticoat but strung together with tapes. This was tied on at the waist in a similar manner to previously and was thus an articulated panier. To negotiate an entrance the lady need only lift her skirt upwards with her elbows or by putting her hands through side pocket slits to raise the panier upwards so reducing its width.

The gown styles worn over these panier skirts changed as the form beneath developed. The typical fashion of the 1720s was the *contouche* or *sacque* – in English, sack – gown. This had evolved from the house dress worn for relaxation a few years earlier. It had a fitted waist in front but flowed loosely over an immense circular hoop at back and sides. The neckline was low and wide, the bodice defined with a stomacher and *échelle* in front. Sleeves were elbow-length with flared frill behind – the pagoda sleeve. From about 1730 evolved the *robe à la française* or, in England, the so-called 'Watteau' gown. This appears to be something of a mis-nomer because the gowns depicted by the painter Watteau are mainly of the earlier fashion. In the new style the front of the bodice was little altered but the back was designed in large box pleats which extended from neckline to hem. Sleeves ended in a cuff at the elbow from which depended the lace flounces of the chemise. In France these gowns went by various names: *robes battantes*, *robes volantes* etc. Despite the change in panier shape, the *robe à la française* continued in fashion until after 1770 (plates 21, 22, **140–142**).

Out-of-doors, for much of the year, because of the layers of petticoats, a covering was only needed for the upper part of the body. Scarves and capes were worn, the material varied according to season. In summer these would be made from lace, silk or tulle. Warmer winter wear would be of velvet or cloth, fur-edged and lined and would be longer, worn with or without a hood (**140**).

Unlike the men, women did not wear wigs at this time. Their coiffure was neat and small, decorated simply. A small white cap with frilled edge and lappets and decorated by ribbons was *de rigueur* indoors and out. Shoes, often matching the gown in colour, were made from a variety of materials: kid, satin, brocade, silk, velvet. They were embroidered and decorated by jewelled buckles. In style toes were pointed and high heels curved. High-heeled mules and slippers were also worn (plates 21, 22, **128, 141, 156**).

The most typical feminine accessory was the folding fan. Many of these were exquisitely made and very costly. Sticks could be of ivory, tortoiseshell, mother-of-pearl, gold or silver. Stretched over these was painted vellum, kid or silk. The art of the fan was important to every lady; it was carried and used coquettishly, provocatively, admonishingly, invitingly as required. Women carried hand-

150 White pig-tail wig, *c.* 1740. Painting, English.

151 White tie wig, *c.* 1730. Painting, English.

152 Pig-tail wig, 1745. Painting, English.

153 Black, gold-edged tricorne hat, white tie wig, *c.* 1738–40. Painting, English.

154 White ramillie wig, 1753. Painting, English.

155 Black, gold-edged Kevenhüller tricorne hat, 1750. Painting, English.

kerchiefs, be-ribboned canes, muffs, parasols and wore tiny bouquets of artificial flowers. They used cosmetics freely, applying them more knowledgeably than previously. Face patches were still widely used and perfume generously added. Clothes and personal articles were scented and ladies carried exquisite perfume cases and even wore rings containing perfume. In an age when personal hygiene was not of high standard and dry cleaning not available, such aids were more than necessary.

In the American colonies the well-to-do continued to order their wardrobes from England. On the whole fashions were still closely related to European modes with certain variations according to climate and particular sections of the population. For example, the skimmer hat (or skimmer-dish hat) was often worn, especially by Quaker ladies. This was a broad-brimmed flat, low-crowned hat made from beaver, felt or straw and was worn over a cap. It was based upon the European bergère hat of flat straw, a style popular in the 1750s (158).

156 White lace-edged cap and lappets, 1723. Drawing, English.

157 Negligé cap, *c.* 1755. Painting, American.

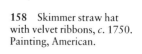

158 Skimmer straw hat with velvet ribbons, *c.* 1750. Painting, American.

159 **Ordinary Dress, 1715–60.** A street scene illustrating dress worn by the general population. *The Enraged Musician*, engraving by William Hogarth, published 1741.

As the middle classes became wealthier and more numerous in Europe so their wardrobes more closely followed those of the fashionable. Quality woollen cloth was still worn but, also more widely, heavy silks and muslins, decorated with ribbons, ruching and fur. For the poor, harsher woollens were the norm but, as the century advanced, cotton became more readily available at a lower price.

The bedgown had originated, as its name suggests, as a loose house gown worn for relaxation by both sexes in the morning at home, having the same function, though less elegant, as the banyan (p. 60). During the later seventeenth century it became solely a feminine garment, the skirt open in front to display a petticoat. The eighteenth century bedgown had become essentially a garment worn in town and country by working women and continued so to be throughout most of the following century. It was a short-sleeved simple garment with bodice and a skirt which was open in front to show the petticoat beneath. A large apron was worn on top of this and the outfit was completed by a kerchief or scarf and a cap. The bedgown could be short or long and was usually made of coarse wool or flannel; the apron, kerchief and cap were of cotton. The traditional outdoor garment was a heavy cloak (often red) usually attached to a hood (159).

CHAPTER SIX

1760–1800

Artificial Extremism to Revolutionary Change

The trend towards egalitarianism, begun so slowly in the first half of the century, accelerated rapidly after 1770. The middle classes adhered much more closely, in their dress, to fashions worn by the aristocracy and, by 1800, a tentative dilution had become apparent in the superb standards of quality in fabrics, decoration and making up just as, at the same time, was happening in the applied arts of the interior decoration of buildings. This was the inescapable price later to be paid for the sharing of the beauty, talent and wealth in life by an increasing proportion of peoples. To provide the quantity needed to those desiring and able to pay for articles of elegance and beauty, manufacturing industry had to become streamlined. Individual craftsmanship had begun to evidence an, as yet, tiny diminution in its standards.

Together with this egalitarianism came the beginnings of a gradual change in the position of women in society. Their importance increased as did their influence. In fashion the outward sign of this was in the changing positions in dress in the relationship of men and women. For centuries man had been the more gloriously apparelled of the sexes. His were the most brilliant colours, the richest ornamentation, the most elegant figure-revealing line and the most beautiful of fabrics. During the eighteenth century this had slowly changed and men began to take second place as the more splendidly attired sex, wearing darker, less decorative materials and more severely cut garments. It was a process which was to culminate, in the later nineteenth century, in a male dressed in sombre black and grey, relieved only by touches of white at neck and cuff.

Following the French modes, eighteenth century aristocratic feminine dress was still, in 1760, characterized by exquisite, daintily patterned fabrics, elaborately ornamented all over by ruching and bows, ruffles and flouncing. The silhouette was artificially constrained and distorted with immense wigs, corseted waistline and paniered skirts.

The artificiality of these excesses peaked in France around 1780 but, before this, an alternative mode was being established in England. Worn by both sexes, this was a more comfortable and practical version of the current fashion. It was from England that the hooped skirts and tall wigs disappeared first. The more egalitarian, democratic society pertaining in England was reflected in what came to be known in Europe as the *mode à l'anglaise*. It was still elegant but was much more natural in line and form.

Varied reasons were put forward in Europe to explain why it was, at this time, only England which challenged French supremacy in fashion in the years 1770–90. It was suggested, for instance, that the English were devoted to sport, to hunting, shooting and fishing and that the landed gentry found the overdressed artificial French styles unsuited to these pursuits; it was also, of course, cold and wet in England, a climate also unsuited to the wearing of silks and satins. These suppositions took little cognizance of the fact that silks and satins had been worn for centuries in England as well as in the rest

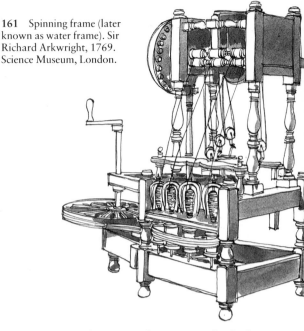

161 Spinning frame (later known as water frame). Sir Richard Arkwright, 1769. Science Museum, London.

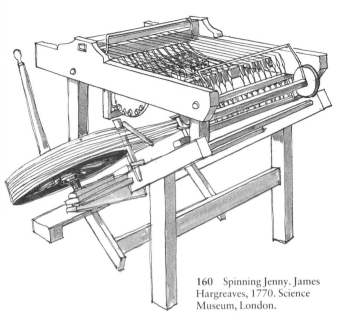

160 Spinning Jenny. James Hargreaves, 1770. Science Museum, London.

of Europe also that the landed gentry represented only a section of the wealthy classes. These views may be likened to a similarly fallacious European opinion, held yet today, that England, especially London, suffers a permanent, damp fog. It seems more likely that these more natural styles evolved because of the characteristic English common sense and a refusal to accept extremism whether in politics or dress.

Whatever the reasons for these simpler styles, they were soon being emulated by other European countries, particularly those further north such as Germany and Scandinavia. Eventually, even in France, 'Anglomania' in dress was enthusiastically accepted as *la mode*.

The outbreak of the French Revolution in 1789, the subsequent short-lived régimes which followed, quickly changing from monarchy to republic to empire, brought economic and social upheavals which were reflected in fashion, each new mode quickly replacing the previous one. The simplicity of the *mode à l'anglaise* of the years 1770–90 had only foreshadowed the extreme plainness and décolleté lines of the 1790s.

The effects of the French Revolution shocked and galvanized society all over Europe. With the later French wars and

conquests under Napoleon French fashions once again became dominant in Europe. Only England, apart and protected by her navy, continued her own way, her fashions reflecting but complementing those of the French. It was in these last years of the eighteenth century that English masculine tailoring became supreme. While Paris remained the centre of feminine fashion, London became established as the centre for men's dress. Tail coats, waistcoats and breeches required fine tailoring for the fitted forms now fashionable and English tailors were then the best in the world.

Textiles and the Industrial Revolution

Between 1760 and 1800 Britain's pre-eminence in the Industrial Revolution was reaching its height and nowhere was this more apparent than in the textile industry. All the necessary processes for producing finished cotton, wool, linen and silk were, during these years, gradually transferred from hand processes to machine ones. By the 1780s the need to increase production in order to supply a larger population, and one materially better off and so able to afford to purchase a greater variety and quality of textiles, had become an urgent problem.

162 Sir Richard Arkwright. Engraving, Science Museum, London.

163 Carding engine of the type designed by Arkwright, *c.* 1775. Science Museum, London.

Combined with pressure from hand-workers for higher wages, attempts redoubled to make machines which would carry out these tasks.

In the cotton industry in particular, the triangular trade between Britain, Africa and the New World increased greatly and several ways of mechanizing the cleaning of the American raw cotton were devised in order to enable the plantation owners there to speed up transportation and so reduce costs. Batting machines were designed which opened up the cotton pods and disposed of the seeds. The seedless cotton could then be compressed into smaller bales for shipment. In the 1780s scutching and blowing machines were devised which broke up the cotton bolls then removed the dirt particles by passing a current of air through the raw cotton. A notable milestone there was Eli Whitney's cotton gin (abbreviation for engine) of 1794. This machine, improved two years later, enabled one man to replace fifty men who had been previously employed to hand-operate the roller gins.

After cleansing, the most important preliminary textile processes before spinning are carding and combing; these disentangle and straighten the fibres. Machines for carding cotton were developed, notably Sir Richard Arkwright's carding engine of the 1770s (**162, 163**). Hand-combing was hard, skilled work and, in these years, combers took advantage of their essential position and repeatedly struck for higher rates of pay. Under pressure, employers sought a machine to replace their rebellious workers. Edmund Cartwright supplied this in his wool-combing machine of 1792. Its products were inferior to those of hand-combing but later, successful inventions followed in the early years of the nineteenth century.

By 1760 the mechanization of weaving was causing hold-ups as hand-spinners could not produce sufficient yarn to supply the looms. The first successful spinning machine devised to solve this problem was James Hargreaves' 'spinning jenny'* of 1764 (**160**). This had eight vertical spindles operated by eight driving bands so spinning eight threads simultaneously. By 1766 16 threads were being spun but a weakness of the design was that the yarn produced was insufficiently strong for use as warp threads. It was Sir

---

* 'Jenny', like 'gin' and 'ginny', is a colloquialism for engine and not related, as is sometimes stated, to a woman's name.

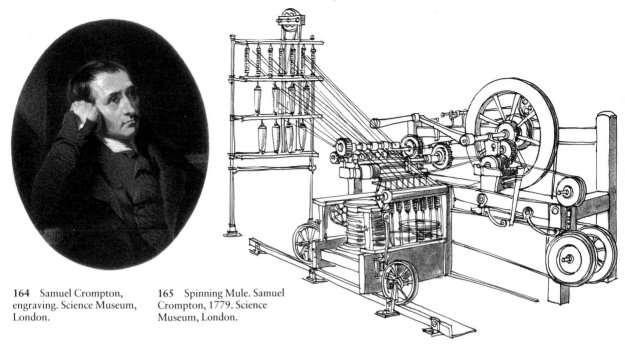

164 Samuel Crompton, engraving. Science Museum, London.

165 Spinning Mule. Samuel Crompton, 1779. Science Museum, London.

Richard Arkwright's spinning frame of 1768 (**161**) which, making use of rollers to draw out the rovings before they were passed to the spindle, overcame the difficulty. In 1779 Samuel Crompton (**164**) devised the best of these machines which would produce softer, finer yarns and, eventually, operated a thousand spindles at once. Crompton's machine was known as the 'spinning mule' because it was a cross between Arkwright's and Hargreaves' designs, containing the best features of both (**165**).

Attempts to design power looms for weaving had been made, not successfully, since the sixteenth century. In this field it was Dr Edmund Cartwright who finally succeeded in designing a practical power loom to weave cloth of adequate widths. In 1786, in cooperation with Manchester cotton manufacturers, he produced an improved version.

In all these textile fields the great majority of inventors of means of mechanizing the processes came from Britain and, especially, Scotland. In all cases great industrial unrest was caused as hundreds of hand-workers were gradually replaced by a far smaller number of machine operators. Machines and workshops were attacked and destroyed and

minders and inventors were physically assaulted but, in the end, the machine prevailed. The replacement of handwork by mechanization did not create the same level of unemployment that it has done in the twentieth century, partly because of the rapidly increasing indigenous population and partly because of the equally rapidly expanding overseas markets then becoming available. Rural unemployment was created as the cottage industry gave way to town factories and urbanization was the result which caused great rural distress in the flight from the land but, within the country as a whole, unemployment was not created.

Machines were originally worked by hand then by horse power or, in suitable parts of the countryside, by watermills. The development of the steam engine in the 1770s created a revolution of its own and steam remained the dominant power source for much of the nineteenth century.

Fashion Journals

The fashion journal, which appeared in the second half of the eighteenth century, was a publication which gave news and illustrations of fashions which were being worn and others which were new and likely to become fashionable; it was thus an advance upon the earlier fashion plate. In the eighteenth century it was the English particularly who provided such publications, the chief of which was the *Lady's Magazine*, dating from 1770. This was published first in black and white, later in colour. Between 1770 and 1800 a number of such journals appeared, illustrated by good artists and giving reliable drawings of the leading fashions of the day. Typical of the best of such publications was the French journal *Le Cabinet des Modes* and, at the end of the century, the German *Gallery of Fashion*, begun in 1794 by Niklaus Wilhelm von Heideloff from Stuttgart who had worked for Ackermann, the bookseller and publisher of quality prints. *The Gallery of Fashion* was a superb production on fine quarto-sized paper. Its annual subscription was three guineas, despite a limited issue of some twenty plates per annum. On each of the plates was engraved two or three figures, showing accessories also, and giving descriptions of the garments. They were a record (highly prized today) of existing, not future, modes.

Men's Dress

Between 1760 and the outbreak of the French Revolution in 1789, fashionable men continued to wear the same three basic outer garments – coat, waistcoat, breeches – but the materials, decoration and cut of the first two of these gradually altered. (plate 25, plate 27). The trend was for colours to become more muted, fabrics to be heavier and less opulent (wool largely replacing silk, satin and velvet for everyday wear) and ornamentation to become more restrained. In cut, sleeves narrowed and cuffs and pocket flaps became smaller. The front edge buttoning of the coat, originally full-length, now only extended to the hips. The whole cut of the coat and waistcoat was slenderer, the coat worn open and tails cut back sleekly on the hips (**166, 169**). As wigs became smaller and, eventually, natural hair styles resumed, a

166 Grey velvet coat with silver stripe, rich embroidery on pockets and edges. White satin lining. Waistcoat embroidered all over. Breeches to match coat. White stockings, black shoes. Cane. White tie wig. Actual costume. Rijksmuseum, Amsterdam.

167 Brown jacket. Red and brown striped waistcoat. Grey-blue trousers. Black hat. White shirt. The actor Chenard dressed as a *Sansculotte*. Painting by Boilly, 1792. Musée Carnavalet, Paris.

168 Dark green coat, the edges embroidered in white and shades of pink. Red silk caped cloak. White powdered wig. White stockings, green breeches, black shoes. Actual costume. Museum of Costume, Bath.

169   French fashionable dress at the Palace of Versailles.
A   Polonaise gown. Decorative hat over cadogan wig. 1781. Bibliothèque Nationale, Paris.
B   Plum-coloured satin coat, waistcoat and breeches. Embroidered in colours in silk, a floral design. Powdered wig. White stockings, black shoes. *c.* 1781. Actual costume. Musée du Costume de la Ville de Paris.
C   Dark satin pelisse with fur edging and lining. White decorative cap, baigneuse style. Powdered wig. Satin shoes. 1778. Drawing. Galerie des Modes et Costumes Français.
D   White satin gown with gold decoration, fringe and tassels. White coiffure with plumes. *c.* 1775. Portrait of Queen Marie Antoinette by Madame Vigée-Lebrun, Palace of Versailles.
E   Beige patterned velvet suit with coloured silk embroidered panel edging. White powdered wig. White stockings, black shoes. *c.* 1770. Actual costume. Musée du Costume de la Ville de Paris.

small collar and revers were introduced. In the 1780s the simpler English styles strongly influenced general fashion. In these the coat was very slimly cut and the waistcoat ended in a straight horizontal line at waist level; sometimes it had revers and was of plainer material than hitherto (**170, 171**).

Outside France, men's dress of the 1790s altered slowly, the trends of the eighties continuing. English styles were paramount in

masculine wear and movement was towards social equality expressed in the attire and a diminution of privilege; this manifested itself in greater severity and plainness in style, materials and colours. Steel coat buttons were fashionable. Waistcoats were often horizontally striped (**170**).

In France changes of style were abrupt, frequent and acute. In the early years of the Revolution people did not dare to wear items

170　Striped faille coat in light and dark green, steel buttons. Cadogan style white wig. Plain white breeches and stockings. Fawn waistcoat. Black shoes. Black bicorne hat with gold braid and lace. Actual costume. Musée du Costume de la Ville de Paris.

171　Red coat. White and gold striped waistcoat. Gold breeches. Stockings striped in gold and white. Black slippers. Black hat over grey powdered hedgehog wig. Painting. Musée Communal, Brussels.

172　Incroyable dress, 1797. Exaggerated style of coat with large revers worn open and flowered waistcoat with similar revers. Bicorne hat over long flowing hair. Tight breeches, striped stockings. Slippers, lorgnette, cane. Lithograph, Wenzel Pobuda.

173　Pale grey cloth redingote, light breeches, top boots with turned-down cuffs. Felt hat and cane, 1780. French fashion journal.

of dress associated with the former aristocracy. In men's attire, breeches and stockings were automatically linked to court dress so a longer pantaloon or trouser was adopted together with long socks. The aristocracy contemptuously dismissed wearers of this attire as *sans-culottes*, literally 'without breeches'. The name survived but most people deemed it politic to avoid controversy and the possibility of offence so played safe.

The early years of the 1790s in France permanently affected men's dress in Europe at least until well into the twentieth century. The influence of aristocratic society upon dress was replaced by that of the political assembly. Its members wore black: austere and plain. After a few years colours returned

and, under Napoleon, luxury and *culottes* came back also to the French court but dark colours for men's dress comprised a more important part of the masculine wardrobe for over a century.

In the early years of the Revolution it was considered fashionable to dress in accord with the new democratic ideal of 'liberty'. Clothes should be simple and unadorned. The basis of design was that of ancient Greece, 'birthplace of democracy'. After the execution of the King in January 1793, there were attempts to design a costume suited to everyone. Such styles were created by the intelligentsia, painters such as David for example, and were based upon the normal attire of a labourer with an overlay of clas-

174 Dark beaver hat with ribbon and buckle, cadogan wig, *c.* 1787. Actual garment, English.

175 Napoleon-style coiffure and high collar. Portrait, French, *c.* 1799.

176 Felt brown hat, cord trimming, 1790–5. English portrait.

177 White powdered pig-tail wig, *c.* 1768. English drawing.

178 Black felt bicorne hat with gold trimming, 1798. English portrait.

179 Man's negligé cap, 1760s. English portrait.

sical, i.e. ancient Greek, dress. They were, therefore, neither genuinely plebeian nor attractive or sensible; there was an air of unreality about them, almost musical comedy. Typical was the outfit with loose trousers and the short jacket called a *carmagnole**, a red cap and French sabots (**167**). Another was of a long Greek chiton with draped himation on top accompanied by the wearing of a soft woollen cap. A third version had a knee-length belted chiton worn over fitted trousers, these tucked into short boots and accompanied by a round cap and a cloak.

Such attempts to make everyone dress alike according to a misinterpretation of a concept of two thousand years earlier and in a very different climate were clearly doomed to failure. An intentional levelling down in dress could not be long maintained in a country so noted for the individuality of its people and with an upper class so accus-

* Named after a garment worn by workers in Carmagnola near Turin.

tomed to a high distinctive mode of life. After the end of the Reign of Terror in 1794, people wanted to forget, to relax and to enjoy stability in life once more. The years of the Directoire (1795–9) witnessed once more the publication of fashion journals and the various forms of government-inspired patriotic dress were set aside. The fashions worn elsewhere in Europe returned to France (plate 25, **184**, plate 27). Only the young enthusiasts, the dandies, known as *incroyables*, pursued a more extreme course. They cut their hair raggedly short and topped this with an extravagant bicorne hat. Their coats had high collars, immense revers and flared skirts. Their breeches were excessively tight in order to display the masculine leg line (**172**).

After 1760 most men abandoned the wearing of wigs and reverted to their own hair, dressed and powdered as a wig. The style of the late 1770s was the *peruke à l'hérisson*, the hedgehog wig, in which the hair was cut spikily and short all over the head but maintaining a queue at the nape (plate 25). After 1780 hairstyles were fairly short, simply and naturally coiffured. With these shorter hairstyles the small tricorne hat was adopted and this soon, after 1775, gave way to the two-pointed bicorne (**170**, **178**). From the 1780s the English style of tall-crowned hat of beaver, felt or fur, with ribbon and buckle was the predominant mode for the rest of the century (plate 25, **171**, **173**, **174**, **175**, plate 27).

English fashions also influenced men's footwear in the later eighteenth century. This was in the return to the popularity of the leather boot which replaced shoes for fashionable outdoor wear. This was a revival of the seventeenth century mode but, unlike the soft leather of the Cavalier boot, these styles were of hard, polished, usually black leather (**201**, **202**). Indoors, shoes were usually of a slipper style, cut low in front, decorated by a simple bow or buckle; they were almost heel-less. (plate 25, plate 27).

Women's Dress

Until about 1780 the French feminine mode continued to be for an artificial silhouette, the slenderized waist provided by tight lacing and the bodice, with corseting restricting the rib cage, formed in a straight, even concave line, then rising to a full, high bosom above. The décolleté neckline was edged by lace frilling or a soft fichu. Panier frameworks continued to be worn under the very full skirts in which the overskirt was looped up and back to fall down to a train; the shorter underskirt displayed a dainty toe. Gowns were made of silk, satin, taffeta or brocade. By the 1770s decoration was lavish, characterized by festoons of flowers, flounces, ribbon bows and loops and quantities of lace and tulle (plate 21, **169D**, **180**).

In the 1770s the *robe à la française* style, with its oval panier form and pleated back to the gown was reserved more and more for court dress and formal wear. The paniers extended widely at the sides and corseting was strict. For more normal wear several alternative panier styles appeared. Most of these derived from eastern Europe and were French versions of what was believed to have been worn in these areas. Most popular was the *robe à la polonaise* (though not a style worn in Poland), a vogue of about 1773–85. Very waisted and tight-bodiced, the contrastingly full overskirt was drawn up by interior cords to create three draped swags of fabric worn over three small paniers. These swags were edged with pleating or

180 Cream-coloured cotton dress embroidered in brown, red and green. Green ribbon bows. Natural hair with coronet of small pink flowers and green leaves. Black neck ribbon with silver jewel, 1777–80. Actual costume. Schweizerisches Landesmuseum, Zürich, Switzerland.

181 German outfit of flounced dress with fitted fur-edged jacket. Fichu. Straw hat. Satin shoes. Engraving by Chodowiecki, Dresden Print Room, 1770.

182 Fur-edged velvet pelisse and fur muff. Flounced gown skirt. Silk calash, 1775. French fashion journal.

183   White silk dress decorated by silver fringe and sequins. Overdress of olive green decorated by embroidery in a spot pattern, 1799. Actual costume. Rocamora Costume Museum, Barcelona.

184   Grey silk coat with steel buttons. Breeches to match. Lace jabot and sleeve ruffles. White stockings, black slippers. Natural hair. 1795. Actual costume. Rocamora Costume Museum. Barcelona.

185   Plain light-coloured coat over striped waistcoat. Dark breeches. White stockings, black shoes. White lace-edged collar. Natural hair. 1790. Portrait of Francesco di Borbone as a boy by Madame Vigée-Lebrun. Galleria Nazionale di Capodimonte, Naples.

186   Small boy in a skeleton suit with white frilled-edge collar and waist sash. Black shoes. 1785. English portrait.

187   White muslin dress embroidered in coloured silks. Border hem in classical pattern. Stole striped in yellow and tan with tan fringe, 1798. Actual costume. Rocamora Costume Museum, Barcelona.

flouncing and decorated by ribbon bows. The rear swag was larger than the side ones. The underskirt was now short enough to clear the ground – there was no train – and display shoes and ankles. Other variations included the *robe à la circassienne, à la levité, à la levantine* and *à la turque*. In these there were small differences in sleeve styles, peplum waists and skirt draping. All this period several layers of petticoats were worn with the panier frameworks (**169A, 181**).

Meanwhile, during the 1770s, the softer, less restrictive English styles were being introduced (except in France) to wider and wider areas of Europe and, after 1775, even some French ladies were becoming aware of their attractions. Such a style of gown, known as *la robe à l'anglaise*, was far more comfortable and, especially in summer,

much cooler. The panier underskirt was abandoned and, since the fullness of the skirt was concentrated at the back, this fabric needed support only from a bustle which was a simple pad resting upon the buttocks and tied on round the waist. Fewer petticoats were needed and the rigidity of the corset had been considerably relaxed. The gown still had a fitted bodice but with a higher waistline. The full, long skirt was ground-length; it was often open in front to display the underskirt and was very plain, usually decorated only by a hem flounce. Sleeves were fitting. The décolleté neckline was edged by a soft, white fichu which, in the 1780s, became very full to accentuate the high breast line: it was called the 'pouter pigeon' line (plate 23).

The French styles of the 1780s were in a transitional phase between the artificiality of the 1770s and the total contrast when every-

188 White powdered wig decorated with ribbons, jewel and ostrich plumes, 1780. Swedish portrait.

189 White cap, baigneuse style. Engraving from Galerie des Modes. 1780.

190 Straw hat with ribbons and bows, lace edging. Natural hair. English portrait, c. 1786.

191 White cap, butterfly style, French, 1776.

192 Cap and ribbon. English mob cap style, drawing.

193 Straw hat with flower decoration over white cap with ribbons. Plumes. Natural hair. French fashion plate, 1785.

194 Powdered tall wig with side curls, the back arranged in cadogan style. Decoration by ribbons, flowers and plumes. French drawing, 1775.

195 Straw chignon bonnet decorated with ribbons. Natural hair. French fashion journal c. 1800.

thing which had characterized these styles was swept away in the Revolution. The English *robe à l'anglaise* was the strongest influence, French ladies sensing that such modes were in keeping with the Rousseau-inspired 'naturalism' then prevalent in France. As in England, a waist-length jacket often accompanied these gowns with their fichu-covered necklines and long, slenderer skirts with trains.

The trend towards simpler gown styles was accompanied by one preferring lighter fabrics. Heavy satins and silks gave place to muslin, cambric and linen. White or light colours were fashionable as were sprig and spot patterns. Marie Antoinette's playing at 'milkmaid activities' led to the wearing by the aristocracy of such fabrics earlier believed to

196 Black hat, ribbons and plumes over powdered hedgehog wig. Gown striped blue and white with blue neck scarf and white fichu. Gold stole. Black velvet neck ribbons. Mrs Siddons portrait by Gainsborough, National Gallery, London, 1784.

have been suited to the 'peasantry' and these were especially adopted for caps and aprons to complete the ensembles. A style known as the *chemise à la reine* was based upon a type of gown worn by the queen. This had a ruffle-edged neckline, a high-waisted sash and a full, long skirt with hem flounce.

Though, in France, the effect of the Revolution on women's fashions was marked, it was less so than on men's; women were, at least prior to the twentieth century, less likely to follow a political cause; they were also more individualistic. For them, femininity, their attractiveness to men and their loyalty to husband and family were stronger motives than support for a movement towards social equality and political freedom. They had joyfully abandoned the shackles of corset, panier and layers of petticoats. Their only contribution towards the political themes of the day was to adopt the then French support for 'democracy' by wearing supposedly ancient Greek dress. This cult for emulation of the classical world led to the adoption of Greek classical motifs – the fret pattern and anthemion designs used especially on garment edging – and to classical hairstyles.

Fashionable feminine attire of the 1790s was then a blend of a development from the English modes of the eighties together with the more classical form from France. Some ladies – generally the younger and more fashion conscious – pursued this road more vigorously than the more conservative-minded. Few garments were worn. The corset and bustle were abandoned and one thin petticoat was considered adequate. Under this was a simple chemise and, possibly, stockings. Fabrics were thin: muslin, tulle, cotton, gauze. Colours were light or white. Fabrics were plain or very daintily patterned; polka dot spots were popular. It was presumed that, since surviving classical statuary in marble was white, that was how ancient Greeks dressed, an opinion which we now know to be erroneous.

The style of the Directoire gown was in stark contrast to that of the 1770s. The undecorated neckline was cut very low and wide. At the same time the waistline rose to be just below the breasts so giving a bodice only three to four inches deep. Ribbons often delineated the breasts and a dainty girdle encircled the 'waistline'. The skirt fell long and loose in soft folds from here to a train at the rear. Until about 1800 garments became fewer and fabrics thinner. Such attire may have been suitable for much of the year in Greece but was certainly not so in northern Europe. Ladies shivered. They tried to keep warm by wearing a thin negligée-type overgown or a three-quarter length tunic of velvet or wool. They draped themselves in stoles and shawls of cashmere or silk; these varied greatly in size and shape. They were fringed or tasselled at the edges and were often the main note of colour and pattern in the costume (**182, 187,** plate 26).

Outdoors in the early 1770s the multi-purpose cloak or cape was tending to be replaced by a *pelisse*. This velvet or satin garment, half-way between cloak and coat, was probably of eastern origin. It was fur-trimmed and, in winter fur-lined. It had a large collar and slits for hands in front (**182**). After 1775 short jackets or long, fitted cloth redingotes provided alternative wear with the simpler English and Directoire gowns.

The complete contrast between styles of the 1770s and those of the 1790s was nowhere more notable than in the realm of the coiffure and headcoverings. Whereas men had worn immense periwigs from the late seventeenth century onwards, the styles gradually diminishing and finally disappearing in the 1780s, the history of elaborate feminine coiffures was in reverse order. Until 1750 short natural hair, dressed simply, had prevailed, the interest being concentrated on the elaborate dresses. From about 1750 this neat small coiffure disappeared. At first the hair was grown longer and dressed more elaborately. It was treated with pomatum* and powdered white.

From about 1760 the coiffure grew larger and in the 1770s, reached its apogee. The erection was very tall, false hair or a complete wig being adopted as necessary. It was decorated profusely with pearl ropes, flowers, feathers, ribbons and a variety of

---

* This concoction was the eighteenth century equivalent of hair lacquer and became increasingly necessary as styles were ever more complex.

198 Pink satin lady's shoe with coloured silk embroidery, 1780. Musée du Costume de la Ville de Paris.

199 Black silk lady's shoe with diamanté buckle, 1780. Rocamora Costume Museum, Barcelona.

200 Brown and cream satin lady's shoe. Italian heel.

197 Boy in skeleton suit with white collared shirt, white socks and black shoes. Black hat. Engraving after W. Bigg (*see* Fig. 204).

201 Black leather top boot with buff leather cuff. English, Central Museum, Northampton.

202 Black Hessian boot, Central Museum, Northampton.

other ornaments. Ringlets fell over the shoulders and on to the breasts, great sausage curls decorated the sides and the back was dressed in the masculine cadogan style. Extreme versions of these fashions were adopted for formal, especially evening, functions. Such erections had to be dressed by hairdressers, several hours being needed to create such artistry and, needless to say, the creation was not too frequently dismantled. The constant application of pomatum and rice or wheat powder created a verminous condition which must have been profoundly uncomfortable (**169D, 188, 194**).

From about 1780, as in men's dress, the simpler hedgehog style of wig replaced such complex erections (**196**) and, in the 1790s, natural hair, dressed in classical chignon or short curly styles was fashionable. These styles were decorated with ribbon banding and plumes – an immense contrast to 20 years earlier.

Women still wore caps indoors and out for much of the eighteenth century (**191**). As the coiffure became larger, in the 1760s and 1770s, the dainty caps were replaced by extravagantly larger overdecorated ones with an abundance of ribbons, lace and flouncing. They went by a variety of descriptive names, indicating their origins but not their later functions: *baigneuse, dormeuse* etc. (**189, 192**). Hats were worn outdoors on top of the caps, especially from the 1770s onwards. Those of the earlier years were small and dainty, perched on the forehead at an angle (**193**) while, in the 1780s, the large-brimmed English styles became the mode, ornamented with a profusion of flowers and ribbons (**190**). Directoire hats were of a wide variety of designs, often tall and now much smaller.

A fashionable outdoor covering for the elaborate wigs of the 1760s and 1770s was the calash (calèche) which was a large, articulated hood made as a hooped frame covered in ruched and padded silk. This could be pulled up or lowered over the coiffure as required in the manner of a perambulator hood. It was tied under the chin by wide ribbons (**182**).

Women's shoes had pointed toes and high curved heels until after 1775. They were of satin, silk or velvet, richly embroidered and decorated by jewelled buckles and lace; often they matched the gown. With the shorter skirts of the 1770s they became more important as they were visible (**198, 199, 200**). They were worn with coloured stockings. After this heels became gradually lower and, after the Revolution, the heel-less slipper, tied on with ribbons, became the mode as also was the Greek style sandal.

A heavy use of cosmetics and perfume as well as application of face patches continued until the simpler modes of the 1780s; a more natural skin care practice followed. With the introduction of simple gowns of thin material a handbag or reticule became a necessity – pockets had been hidden in the skirt folds before this to contain keys, cosmetics etc. The reticule hung over the arm by handles (plate 26). Such bags were decoratively embroidered with jewels and beads. Fans were still carried and used as were parasols. Large fur muffs became most important for warmth in the winters of the 1790s (**182**). Jewellery was worn in abundance all through the eighteenth century but later designs were less elaborate and ostentatious.

Fashion Designers

Although France had led the world of *la mode* since the time of Louis XIV, the names of leading designers had not been especially noted. Tailors and dressmakers were, by tradition, mainly men but it was in 1675 that women dressmakers successfully petitioned the king to be permitted to make feminine underwear, skirts and petticoats, peignoirs and accessories on the grounds that this would be in accord with feminine modesty. The feminine dressmakers then founded their own corporation and guilds.

The first designer with marked influence, whose reputation is well known, was also a woman: Rose Bertin from Abbeville. She was a milliner, a vitally important profession in the 1770s when overdecorated coiffures were surmounted by elaborate caps and hats. Madame Bertin was highly successful in this field so came to Paris where she set up her salon in the fashionable Rue Faubourg S. Honoré in 1773. Here her eye for design and colour quickly made her indispensable to the Parisian aristocracy and she became milliner and dressmaker to the Dauphine, soon to be Queen Marie Antoinette.

The Revolution brought an end to Rose Bertin's career in France. She went to Germany where she was patronized by French émigrés but, on her return to France in 1800, she failed to adapt to the new modes and died in obscurity in 1812. The rising star was then Louis Leroy who, before the Revolution, was also a designer for the aristocracy, a coiffeur, milliner and tailor. Unlike Madame Bertin, he remained in France and soon, having curried favour with the new régime, was rewarded by being asked to design clothes for members of the Convention.

Children's Dress

For centuries children's dress had taken the form of a miniaturized version of that worn by their parents (plate 22) but it was in the 1770s that this custom began to change and garments for children show a divergence from adult attire; indeed, in many aspects the child's clothes became the prototypes of designs adopted later by the adult world.

The liberalization of thought and the ideas and themes of philosophers such as the seventeenth century John Locke and the eighteenth century Jean Jacques Rousseau were bearing fruit at this time but it was not until the Revolution that adult dress in France underwent such a *volte face* away from artificial overdecoration towards modified classicism. In children's dress this development towards greater suitability and freedom of attire began earlier especially in boys' wear.

Baby boys continued to be dressed in petticoats and skirts (plate 24) but the five-year old, when breeched, instead of being put into knee breeches, coat and waistcoat was, from the late 1770s, dressed in a skeleton suit (skeletons). This outfit, which was much more comfortable, consisted of ankle-length, loose-fitting trousers, generally made of cotton materials, which buttoned on to a soft, frilled shirt or a short, fitting jacket.

15   The man wears a short silk jacket and petticoat breeches (rhinegraves) decorated with satin ribbon loops, a lace cravat and knee falls. His curled hair falls softly upon his shoulders. His felt hat is ornamented with ostrich plumes. He carries a be-ribboned fur muff. English Restoration dress from a painting, 1660.

16   A dark overgown with embroidered silk collar. A lighter silk undergown with white silk sleeves and lace cuffs. Ribbon bows. Pearl necklace. From an engraving by Aubry, c.1650. Nuremburg Germanisches Museum.

17   A fur-edged and linen samare showing the Dutch influence on American Colonial dress of 1660. Silk gown with gold embroidery. Silk undergown, embroidered all over. Heavy silk hood and face mask. Fan. From American portraits.

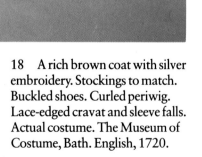

18   A rich brown coat with silver embroidery. Stockings to match. Buckled shoes. Curled periwig. Lace-edged cravat and sleeve falls. Actual costume. The Museum of Costume, Bath. English, 1720.

19   Velvet coat with silk embroidered cuffs. Velvet breeches, silk stockings. Leather shoes with jewelled metal buckles. Powdered tie wig.

20   Velvet coat with gold buttons and passementerie. Large buttoned back decorative cuffs. Silk brocade waistcoat. Velvet breeches, silk stockings. Leather shoes with jewelled metal buckles. Felt tricorne hat. Powdered tie wig. Silk shirt and ruffles. Cane. Sword. Painting Ca' Rezzonico, Venice. Italian dress.

21   Robe à la française made of brocaded
silk with rococo and floral motifs. Gold lace
at neck and shoulders. Pagoda-style sleeve
with ruffles (engageántes) beneath.
Powdered hair. French gown. Bayerische
Nationalmuseum, Munich.

LE DÉJEUNER BY FRANÇOIS BOUCHER, 1739

22   A domestic breakfast scene. Both women are
wearing the robe à la française and their neat coiffures
are unpowdered. Both children wear caps and
dresses. The child on the right also wears on his head,
on top of his cap, a padded covering known in
England as a 'pudding'; this was for protection in case
he should have a tumble. Louvre, Paris.

23   Walking costume c.1785. Robe à l'Anglaise in striped satin. Jacket with small bustle. White, embroidery-edged fichu and wrist frills. Cream silk-covered hat with striped ribbons and white draped crown. French gown. Boston Museum of Fine Arts, USA.

24   Portrait by Duprat of the Duke of Monferrato as a small boy, 1764. Velvet and satin dress. Muslin cap. Italian, Palazzo Reale, Turin.

25   Silk coat with striped collar and revers, buttons covered by same material. White waistcoat with sprig pattern embroidered in colours. Stockinet breeches, silk stockings, leather slippers. Hedgehog wig, felt hat. Actual costume, French, 1780s. Victoria and Albert Museum, London.

26   Silk gown with appliqué embroidery. White kid
gloves. Silk turban with plume. Embroidered kid
reticule. Actual costume, Musée Historique des
Tissus, Lyons, c.1797.

27   Striped silk coat and waistcoat.
Stockinet breeches. Silk stockings.
Leather shoes. High collar with cravat.
Felt hat, cane. Actual costume, Victoria
and Albert Museum, London, 1790–5.

28   Day dress with fringe and cord trimming. White tulle 'betsie'. Long kid gloves. Satin slippers. Actual costume *c.*1815. French. Musée du Costume de la Ville de Paris.

29   Day dress of tail coat, waistcoat and strapped pantaloons. Stand-up collar and cravat. Top hat and gloves. Leather boots and cane. 1815. Italian. Corriere delle Dame, Milan.

203 Dorsetshire
peasants wearing smocks.

The trouser design was derived from the country peasant type and its introduction for children's fashionable dress ante-dated that of trousers for this purpose for men by a generation. The attire of the skeleton suit was completed by white socks, flat-heeled black shoes and a broad-brimmed hat. Sometimes a waist sash was worn. This remained the standard oufit until about 1830 (186, 197, 204).

A parallel revolution took place in the dress of little girls where the change from constricted waists and layers of petticoats to high-waisted simple dresses ante-dated the adult changes on these lines. Ankle-length dresses were white or light-coloured; they had short sleeves and a sash encircled a high waistline.

American Dress

The American Revolution affected the attitude there to dress. During the years of struggle and war which led to Independence, of necessity restrictions had been placed upon the importation of goods of foreign manufacture. Home-produced fabrics were being used for the making of garments and luxurious attire was eschewed. A simplicity and plainness of costume, out of tune with the current European fashions, resulted. After the Declaration of Independence and the end of the war with England, the majority of Americans did not return to ordering their clothes from the mother country. Paris became and remained the chief source of fashion for well-to-do Americans.

Clothes for the Ordinary Man and Woman

The cotton revolution in England transformed the wear of the ordinary man and woman. Here was a fabric which was less costly to purchase, which was available in quantity in the shops to be made up at home into attractive garments. Moreover, particularly from about 1780 onwards, it was eminently suited to the newer, simpler styles. Even more to the point, cotton is a fabric

204 'Black Monday' or the Departure for School. Dress for schoolboys. Note the difference between the younger boy who wears a skeleton suit and the older one who is dressed in adult attire. Engraving, 1790.

which can, without harm, be washed frequently. Before its advent so many fabrics, worn by nobleman or peasant, were unsuited to being washed; velvet, brocade, silks and fur linings could not be washed and woollens shrank and became felted. So, washday at home had, prior to the eighteenth century, been an infrequent event, taking place every two or three months. By 1750 it took place, in a large household, monthly or even fortnightly. The washing, pressing and ironing occupied nearly a week.

That characteristic garment of the countryman, the smock, was also given a boost by the availability of cheap cotton. It became a kind of rustic uniform in the second half of the eighteenth century and remained so for much of the nineteenth. Smocks were made in various colours. Sunday best ones – often made from fine linen – were termed smock-frocks. The smock was a full garment with round neck opening and long full sleeves (**203**). It was slipped on over the head on top of other garments. For women the bedgown continued to be worn.

During the later eighteenth century ready-made clothes became available. At this time these were ill-fitting and of poor quality; they were advertised for purchase by working class men and women; the middle classes would not deign to buy them.

CHAPTER SEVEN

1800–1830

Classicism to Romanticism

A steady decline in national influence upon fashionable dress took place during the whole of the eighteenth century and by the early 1800s it was negligible: an international style had evolved. Local and national characteristics still moulded peasant dress and, to a lesser extent, that of the bourgeoisie where climate, occupation and locality continued to produce a myriad variations upon the main theme.

For the whole of the nineteenth century fashionable dress, worn by the aristocracy and upper middle and professional classes, was dominated by France for women's designs and by England for those of the men. French modes had been of paramount influence since the time of Louis XIV but, by the early 1800s, the combination of circumstances of the unification of Europe (England excepted) under the dominance of Napoleonic France and, in the years 1814–15, the considerable numbers of English tourists flocking to Paris while Allied armies were in occupation, led to an immense popularity for French fashions; these were what was considered to be *chic* for elegant ladies.

The years 1800–1830 were those which established the English gentleman as the best-dressed and best-mannered in Europe. The noted English elegants of these years, imperturbable, ironic, graceful, were models for aristocratic bearing and behaviour. Best known of these dandies was George Bryan Brummell (1778–1840). Reputed since his youth as extremely fastidious in dress, he deeply impressed the Prince Regent who

sponsored him to become a leading light in Brighton society. However, there was nothing flamboyant about his dress. 'Beau' Brummell wore garments in subtly coloured fabrics with a minimum of decoration but these were superbly cut and made. Typical was his blue tail coat with brass buttons worn over a fawn waistcoat accompanied by light-coloured buckskin pantaloons and elegant black boots. For evening wear his waistcoat was white and pantaloons of blue stockinet strapped over black slippers. He certainly helped to popularize the wearing of trousers instead of knee breeches.

Textiles

The textile industries of all western European countries began to flourish and expand after the upheavals of the Napoleonic wars. Mechanization increased output and steam power was introduced. England was the leader in this textile revolution and so the most prosperous country, London becoming the chief economic centre. Trade overseas to the Americas, the Indies, the Far East and Australasia expanded explosively and British fabrics enjoyed world-wide sales and dominance.

The most important technical advance of these years, though, came from France. This was the successful development of pattern weaving on the punched-card system – a method adopted in a different age to become the basis of the early computers. The French had invented a punched-card method as early as 1725 but it was not until 1801 that Joseph

205 Joseph Marie Jacquard. Engraving. Science Museum, London.

Marie Jacquard (1752–1834) produced a practical and satisfactory apparatus which made it possible for all the necessary motions of the loom to be controlled solely by the weaver. The pattern to be woven was drawn on squared paper and from this the punched cards were prepared. The warp threads were then forced mechanically to follow this pattern by means of the holes punched in the cards. The Jacquard attachment was intended for use in the silk industry where as many as 1200 individual cards controlled the raising and lowering of several hundred warp threads. The attachment, for hand or power looms, was later adapted to weave other fibres. Jacquard's invention was taken over by the French government in 1806 and a royalty and pension were paid to the inventor (205).

Fashion Journals

The nineteenth century was the heyday of the fashion journal, hand-coloured and, until after 1830, mainly produced in France and England. Notable were *La Belle Assemblée*, *Le Bon Ton* and *La Mode* from France and *The Lady's Monthly Museum* and *The Ladies' Monthly Magazine* from England with, from Milan, *Corriere delle Dame*. It was by means of such journals that information about current styles was disseminated throughout Europe and north America.

Men's Dress

The important change in these years was the gradual adoption of pantaloons to replace the wearing of knee breeches and stockings, a custom which had persisted for so long. There was strong opposition, particularly in fashionable circles in England and France, to the ousting of breeches from customary wear but by 1820 the changeover was virtually complete. It will be remembered that in children's dress trousers had replaced the wearing of knee breeches in the 1770s (p. 80) but adult males were slow to copy this fashion.

The word pantaloon had a long history. It had been in use in the sixteenth century – Shakespeare had referred in *As You Like It* to the 'leane and slipper'd Pantaloone' when he was discussing the seven ages of man. In Italian comedy, Pantalone was an elderly character who wore such fitting trousers. After the later seventeenth century the word went out of use until its revival about 1790 to describe a tight-fitting trouser worn at the time of the French Revolution (p. 73). The typical pantaloons of the early nineteenth century were usually made from an elastic-type of material such as stockinet or soft doeskin. They were light in colour: white, lemon, beige or grey were preferred. Also fashionable were those cut from a nankeen fabric which was a strong cotton imported from Nanking in China. Early pantaloons were leg-hugging, extending to just below the calf and worn inside tall boots. Gradually these were worn longer so that by 1817–18 they reached down to the ankles where they

206 Grey tail coat. Fawn pantaloons and black boots. Black top hat. Gloves. Fob watches. French costume, painting, Louvre, Paris, 1819.

207 Brown cutaway tail coat. Fawn waistcoat. Spotted fawn cravat, white collar. Black top hat. White trousers. Pink striped socks. Black boots. Brown gloves. Cane. Austrian fashion plate, Wiener Moden, 1826.

208 Dark blue tail coat with black collar. White waistcoat, cravat and collar. Grey pantaloons. Mauve striped socks and black boots. Cream gloves. Black top hat. Austrian fashion plate, Wiener Moden, 1826.

209 Sea-blue cloth redingote with black braid and tassel fastenings. Black top hat. Black and white stock and white collar. Grey trousers, black boots. Light grey gloves, cane. Actual Polish costume. Narodowe Museum, Cracow, Poland, c. 1830.

were fastened by buttons or a buckle. By 1820 they were still fitting but were longer still and were strapped under the instep to hold them down (206–209, plate 29).

The tail coat had become *de rigueur* in these years. Two styles predominated at this time. One was double-breasted, cut away square in front at waist level and descended at the back to knee-level tails. The other was single-breasted then was cut away, curving snugly round the hips to shorter, rounded tails at the rear. The cut and style of these coats altered gradually but significantly over these three decades. In the early years coat collars were high, boned up to the ears, lapels were large, body and sleeves were fitting. As time passed sleeves became fuller, especially on the upper arm and the material was pleated or gathered at the shoulder into the armhole. The collar became lower and simpler; a shawl design became fashionable.

Coats were very waisted – corsets were adopted by many men in order to achieve the desired silhouette – but, in contrast, were padded on the chest and hips to accentuate this. Materials were becoming heavier, usually wool or cloth, and colours were darker browns, greens or blues (206–209, plate 29).

Waistcoats followed the line of the coat. They were white or light in colour and might be striped or spotted in pattern (207, 208).

There were three chief styles of overcoat. The dress mode for town wear was still the redingote. Usually double-breasted this was waisted with knee-length flared skirts. The cold weather travelling design was the long, voluminous Garrick which had collar, cuffs and several shoulder capes. The third style was derived from military dress in eastern Europe. It had a high or stand-up collar and across the chest in rows were braided and

210 and 211. 210. Walking dress in pink muslin trimmed with white lace. White muslin pelisse with yellow sarsnet trimming. Straw hat. 211. Full dress in satin and muslin, long train. Green trimming. White crêpe cap with flowers. Buff gloves. Fashion plates from *Cabinet of Fashion*, 1806.

212 Dark spencer with piped decoration. White spotted dress with lace flounce. Bonnet to match spencer. Lace and plume decoration. Italian fashion plate, *Corriere delle Dame*, Milan, 1818.

213 Hussar velvet jacket with braid and fur decoration. Silk gown. Fur muff. Velvet hat with plumes. Laced slippers. French costume, painting, 1813.

frogged button fastenings. A new material was introduced at this time. This was a waterproof fabric deriving from the researches of a Scottish chemist Charles Macintosh who cemented two layers of rubber together with naphtha between and incorporated this into woollen travelling coats (**209**).

Prior to the nineteenth century there had been no particular form of dress for evening to differentiate it from day wear; it was simply a richer, more colourful and ornamented version. By 1820, though, the evening attire in black was being introduced. It consisted of an elegantly cut slim version of day-time pantaloons and tail coats worn with a white or coloured waistcoat.

In men's linen, collars were attached to the shirt and, in the early years especially, were turned upwards to cover part of the cheekbone. The white silk or linen cravat could be tied in various ways. Sometimes a black satin cravat was wound round on top of the white one making the neckwear appear somewhat bulky.

Men's hairstyles were fairly short, naturally curled or waved. As time passed hair was worn longer and curls were arranged over the ears. Beards were unusual but curled side whiskers were fashionable. The top hat had been introduced in the early years of the century but did not finally oust the tall felt English hat from fashion until about 1820. After this it became the nineteenth century hat, worn on all occasions and, strange as it seems today, by all classes of the population. The shape of the top hat varied over the years though. At this time it had curved sides, an upswept brim and was not overly tall (**206–209**).

Throughout this century men wore boots rather than shoes. At first these were high and stiff, pulled on over the stockings or

214 White satin ball dress with gold metal embroidery. White slippers and gloves. Circular white lace fan. Deep red leaves as hair decoration. French actual costume. Boston Museum of Fine Arts, USA, 1820–5.

215 Cream dress with open lace-work overlay. Self-coloured ribbon ornamentation on bodice and skirt. White gloves. Flowers in hair. Actual Spanish costume. Rocamora Costume Museum. Barcelona, Spain, c. 1820.

216 Bride's white satin wedding dress with white gauze trimming. White veil and gloves. Flowers in hair. White slippers. Actual Dutch costume. Kostuum Museum, The Hague, 1825.

217 Promenade dress of blue wool decorated with satin. White collar. Embroidered reticule. Bonnet with striped ribbons and flowers. Gloves. Actual Swedish costume. Nordiska Museet, Stockholm, 1830.

pantaloons. From about 1820 softer boots were donned under the pantaloons and, with the passing of the years, became much shorter. They had narrow square-ended toes. For evening and indoor wear slippers were the norm; these had ribbon bows on the instep (206–209).

With the early style fitted pantaloons fob watches were fashionable, each depending from a ribbon or strap just below the waist on each side. Often only one watch was genuine, the other was a dummy known as a *fausse montre*. Snuff was still taken and beautiful boxes were concealed in waistcoat pockets. A cane would normally be carried out-of-doors by gentlemen.

Women's Dress

The story of feminine fashion in the nineteenth century presents a marked contrast to that of the men. While masculine clothes were becoming heavier, more formal, less decorative and colourful and were settling in towards slower and less fundamental changes, feminine modes changed frequently, each style lasting a much shorter time than hitherto. The form, colour, ornamentation and fabrics used became increasingly varied as the century advanced; each decade presented something different. Students of costume are able easily to date a fashion by its silhouette alone. The nineteenth century is known for its eclecticism in all the arts, a regurgitation of almost every feature of design so far presented. Costume is less eclectic and though some styles can clearly be recognized as having been derived from past modes the nineteenth century version is different, owing these variations to a period when life was unlike that of any previous age. This was the era of industrial-

218 White cotton dress with white stitched embroidery. White ruffles and pantalettes. Embroidered velvet reticule. Actual Swiss costume. Bernisches Historisches Museum, Berne, Switzerland, c. 1805.

219 Skeleton suit with white shirt and socks. Black shoes with buckles. Black hat with ribbons and plumes. French painting, 1815–20.

ization, urbanization, rapid increase in population, especially in cities. The way of life had fundamentally changed. It had become more varied with the advent of improved means of transport, of different forms of housing, of a longer expectation of life and of a higher standard of living for many. The clothes of the time reflected all this. Designs included garments for new forms of sport and leisure activity, for seaside and country holidays, for travel, for town and country wear. Men's wear reflected this also but to a much less marked and varied extent.

Fashions of the first decade of the new century continued in much the same vein as those of the late 1790s. The classical influence persisted in the simple draped lines of the gown of white or light colours and with a minimum of decoration and underwear. The fabrics from which these gowns were made were thin, notably tulle, batiste, lawn, muslin, gauze and taffeta. Decoration, generally embroidered, was confined to hems and necklines. In style, the high waistline just under the breasts persisted as did the low, wide neckline. The walking dress hemline reached the ground and, for evening wear, a long train was added (**210, 211**).

To provide extra warmth a wide variety of shawls and stoles were available and these were draped in differing ways. They came in all shapes and sizes – square, rectangular, semicircular – and, in contrast to the gowns, were often richly coloured and decorated, their edges fringed or tasselled. Alternative means of keeping warm were provided by the waist-length spencer with puff and long sleeves, the open coat of three-quarter length, the pelisse and the tunic or overdress. The tunic usually came down to the knees and was of heavier material than the gown such as velvet or heavy satin and it was decoratively embroidered round the hem and down the centre front.

Between 1810 and 1820 fashions gradually changed. Fabrics became more varied, including brocades, wool and heavy silks. Colours were varied, also stronger. Decoration was more widespread. The silhouette changed too. Day dresses had higher necklines and at the throat it was fashionable to wear a ruffle called, in England, a 'betsie', after the ruffs of Elizabethan times. The waistline descended slightly and the hemline rose to clear the ground, the train being abandoned. The short, spencer-type jacket

220 Pale green dress with black and white stripe. Black velvet sash. Actual Swiss costume. Bernisches Historisches Museum, Berne, Switzerland, 1805.

221 Wool jacket and trousers. Shirt ruffle at neck. White socks, black slippers. English drawing, 1811.

222 Straw bonnet, gipsy style, with veil and scarf tie. Fashion plate, 1808.

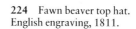

223 Coat with shawl collar. French painting, 1830.

224 Fawn beaver top hat. English engraving, 1811.

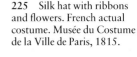

225 Silk hat with ribbons and flowers. French actual costume. Musée du Costume de la Ville de Paris, 1815.

226 Black felt bicorne hat edged with gold braid. English drawing, 1807.

227 Straw bonnet, beehive style. Flower decoration, ribbon necktie. French fashion plate, 1803.

228 White silk hat with white lace trimming and flowers. French fashion plate, *La Mode*, 1830.

continued in fashion but for colder weather a long coat was adopted which had a collar and fur trimming. The typical long sleeve of this time, whether for dress or coat, had a puff at the top then was fitting to the wrist. For evening wear a short puff was usual then long gloves to above the elbow. Evening necklines were décolleté (**212**, **213**, plate 28).

After 1820 the waistline gradually returned to its normal level. When this position was reached, about 1826, the natural instinct to slenderize it re-asserted itself and this was accentuated by a tightly pulled wide belt. Simultaneously the skirt became shorter, to ankle-length, and fuller. This larger skirt area then lent itself to further ornamentation which was provided, generally at the lower part, by ribbon bows, flowers, flounced and scalloped fabric. The day-time neckline was fairly high, often with a collar. In the evening it was décolleté, almost off the shoulder. Sleeves became fuller and the leg-of-mutton style (gigot in France) began to be established by 1830. This was very full on the

upper part then fitting from elbow to wrist. The shoulder line was then sloping, the width accentuated by the full stop to the sleeve (**214**, **217**).

The association of white as a colour symbol for a bride, as well as denoting innocence, was gradually accepted as a tradition from the late eighteenth century. Partly this was because many gowns were white anyway and partly because the weddings of royalty and the aristocracy were often attired in white or silver. By 1800 white was thought to be ideal for the wedding gown and, in 1813, the first fashion plate of a white wedding dress appeared in the *Journal des Dames*. It was from this time onwards that the white wedding with its specially designed gown for wear on just one occasion became customary (**216**).

It was in the early years of the nineteenth century that more frequent references were made in journals to the wearing of drawers – or pantaloons as they were often called – by women. Their use had become necessary

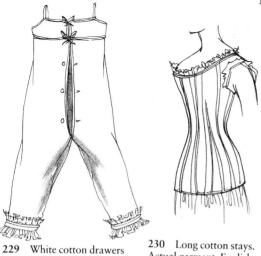

229 White cotton drawers with muslin trimming. Actual garment, English, 1815–30.

230 Long cotton stays. Actual garment, English, *c.* 1810.

because of the fashion for thin dresses. Such drawers were at first made from linen, cotton or muslin but, as the fashion for thin dresses continued, European winters forced women to seek warmer underwear and silk and wool were also used. Such warmer drawers were full and long, extending from a bodice held up by shoulder straps to the knee or calf. For summer wear waist to knee designs were more usual (**229**).

Until the late 1820s corsets were only adopted by older and more corpulent women. Simple girdles and soft long stays which did not accentuate the figure were fashionable. It was only when the waist returned to its natural position that a shorter, more waisted design was reintroduced (**230**).

Classical hairstyles were in vogue in the first decade of the new century. These were either short and curly or in longer chignon modes. Nets, ribbons and combs held these coiffures in place and turbans and scarves, with ostrich plume decoration, were fashionable headcoverings. After this hairstyles became longer and bonnets and hats were the mode. Towards 1830 the coiffure was more elaborate and both bonnets and hats became very large (**210–17, 222, 225, 227, 228**).

A reticule hung over the arm was still essential because of the simple thin gowns though pockets in the skirt seams reappeared in the late 1820s. Other important accessories

included a fur muff, a parasol, a fan and gloves (**213, 214, 217, 231, 235**).

Children's Dress

This changed little during these years, the younger boys wearing a skeleton suit with frilled shirt or trousers with waist-length jacket and the older ones adopting adult wear. Girls' dresses were still simple, a sash marking the high waistline. After 1820 skirts became much shorter so that the pantaloons which they had adopted, even before their mothers had done, were visible below the skirt hem down as far as the ankles. Shorter versions, called pantalettes, were merely leglets tied on by tapes at the knee. Both types were trimmed at the bottom with frills and ribbons (**218–21**).

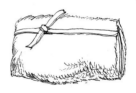

231 White swansdown muff with white ribbon. Actual item, Dutch, *c.* 1810.

232 Black leather Wellington boot. Actual item, 1820.

234 Blue satin slipper. Actual item, Rocamora Museum, Barcelona, Spain. *c.* 1820.

235 Embroidered and painted white satin muff. Actual item, English, 1800.

233 Blue fabric slipper with silk ribbons. Actual item, English, 1828–30.

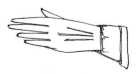

236 White kid glove. Actual item. French, *c.* 1810.

CHAPTER EIGHT

1830–1865

Industrial Prosperity

Despite recurrent conflicts and social unrest in Europe, these years were a time of increasing prosperity and, for the upper classes, luxury in dress was evident. As time passed, changes in fashion, particularly in feminine attire, succeeded one another more rapidly. For both sexes there was a greater variety in clothes regarded as essential wear for different times of day and for different events and functions, the complete costume being changed several times a day.

By the 1850s the leading nations in Europe, also America, were wealthy, their prominent citizens dressed elegantly in quality fabrics. The Second Empire in France, under Napoleon III and his empress Eugénie, led the fashionable world. These were the years of crinoline skirts, requiring vast quantities of material and decoration to make them up (242). At the same time, men's dress became more formal and stereotyped, its fabrics heavy, its colours sombre (246). In this contrast the dress of the sexes acted as a foil one to the other. Not since the time of Elizabeth I had feminine attire been so weighty, so elaborate, so hot, so uncomfortable but elegant and impressive it was indeed.

It was now not only the aristocracy which could dress in such luxurious garments. Quality fabrics and dressmaking were becoming available to a middle and professional class which was increasing rapidly in numbers and wealth. A number of related factors were responsible for this wider availability, for instance, industrialization, mechanical invention, the spread of great empires,

the population explosion, the establishment and development of marketing.

Textiles

An important factor in the increased availability of quality clothes was the rapid development of the textile industry. In major countries all over the world industrialization of the production of textiles was expanding, bringing further mechanization to all the traditional processes – preparation, spinning, weaving, dyeing (237). At the same time there was a marked expansion in the production of the raw materials for this industry. This was especially so in the realm of wool where the merino sheep – crossbred and developed over the centuries in Europe – was introduced into the Americas, South Africa and Australia. In South America and Australia in particular, enormous quantities of fine wool were produced. In Australia expansion had been especially rapid and, from the 29 sheep exported there in 1788 the national flock by 1860 numbered 20 million head. The finest wools were shipped from Botany Bay so lending the name to Botany wool which became a synonym for such quality yarns.

Aniline Dyes

For many years attempts had been made to create synthetic dyes, so extending the colour range. It was Sir William Henry Perkin in England who made the first of these dyes, called aniline, in 1856. The chemical base aniline had been obtained earlier, its name

91

237 Factory use of mechanical textile processes, 1835. Carding, drawing and roving. Science Museum, London.

derived from the Sanskrit word for the indigo plant. Since the days of Perkin these dyes have been made chiefly from coal tar and are often so-called. Perkin named his first dye mauveine. Soon afterwards further research in Europe brought forth several more colours, named magenta, fuchsia, alizarin. All were brilliant but all tended to be fugitive to light. In costume, as in interior decoration, the availability of such strong, bright colours lent specific character to the designs of the rest of the century.

Design and Manufacture

In the actual making of clothes important developments were taking place at different levels in the process of production. At the upper, design end was the advent of *haute couture*, in the marketing stage the establishment of department stores and, for the bulk of the population, a great expansion in ready-made garments, such expansion being made possible by the 'sweat-shop' techniques.

Haute couture had its beginnings in the mid-nineteenth century. Until that time dressmaker or tailor designers had controlled the design and production of ladies' garments, creating one ensemble, bespoke, for one individual client. In *haute couture* models are created by the designer, bear his or her name and are protected by copyright from indiscriminate reproduction. The official definition given by the *Chambre Syndicale de la Couture Française*, founded in 1885, is: '*Haute Couture* is any undertaking whose most important activity consists in creating models with the object of selling them to a professional clientèle which thereby acquires the right to reproduce them. An *Haute Couture* concern of this nature also reserves the right to repeat these models for private customers.' France, and particularly Paris, was the natural source for *haute couture*. The Parisienne had always possessed an intense interest in clothes and personal adornment. This absorption has attracted craftsmen in the world of dress to come to Paris so that the designer has found such expertise to hand when he has needed it. In French, the word *couture* means sewing; a *couturier* is a male dressmaker, a *couturière* a feminine one. An *haute couture* establishment therefore is a first class designing and dressmaking concern. Because of all this, there is a certain irony in the general acceptance that Worth was the first *haute couturier*, for Worth was an Englishman.

Charles Frederick Worth was born in 1825 in Lincolnshire. His father was a lawyer but so impoverished through gambling that the young Charles went to work, at the age of eleven, with a printing firm to help to support the family. Later he worked for eight years at Swan and Edgar's department store in London but, deciding firmly that his future lay in the design and handling of fashion garments, he set off for Paris at the age of twenty. Here he learnt French and worked his way up in the fashion trade until, in 1858, he set up his own establishment and his home in the Rue de la Paix. Here he quickly built up a good clientèle and became the first couturier to use live mannequins to display his creations. His fame was assured in 1860 when Madame Worth showed some of her husband's designs to Princess Pauline de Metternich, wife of the Austrian ambassador. The princess ordered two gowns and soon, having seen them, the Empress Eugénie was so enchanted with them that she became Worth's most famous patron.

Worth was not the only *couturier* in his day in Paris but he was the most influential. He is credited with introducing, among other designs, the ankle-length dress for walking, the slimmer crinoline skirt of the 1860s and the flattering princess line of gown which had no waist seam.

The quality of ready-to-wear clothes was now improving and, for the majority of people, these had become acceptable. By the 1830s finished, attractive mantles and cloaks were available and soon it became possible to buy a fashionable dress partly-made. This was cut out, the skirt finished and the material supplied for bodice and sleeves which then had to be personally fitted

238 Thimmonier's chain-stitch design, 1830.

239 An original Elias Howe lock-stitch machine, 1846.

240 The original design of Singer machine, 1851. Lock-stitch type. All three machines drawn from actual equipment.

by a dressmaker. It was, however, well into the 1860s before middle class women, in general, purchased ready-made clothes and professional men continued to have their wardrobe made to measure (bespoke) until the mid-twentieth century.

Marketing

With the techniques and machinery developed as a result of the Industrial Revolution, the mass production of clothes for a wide market had begun. For such production to be successful, mass retail outlets were needed and it was for this purpose that the department store was introduced. In France the Ville de France opened in Paris in 1844.

241 Costume in London 1830–1840
A Dark coat and cap. Light trousers, collar and bow. English fashion plate, 1830.
B Museum of Costume, Bath. Gold embroidered dress. White muslin and lace pantalettes. Bonnet with ribbons, *c.* 1829–30. Actual costume, English.
C Dark blue velvet cloak with open sleeves, grey fur collar, edging and muff. Pale blue satin dress, bonnet and ribbons. Spotted veil. Light gloves. English fashion plate, 1840.
D Dull purple cloth overcoat with shoulder capes. Silk bonnet with ribbons and plumes. Black fur muff. English fashion plate, 1835.
E Grey Garrick overcoat, light trousers. English fashion plate, 1830.
F Red cotton shawl with white muslin flounces. Spotted pink dress with white flounces. Parasol. Silk bonnet with plumes and ribbons. English fashion plate, 1838.
G Dark grey cloth overcoat with black velvet collar. Grey beaver top hat. White buckskin trousers, black boots. English fashion plate, 1830.
H White dress decorated with embroidered flowers in red and blue. Black velvet shoulder cape, embroidered in colours and edged with black lace. Dark brown silk bonnet with brown and white lace with flowers. English actual costume, Museum of Costume, Bath, 1837.

This was followed in 1853 by Grand Halles and in 1860 by Bon Marché. The example of Paris was followed in other major European cities. Two very early stores in England were Kendal-Milne and Faulkener in Manchester (1836) and Bainbridge at Newcastle (1845). In London's West End Swan and Edgar, Dickens and Jones and Peter Jones all expanded in the years 1855–75. In America Macy's of New York became a department store in 1860 and Stewart's in 1862. All these stores sold not only the Paris modes from the great fashion houses but also popularized simple practical garments for everyday wear.

242 Note: the gentleman's black evening suit, white collar and tie and long side-whiskers. Ladies' gowns worn over crinoline petticoats, now with flatter fronts, ornately decorated with ruching and flowers. Low necklines and short sleeves for evening wear. Engraving from the *Englishwoman's Domestic Magazine*, 1863. Fashion Research Centre, Bath.

Sewing

Hand-sewing, whether for repair and alteration of garments or for the making of new ones had been the work of women throughout the, centuries. Attractive, decorative sewing had been carried out by the ladies of the household, basic dressmaking and repair by those employed to do this. As long as the size of the population remained small and was spread evenly across country and town such work was not too onerous but from the beginning of the nineteenth century when, due largely to improved medical knowledge and better hygiene, the population of Europe and America increased rapidly, the labour of home sewing for large families became burdensome. By the 1840s this pressure had grown as a result of the increased number of feminine garments worn – chemise, pantaloons, many petticoats, corset and cover and, on top, an increasingly elaborate style of gown, jacket and outer wear. The rapid rise in numbers of people led to greater poverty, especially in towns to which country people had come in search of work. By mid-century many women were working excessively long hours, not just at home, but also in the 'sweat-shops' of the day, where they earned a pittance to help to keep them alive. Conditions in such workshops were very bad – an extremely low level of illumination, lack of heating, draughts or a stale atmosphere.

The appearance in 1851 of the most effective sewing machine to date, that designed by Isaac Merrit Singer, was opportune indeed (**240**). Its availability coincided with the need to handle the yards of sewing required for the crinoline skirts which reached their maximum circumference in the years 1858–60.

Attempts to produce a machine to sew had lagged behind the successful mechanization of spinning and weaving processes. This was not for lack of trying but because of the

243 Black cloth evening cloak with velvet collar and red silk lining. Black top hat and slippers. French fashion plate, 1835.

244 Evening dress. Black tail coat and trousers. White waistcoat, shirt, cravat, collar and gloves. Black shoes. 1850. French fashion plate, *Les Modes Parisiennes*.

245 Dark maroon coat, fawn waistcoat. Black and white stock and white collar. Fawn trousers, white spats, black boots. Black top hat. 1839. German costume. Portrait by Krüger of Baron von Arnim. Till 1945 in the Royal Palace in Berlin.

246 Black frock coat with dark grey trousers and light grey waistcoat. Black stock, white collar. Black top hat and boots. 1832. Russian costume. Portrait by Tschernelow of Schukovska.

extreme difficulty of reproducing mechanically the action of a hand-sewer, namely to pass a needle and thread through material and back again from the other side. Several not very successful machines had been designed and made since Thomas Saint's 1790 invention in England but it was the Frenchman Barthélemy Thimmonier who produced the first satisfactory mechanism to sew. The incentive for this came not from a desire to relieve home seamstresses throughout Europe but the French army's need for mass production of uniforms (**238**).

In order to simulate hand-sewing, different types of action were evolved in the several machines designed in Europe and America. There were three types of stitch: the single chain, the double chain and the lock stitch.

Thimmonier's sewing machine of 1830 was of the first type, having a single thread held by a looper as the needle rose and fell, each stitch being secured by the one before. More satisfactory were the other two systems which used two threads and the lock stitch eventually became accepted as the best. In this there is a needle thread above the fabric and a bobbin thread under it. The two are locked together at each stitch by the upper thread being passed round the lower, so tightening it into position. The lock stitch design was developed chiefly in America, first by Walter Hunt (1832–4), then Elias Howe (1846) (**239**) and, best known, Singer (**240**). Before long Singer machines were operating in several countries, revolutionizing the ready-to-wear clothing market.

247 Dark brown tweed sack coat with braid edges. Brown and white check trousers. Dark brown waistcoat. Black bowler and boots. Bow tie, light gloves. English fashion plate, 1864.

248 Fawn Taglioni style of overcoat worn over coat with braided fastenings. Fawn trousers. Black stock, white collar. Black top hat and boots. Fawn gloves, cane. Italian fashion plate, c. 1840.

249 English style short overcoat of dark blue cloth with velvet collar. Plaid tweed trousers over black boots. Top hat, gloves, cane, 1845.

250 French polonaise-redingote cloth overcoat from portrait, 1834. Fur collar and braid trimming.

Men's Dress

The trend in these years was towards heavier, formal garments from which colour was gradually deleted. By the 1850s the typical stereotyped masculine attire was established, an appearance of severity in shades of white, grey and black which, in England we characterize as Victorian but it is a picture equally representative of the rest of the western world.

The most typical garment was some type of coat with tails or skirt. By now this appeared in three forms: the tail coat, the frock coat and the cutaway. The tail coat continued in fashion for town wear until about 1860 but was seen less often after 1855 (**245**). Like the other coats it was made of black or dark cloth with collar and revers buttoned high on the chest. The tails were knee-length or slightly shorter. The style survived as evening dress 'white tie and tails' until the mid-twentieth century. The black tail suit had become an evening dress uniform by the 1860s. It was made from worsted with black silk-covered revers and braid outside seams to the trousers (**242, 244**).

The frock coat continued to be worn as formal city attire into the early years of the twentieth century. At this time it was the chief town coat. Its full skirts reached to the knee, level all round and there was a vent at the back. The skirt was seamed at the waist. The coat was double-breasted and most often worn open (**246, plate 34, plate 35**).

The third design, the cutaway, had largely

replaced the tail coat by the 1850s. It was the preferred wear for less formal occasions and was popular with younger men. It was single-breasted and the skirts were cut back in front to rounded short tails (plate 31).

In the 1850s a short coat was introduced for very informal wear – indoors, the country or on holiday. It was made of black or dark cloth and was worn with trousers of a different material; these were usually checked, plaid or striped. These garments were known as sack coats because of their shapeless, ill-cut form but by the 1860s were better fitting and became accepted for informal street wear. In style they were single-breasted and had a high-buttoned small collar and revers with only the top button generally fastened. Some designs were braid-edged and had velvet collars (**247**).

Pantaloons had now become trousers which were less tightly fitting so did not need to be strapped under the instep of the boot. They either matched the coat in colour and material or were plain or striped in grey. The waistcoat, cut straight across at the waist in front, was usually light-coloured or white. By mid-century the fob watch had been replaced by a gold watch and chain suspended across the waistcoat front. In shape these body garments continued to be waisted in the 1830s and early 1840s with some padding on the chest and at the shoulder. After this a natural figure became the mode in a more formal masculine appearance (plate 31, **243–250**).

From about 1840 there was considerable variety in outer wear for men. The voluminous, caped Garrick overcoat was still widely worn for travelling in cold weather (**241E**) and the more fitting redingote style in dark cloth for town (**241G, 248, 250**). Alternatively men could also wear shorter hip-length coats with fur collars and patch pockets (**249**). In the evenings it was fashionable to wear a long cloak or cape which might be lined with coloured silk – plain or quilted – or fur (**243**).

Shortish hairstyles covered by top hats were the norm for town and formal needs. A characteristic feature of the years from about 1845 was exceptionally long, bushy side-whiskers. These were grown on the cheeks and jaw but left the chin free. Various names were applied to these whiskers, names which differed from country to country. In England they were referred to as Piccadilly Weepers, in France cutlets and in America either dundrearies after Lord Dundreary, a character in a play, or burnsides after General Burnside. Similarly, the American term for side-whiskers is sideburns (**242, 267, 268**).

The top hat, the accepted form of head-gear for these years, changed shape and the material from which it was made over the period. The 1830s version had curved sides, was of moderate height and had a curling brim; it was made of white, grey or fawn beaver. By the 1840s it had a narrower brim and was usually black, of beaver or silk. The mid-century style was the stovepipe version which was tall and straight-sided (**241G, 263, 267, 268**, plate 31. A collapsible black silk opera hat was patented in 1837. This could be flattened by an internal spring so that it could be carried under the arm. It was called the gibus after the Parisian hatter who invented it. An alternative hat, for informal wear, was introduced in the 1850s. This was the bowler or billycock named, in England, after its original hatter William Bowler. It was a hard felt, round hat with rolling brim made in black, brown or grey. The bowler went by other names outside England: a derby in America, after Lord Derby, and in France, a *melon* (**247**).

Neckwear gradually became less obtrusive. By mid-century collars were detached from the shirt and were stiffly starched. The cravat became smaller and, by 1850, was usually replaced by a necktie which was made up into a flat scarf, its ends crossed over in front and fastened in position by a decorative pin (**263, 267, 268, 270**).

Rules of etiquette were as strict for gentlemen as for ladies. This applied particularly to the wearing of jewellery and accessories. Gloves must be worn at all times. At a dance these must be white and must not be removed. A hat must be worn or carried and there were specific customs regarding where this should be placed while the gentleman was being entertained or at a ball. Canes were carried out-of-doors.

Women's Dress

Changes in feminine attire, in silhouette, in style, in colours, fabrics and decoration were more rapid and marked than in that of the men. There is a world of difference between dress of the 1830s and that of the 1860s not only in all these factors but in the underlying causes which were primarily those of the social structure. There was a general and steady trend throughout these years towards a greater weight of material and numbers of

251 *Left:* a promenade dress in blue and white check with black figuring and white ruching. White cambric collar and cuffs. *Right:* a muslin carriage dress, the flounces edged with Valenciennes lace and pink ribbons. Straw bonnet decorated with roses and ribbons. Ladies' Fashions for August from *La Belle Assembleé* of 1838. Fashion Research Centre, Bath.

garments worn, to a complete covering up of the body, towards an artificially distorted silhouette.

The 1830s were years of the Romantic age in literature, painting and the decorative arts. In dress too the feminine romantic theme was clearly stated. The figure shape was a natural one, the waistline where Nature intended it to be, a belt drawn in to accentuate this in a feminine manner. The skirt was a pretty, full shape, pleated in at the waist and extending down to the ankles. The shoulder line was sloping from a high neckline towards the full leg-of-mutton or elephant sleeve; the former was puffed on the upper arm, fitted on the forearm, in the latter the fullness dropped to a lower line so resembling an elephant's ear before being gathered into a fitting wristband. These sleeves reached their maximum width between 1833 and 1835 when they might be padded or fitted with metal springs to maintain their shape. It was fashionable to wear on top of the bodice a cape or a canezou (a shawl-like blouse covering the shoulders and descending in two lappets which were tucked into the belt in front). Colours were now less pastel-shaded than in the previous decade and fabrics more varied, for example, velvet, silk, brocade, wool or gingham (**241, 251, 254, 255**).

By the 1840s this romantic feminism was gradually moving towards the primly correct and sober lady: propriety was all important. Lightness and prettiness had disappeared and women were beginning those long decades of being weighed down by the sheer quantity of clothes. Every part of the body except for the face was decorously covered from high neckline, wrist-length sleeves to ground-length skirt. Despite this all-embracing covering the lady of the 1840s still appeared feminine and dainty. She wore a tight-fitting bodice which had a very slender waist extending to a deep point in front. Her very full skirt was gathered in here. Colours were now darker and stronger. Stripes, checks, plaids and sprig-patterned materials were fashionable and there was a wide range

252 Dark green silk dress and coat, grey decoration and fringing. Pale grey fur muff. Gloves. Bonnet of green silk with white lace trimming. Hungarian actual costume, 1857. Hungarian National Museum, Budapest.

skirt which was its central focus, the rest of the ensemble being designed to show this to advantage. The circular form of this skirt increased inexorably in dimension during this decade. Despite criticism and ribaldry from the medical profession and the cartoonist, its popularity remained unaffected: it was the undisputed status symbol for all classes of the population. The bodice of the day gown was fitted and plain, buttoned up the centre front to a high neckline finished by a small collar. Pagoda sleeves, full at the bottom, were fashionable. The enormous skirt, with its vast quantity of material, provided a blank canvas for decoration. This was lavish, ranging through braid, frogging, fringing, tasselling, ribbon ruching and bows to embroidery. Colours were vivid and strong – the aniline dyes were introduced at the end of the decade – and fabrics were extensively varied (**252**, plate 32).

In contrast, evening gowns had low, wide, off-the-shoulder necklines and tiny puff sleeves. The skirts were popularly designed in many rows of flounces. The overskirt might be looped back at the sides by large ribbon bows to display an even more flounced underskirt. At *haute couture* level, in 1859 the Empress Eugénie of France appeared in a ball gown of white satin designed with a hundred such skirt flounces. Decoration of these evening gowns was most lavish, including artificial flowers and a quantity of ruching and ribbons (**242**).

After two decades of the ever-increasing circular-shaped skirt, a slow change took place in the early 1860s towards a flatter front and sides and a concentration of fullness of material, as well as decoration, at the back. The high neckline was maintained but the princess line, without waist seam, accentuated even more elegantly the slender waist (**242, 256, 257**).

Corsets, Crinolines, Petticoats

These garments were the necessary concomitant to the feminine silhouette of the remainder of the century. With the return in the 1830s to a slender waist at natural level,

of fabrics worn according to season and time of day. These now also included cashmere, alpaca, tulle and muslin, cotton, merino and crêpe (**255**).

Since the beginning of the century there had developed a marked difference, as in men's clothes, between evening and day wear. For evening ladies wore lighter colours, thinner fabrics and gowns had lower necklines and short sleeves. As time passed the décolleté neckline and over-decorated skirt contrasted more and more with the sobriety of the day gown.

Dress of the 1850s was dominated by the restrictive corset and the immense crinoline

some kind of stays were once more worn by many women (**258**). By the 1840s these had developed into a restrictive corset which became more extreme as time passed, a narrow waist being regarded as essential to offset the vast circular skirt. The mid-century corset was short, extending from the breasts to just below the waist; no further length was required due to the fullness of the skirt. The nineteenth century corset was a more sophisticated garment than its sixteenth and eighteenth century predecessors. It was tailored in fitting sections and a front fastening had replaced the back lacing. Whalebone or metal strips were inserted in the seams to maintain the desired shape.

From the 1830s onwards increasing layers of underwear were customary. At first this consisted of a long-sleeved voluminous chemise, drawers and a petticoat. Soon a corset cover was needed to prevent the bones showing through to the gown, then a camisole was added and several waist petticoats to fill out the fuller skirts. Underwear was white, partly starched and was made chiefly from cambric, batiste, calico and flannel. There seemed to be a pathological fear of catching a chill so men, women and children all wore an increasing number of layers of underwear as the century advanced. No part of the body, except the face, should be exposed to the air. These was much coyness about referring to underwear except by euphemisms: underpinnings, unmentionables, undescribables, unwhisperables etc.

From the early 1840s a stiffened petticoat was adopted to hold the skirt out to the desired shape. The material was made from a mixture of horsehair and linen. It was called a crinoline, the name derived from the Latin *crinis*, meaning hair and *linum*, meaning thread. As time passed the gown skirt became fuller and wider so several layers of starched cambric petticoats had to be worn on top of the crinoline but, by the 1850s, even these were insufficient to maintain the shape. A crinoline petticoat was then devised which resembled its predecessors, the farthingale and the hoop, though of

253 Dark blue cloth habit, black top hat with veil. Underneath, pantaloons strapped under boots. English fashion plate depicting riding dress of 1834.

254 White figured dress. White bonnet with tulle, ribbon and plume decoration. Dutch actual costume, 1834–5. Kostuum Museum, The Hague.

255 Green silk and cotton mixture day dress with dark green printed pattern. Deep lavender silk mantelet with fringed edges. Lavender silk bonnet (drawn style) with white ribbons. White silk parasol. English actual costume, 1847–8. Platt Hall Museum, Manchester.

256 Olive green taffeta dress with stripes in black and green. Pale green sash and trimming. Dutch actual costume, 1865. Kostuum Museum, The Hague.

257 Green silk dress over crinoline. Grey paletot trimmed with claret velvet bands and buttons. Shoulder cape attached. Grey velvet bonnet trimmed with claret velvet and grey plume. Grey ribbons. White undersleeves and gloves. English fashion plate of 1860 showing winter promenade costume.

a different shape. It was an underskirt of quilted material with circular whalebone hoops of diminishing diameter inserted at intervals from ground to waist. Unlike the earlier designs the crinoline did not stop at these proportions. Its circumference continued to grow, so did its popularity, until it became so heavy that it was difficult to wear, to move or to sit (259).

Logically, at this point, the design should have been abandoned but, in 1856, the cage-crinoline was patented and, by 1857, was in production. This was a framework of flexible steel hoops joined together by bands of tape or braid which, attached in vertical strips, provided the requisite shape and support without the weight and avoided the need to wear so many layers of clothing. It was taken up with enthusiasm by all classes of women. It was cheap and a great success. The skirt circumference continued to increase. 1859–60 saw the zenith of the circular form after which the shape gradually changed to an oval. Then the front was flattened, also the sides, and the fullness was concentrated at the back. There were several versions of the cage-crinoline. Most notable were the Cage-Américaine, where the upper part was in framework skeleton form and the lower covered in material and the Cage-Empire which was designed to support the numerous flounces of a ball dress and had extra hoops and framework for a train (260, 261, 262).

Several opposition movements arose against the crinoline gown. In America the 'anti-crinoline movement' tried to point out by propaganda, to women who were regarded as silly, what loss of dignity they suffered by wearing such a restrictive garment. Other designs of fashion were proposed, notably the Reform Dress. This was supported and publicized by Mrs Amelia Jenks Bloomer, a mid-western American. The outfit consisted of a jacket and knee-length full skirt worn over full Turkish-style trousers. These trousers were nick-named 'bloomers' were ridiculed by most women who continued to wear the crinoline.

Outdoor Wear

This was extremely varied, according to season and to date. In the earlier years fitted, long coats were in fashion, also jackets and capes. As skirts grew larger, the lower part of the body was so warmly clad that it was only on the upper part that further garments were needed. In very cold weather three-quarter coats were worn but more popular were capes, jackets, mantelets, shawls, berthes and cloaks (241C, D, F, H, 251, 255, 257, plate 32, plate 33).

Hairstyles, Bonnets, Hats

Most elaborate styles of coiffure, piled high on the head, dressed in loops and swirls and decorated with plumes, ribbons and flowers were characteristic of the 1830s. Styles were especially elaborate for evening wear. With the more decorous attire of the 1840s, the coiffure was plainer. There was a centre parting, ringlets at the sides, framing the face, and coiled plaits at the back. As the focus of the ensemble moved to the immense skirts of the 1850s, the coiffure, as in earlier ages of such skirts, became very plain and small. The hair was drawn back primly to a bun at the nape. Towards 1860 the bun became a decorative chignon (264, 271).

In the 1830s bonnets and hats were very large and profusely decorated with ribbons and flowers. As time passed the hat was supplanted by the bonnet which, in turn, became smaller as the skirt grew larger (265, 266, 269, plate 32, plate 33).

Footwear

With the ankle-length skirts of the 1830s stockings were of varied colours and footwear was dainty, slippers for evening and ankle boots for day wear. With the longer, wider skirts, boots were higher, laced or buttoned up the leg and had heels. Slippers were still usual wear with evening gowns but were not visible beneath the long skirts (273, 276, 277, 278).

258 Cotton and boned stays, c. 1830. French, advertisement.

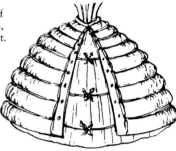

259 Crinoline petticoat of padded horsehair and linen, 1858. French advertisement.

260 Folding crinoline of 1863 made from flexible steel circles, narrow tape and lightweight fabric. *Englishwoman's Domestic Magazine*. 1863 Fashion Research Centre, Bath.

261 Cage crinoline made from steel hoops held together with tapes. French advertisement, 1862.

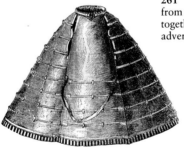

262 The steel bands, tapes and fabric crinoline or jupon, 1863. *The Englishwoman's Domestic Magazine*. Fashion Research Centre, Bath.

263 Beaver top hat, bow tie and collar. French fashion plate, 1849.

264 Ribbon hair decoration. Austrian fashion, 1845. Painting by J.B. Reiter, Osterreisches Museum der Stadt Wien, Vienna.

265 English bonnet in bibi or cottage style. Split straw with floral and ribbon decoration. Gallery of Costume, Platt Hall, Manchester.

266 Silk bonnet with ribbon ornamentation. English fashion plate, 1835.

267 Light grey top hat, side-whiskers, striped neckcloth. French portrait, 1855.

268 Black silk top hat, side-whiskers, silk scarf and collar. English photograph, 1865.

269 Mauve silk gauged drawn bonnet. English c. 1840. Gallery of Costume, Platt Hall, Manchester.

270 Bow tie, stiff collar. English photograph, 1857.

271 Evening coiffure. Pearl rope, rose and plume decoration. French fashion plate, 1859.

Accessories

Gloves were worn always, even at home. Day gloves were short, evening ones reached to at least the elbow. Parasols or umbrellas were carried (**255, 272**) also fur muffs (**252**). This was very much the age of the fan and, as in the eighteenth century, particularly with evening dress, it was an article of expression (**275**). Jewellery was widely worn, especially shell cameos and gold lockets. Small perfume boxes or bottles were carried. Use of cosmetics was frowned upon; it was considered most improper for well brought up ladies.

Children's Dress

Clothes for babies and children followed a not dissimilar pattern from those of adults. From about 1850 a great many layers were being wrapped around the long-suffering baby. The outfit consisted of a chemise, stays to support the spine, a flannel stomach-band, a flannel and several cambric petticoats, a dress, a coat and two caps.

272 Green silk, brass stick and carved bone handle. English, actual parasol, 1840–50.

273 White satin boot, Polish, 1840. Narodowe Museum, Cracow.

274 White cotton canezou, French fashion plate, 1838.

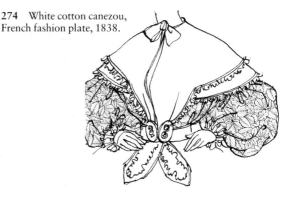

275 Spanish fan, *c.* 1850. Pleated white silk decorated with lace and flowers. Ivory handle. Rocamora Costume Museum, Barcelona.

276 French boot, *c.* 1830. Black velvet embroidered with coloured silks. Musée du Costume de la Ville de Paris.

277 Ladies' slipper, Black figured satin. English, 1830–40.

278 Brown stockinet and leather. Elastic top. English boot, 1851.

279 Man's shoe of brown cloth and leather, 1850.

From about 1840 children's clothes moved once more towards greater restriction and artificiality of form. This was less so for boys but they too were kept in skirts for much longer than before. These skirts were worn over flounced petticoats and displayed beneath lace-trimmed pantalettes or short pantaloons (**283**, **286**). Older boys wore jackets or belted coats together with long trousers or knickerbockers with stockings. Shirts had frilled collars. A peaked cap or a top hat covered the head. Colours tended to follow the adult lead, becoming darker and more sombre (**280**, **281**, **284**, **285**, **288**, plate 30).

From about 1840 also girls, more and more, wore clothes based closely upon the designs adopted by their mothers. By 1850 they were put into boned bodices at the age of eleven and wore a quantity of underwear which included a stiffened or crinoline petticoat. Their skirts became wider and wider but were shorter than adult wear so displaying lace-trimmed pantaloons beneath. The designs of dresses, hair, bonnets and boots were miniature versions of adult ones (**282**, **287**).

Tartan patterns of material were popular for the garments of boys and girls from the 1840s (**286**). By 1850 the vogue for sailor suits for boys had begun, a custom which was to last beyond the end of the century. Such suits had long trousers, a blouse with a large square collar edged in the blue and white stripes and a circular straw hat. The winter version of this outfit would be made of navy serge instead of cotton or linen and a navy cap replaced the straw hat.

282 and 283 The little girl wears a pale grey dress striped in deep pink. Her sleeves, collar and petticoats are white. She has white stockings and shoes. The little boy wears a light grey dress with dark brown velvet banding. His cap is to match. He wears white pantalettes, white stockings and brown boots. His sleeves are white. French fashion plate, *Les Modes Parisiennes*, 1855.

284 Black velvet suit and cap. White shirt. Grey gaiters. French dress, photograph, 1857.

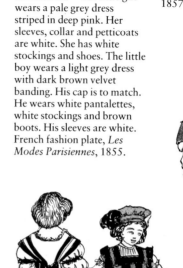

280 French boy, 1844. Black jacket and top hat. White trousers with blue stripe. White blouse. Black boots. Fashion plate.

281 Austrian dress 1835. Golden brown coat with black belt. White trousers. Black boots. Painting of the Eltz family by Ferdinand George Waldmüller. Österreische Galerie in Wien.

285 Black jacket, grey trousers with coloured braces. White shirt and collar, red bow. Black boots and hat. Spanish dress, 1830–40. Painting, Museum for Nineteenth Century Painting, Madrid.

286 Tartan dress over lace-edged white cambric pantalettes. White shirt and stockings. Peaked cap. Stockinet boots with patent leather toe caps. English dress, fashion plate, 1851.

287 Green and fawn shot silk dress with braid decoration. Embroidered white drawers. English dress, 1840. Fashion plate.

288 Brown jacket and trousers. White blouse and stockings. Brown boots. French dress, 1863. Fashion plate, *Le Follet*.

CHAPTER NINE

1865–1890

Expansion of Manufacture and Style

Trends established earlier in the century and described in Chapter Eight intensified and accelerated. Improved medicine and hygiene further reduced early mortality, especially that of infants, so population numbers continued to rise spectacularly. Industrial development in mass-production and mechanization accelerated also but the extensive empires established under the jurisdiction of the countries of western Europe were at their zenith so absorbed the goods resulting from the increased productivity.

The middle classes continued to expand, expecting and receiving a yet higher standard of living. Continued development and mechanization of textile processes produced a marked increase in quality and total production so bringing a wide variety of fabrics within reach of a larger proportion of ordinary citizens.

In Paris Worth still led the way in couture with his innovatory approach. He set the new business pattern by producing model designs not only for private clients, but also for sale to dressmakers, manufacturers and department stores in Europe and America so establishing the system of *haute couture*. He reigned over Parisian couture for nearly fifty years; no other couturier ever gained such complete supremacy. After his death his fashion house continued business in the hands of his two sons Gaston and Jean-Philippe and later was controlled by his grandsons but, despite the experience and superb taste of Jean-Philippe in particular, the inventive genius of the concern had died with Charles Frederick (**310**).

The department store also became fully established. More stores opened and existing ones expanded particularly in the USA which had entered the field later than western Europe but made up for lost time after the Civil War there.

There was by 1865 a tremendous increase in the number of fashion journals being published, now by nearly all the countries of Europe. From 1860 Germany's *Die Modenwelt* was an important journal published in Berlin. It had a wide circulation and was published in fourteen languages under different titles; the English version was *The Season*. Vienna became a fashion centre of importance in the 1870s and, taking advantage of the preoccupation of France and Prussia with war, established journals like *Wiener Mode* and *Wiener Chic* whose circulations were boosted markedly in the 1880s and 1890s. In England two famous publications launched by Samuel Beeton (husband of Mrs Beeton of the *Book of Household Management* fame) were *The Queen* and *The Englishwoman's Domestic Magazine* (**319, 320**). The Americans now began to enter the field and several journals which were later to become world-famous were launched, for example, *Vogue* and *Harper's Bazaar*.

By the 1870s middle class women were also beginning to purchase ready-to-wear garments as these were, by this time, of much higher quality than hitherto. The advent of the sewing machine (p. 95), whose performance had by now been greatly improved, led to a marked extension in ready-to-wear clothes for men. Factories for such manu-

289 London's Riverside, 1870–80.
A Cream-coloured wool dress with plaid skirt draperies. Plum-coloured velvet jacket with grey fur trimming. Silk hat and plumes, gloves. English fashion plate 1877–8.
B Dark grey cutaway coat with lighter grey trousers. White waistcoat. Black stock, white collar. Black hat and shoes. White gloves and spats, cane. English fashion plate, 1874.
C Black silk day dress with white lace neck and waist frills. Hat to match. Actual costume, English. Gallery of Costume, Platt Hall, Manchester, 1872.
D Blue-grey coat with shoulder capes. Dark blue velvet hat with plumes. English fashion plate, 1879–80.
E Deep magenta cashmere day dress with black braid edging and black velvet trimming. Hat to match. Actual costume, English. Gallery of English Costume, Platt Hall, Manchester, 1870.
F Fawn cloth coat with braid edging. Yellow ribbon bow at back. Cream dress with brown accordion pleating. Brown hat with cream ribbons and plumes. Umbrella. English fashion plate, 1875.
G Black cloth coat, grey trousers, white spats, black boots, grey hat. English fashion plate, 1875.
H Grey poplin promenade dress in princess style. Ultramarine blue velvet bows and accordion pleating. Cream straw hat with white plume. Gloves, umbrella. English fashion plate, 1876–7.

facture and stores to sell this wear, which were opened, were primarily to be found in areas of textile manufacture, especially those of wool. In England this was in the north in cities such as Leeds, Bradford and Chester. Sewing machines were purchased in quantity for mass-production manufacture of clothes and the development of the band-knife, which could cut out some twenty to thirty thicknesses of heavy cloth at once, was a great advance.

The trade in recycled textiles and second-hand clothing also increased enormously, mainly for use by the man or woman in the street, as the population expanded explosively. The woollen industry had been

290 Street Attire in 1883. Outdoor scene from the *Young Ladies' Journal* of 1 July 1883. Costume Galleries, Castle Howard, York.

greatly boosted with the invention in 1801 (greatly improved in the 1830s) of a rag-tearing machine known as a 'devil'. Wool rags were fed by rollers into a drum filled with metal teeth which tore up the fabric as it was rapidly revolved. The bulk of the product was then spun, together with a quantity of new wool, and the yarn was called shoddy; yarn made from rags of higher quality being termed mungo. This led to the colloquial use of the word shoddy to mean something of inferior quality. Residue not suitable for spinning was sold as agricultural fertilizer and, later, for providing the wool powder to make flock wallpaper.

Second-hand clothing had been sold by street pedlars for generations but, again, with the rise in population, the trade became greatly expanded and was organized into a widescale development of shops and markets. An extensive export trade developed between the countries of Europe, so bringing different textiles within the reach of all sections of the population.

Men's Dress

As the century advanced a greater variety of clothes were being worn by both sexes; these varied according to season, time of day, whether for town or country wear, and for sport. This range was much more limited in men's wear than in women's.

Different designs of tail coat were part of the wardrobe for formal wear. The more formal of the two, customary for city attire, was the unbuttoned, double-breasted frock coat, usually made of heavy, black cloth (**294**). Also to be seen, though now old-fashioned, was the earlier design (plate 34). The single-breasted rounded tail cutaway design might be of black or grey and was often edged

291   Street scene in London.
A   Plaid Inverness overcoat. Tweed trousers. Bowler hat, gloves. English fashion plate, 1881.
B   Deep purple velvet dress with leg-of-mutton sleeves in paler mauve brocade. Purple velvet hat with ostrich plumes and black spotted veil. Grey gloves, purple umbrella. Actual costume, English, Museum of Costume, Bath, *c.* 1893.
C   Red satin dress with cream lace flounce and darker red hem and ribbons. Green jacket with white fur. Felt hat with ribbons and plume. Fur muff. Actual costume, English, Gallery of Costume, Platt Hall, Manchester, 1886.
D   Sealskin coat trimmed with lighter-coloured fur. Velvet hat with ribbons, plumes and veil. Gloves, umbrella. English fashion plate, 1893.
E   Pink walking costume with lace trimming. Hat with ribbons, plumes and face veil. Gloves. Actual costume, English, Costume Museum, Bethnal Green, London, 1895.
F   Short fawn cloth coat, tweed trousers. Brown bowler hat, lemon gloves. English fashion plate, 1889.

with braid (**289B**, **290**). For less formal country wear the 1860s sack coat accompanying trousers of a different material had evolved, by 1870, into a three-piece suit – known as a lounge suit – with jacket, waistcoat and trousers of matching material. This might be of patterned tweed or dark plain cloth. The suit was still rather loose-fitting but its cut had improved considerably. Revers were still high, the collar small and front edges were rounded off (**290**, **292**).

By 1865 evening dress had become a formal uniform. Coat and trousers were of black worsted, the former a tail coat worn open, the revers silk-faced and trousers with braid outside seams. The waistcoat was white as was the shirt, collar and tie. In the 1880s for less formal wear and when ladies were not present, the dinner jacket was introduced. There is a certain dispute as to whether this garment originated in Monte Carlo, London or New York. In England it was called a 'dress lounge' but in America a 'tuxedo' or 'tux' because it was first worn for small dinner parties in the millionaire district of Tuxedo Park, New York. A black tie was accepted wear with such jackets which have always been more popular in the USA than in Europe due to their greater comfort and informality.

Styles of waistcoat and trousers barely changed in these years. In trouser design the front fall had been replaced by a fly front opening. Black, dark grey or grey striped material was usual.

During the first half of the nineteenth century men had begun to wear an accepted form of dress for sport and games, though, before this time, no special attire had been devised for this purpose. More specific recommendations came in the second half. During the 1880s striped, coloured blazers were worn for playing cricket and these were accompanied by white flannel trousers. For football, players wore jerseys with knickerbockers, long stockings, ankle boots and a pill-box cap. Later the knickerbockers were replaced by knee-length shorts. From the 1870s onwards men tended to adopt blazers with trousers in summer and tweed jackets with loose knee-breeches and long stockings in winter for other games or for holiday or country wear (**313**).

A variety of overcoat styles persisted. In town, a top frock overcoat was fashionable. A fitting coat, this was cut in a similar manner to the frock coat but was worn buttoned and was made from a heavier material (**289G**). There were also longer, heavier overcoats, single- or double-breasted (**295**). Some, like the Ulster, had a shoulder cape as well as a collar. The Inverness was also caped but was very much the travelling winter coat, looser and belted with patch pockets (**291A**, **293**). It was generally made from check, plaid or tweed. For warmer weather short, straight coats were still fashionable.

Side-whiskers continued to be customary but became much shorter and neater as time passed. The top hat was always the formal fashionable wear (**289B**, **G**, **290**, **294**, **295**,

292 Tweed lounge suit with black braid edging. Brown bowler and boots. Gloves, cane. English fashion plate, 1885.

293 Plaid wool Inverness overcoat with hat to match. Plain trousers. Gloves, cane. English fashion plate, 1885.

294 Black frock coat with light grey trousers. Black hat and boots. German fashion plate. Europäische Modenzeitung für Herrengarderobe, Dresden, 1873.

295 Dark cloth overcoat and trousers. Overcoat has muff pockets. Black hat and boots. German fashion plate. Universal-Modenzeitung für Herrengarderobe, Dresden, 1882.

296 Bustle-style taffeta petticoat with 'sweepers'. Manufacturer's advertisement, 1878.

298 Corset, French Fashion Journal, *La Mode Illustrée*, 1878.

300 The 'Lillie Langtry' bustle advertised at 2s 6d. 1877.

302 Corset, 1868, German fashion journal *Der Bazar*.

303 Cotton and framework petticoat bustle, 1884. Many examples displayed in Museum costume collections.

297 White cotton camisole. Manufacturer's advertisement, 1880.

299 Crinolette petticoat. Manufacturer's advertisement, 1873.

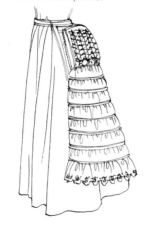

301 Stiffened cotton and lace tournure. Manufacturer's advertisement, 1872.

plate 34, **326**, **331**), but a greater variety of other hats became available. The bowler was very popular (**290**, **291A**, **F**, **292**) and, in summer, the straw boater (**313**); this would accompany the blazer. With tweed jackets and overcoats the peaked cap of matching material was worn; sometimes such caps had ear flaps, deerstalker style, as typified in the Sherlock Holmes stories (**293**, **330**).

Short boots or shoes were usual for outdoor wear. Fashion dictated that, for gentlemen, these were accompanied by spats which were ankle-length, buttoned on the outer side and strapped under the footwear. Low cut slippers were worn indoors and with evening dress.

Neckwear had become less stiff and more varied. With formal attire the stiffly starched white collar was upstanding or winged but, with a lounge suit or holiday attire, a deep, turned-down, soft collar could be worn. Shirts were white with stiff or pleated fronts. Detachable stiff shirt cuffs were commonly worn. Ties could be knotted or bows (**326**, **327**, **330**, **331**).

Women's Dress

The Bustle and Petticoat

The trends begun in the 1840s (*see* Chapter Eight) of wrapping up the body in layers of garments and increasingly restricting the natural form continued and accelerated in these years. The shape of the silhouette changed markedly and more frequently as time passed and the variety of designs of garments increased with specific styles, fabrics and decoration regarded as appropriate for different times of day, season and function.

Whereas the gown styles of the 1850s and early 1860s had been dominated by the crinoline, it was the bustle which was the arbiter of the 1870s and 1880s. In bustle gowns the interest of the design was centred at the back, especially in the skirt. Between 1865 and 1890 the changes of silhouette of such gowns were subtle but continuous.

304 Dark brown silk afternoon dress. Skirt draped up over bustle to display lining of green and copper-coloured floral design. Underskirt of pale copper silk. Decoration of fringe, pleating and bows. Actual costume, Gallery of English Costume, Platt Hall, Manchester, 1875.

305 Brown silk costume with brown spotted velvet and cord trimming, cream lace ruffles. Brown velvet hat, cream plume. Umbrella, gloves. Actual costume, Austrian, c. 1880. Modesammlung des Historischen Museum der Stadt Wien, Vienna.

Between 1865 and 1870 the crinoline form was more and more concentrated at the rear, the front and sides becoming flatter. Between 1870 and 1875 the bustle – the French term, often used, is *tournure* – became more extreme in shape, the skirt draperies being swept up to a horizontal shelf form below the waist at the rear, from which they descended in a cascade of ruffles, pleats and bows to a long train sweeping the floor. After 1875 the bustle form decreased so that between 1878 and 1882 there was no bustle and the hip-line was sleek, the skirt draperies swathed and tied back at a lower level, around the knees. From 1882 to 1885 a new expansion of the bustle shape arose, in a slightly different, slenderer line than before but, after 1885, there was it diminished once more so that, by 1890, such forms had completely disappeared.

As with the crinoline gowns, bustle styles required a structure beneath them to support the immense weight of fabric. Between 1865 and 1875 this was provided by crinoline petticoats in bustle form; these were made of metal band frameworks as before or whalebone was inserted into petticoat seams (**299**).

306 Blue silk afternoon dress with white spot pattern. Apron (tablier) front, bustle. Decoration by blue and black braid and ribbons. Actual costume, 1870, Gallery of English Costume, Platt Hall, Manchester.

These were gradually replaced by a wire basket or horsehair and gauze pad with metal frame beneath, both of which rested upon the buttocks and were tied on round the waist. In the years 1878 to 1882 no bustle was worn but after 1882 it returned but was smaller and neater (**300, 301, 303**). Bustle petticoats accompanied these structures, being worn on top of them or, alternatively, might have the stiffening inserted into them so obviating the need for a separate garment. The petticoats were elaborate, incorporating stiffened ruffles and pleats at the back set in rows between waist and ground. At the hem were sewn pleated or flounced sweepers (*balayeuses*, the French term) which acted as dusters to absorb the dirt and keep clean the gown skirt on top (**296**).

As the crinoline gradually evolved into the bustle fashion, as well as demanding a slender waist to offset the skirt fullness, insisted on slender hips also. Up to 1865 the essential restrictive corset had only reached to just below the waist as the crinoline skirt had obscured the body below that level (**302**). With the bustle line, the corset had to extend over the hips also. The type of manufacture changed too. By 1870 steam moulding had been introduced, a process in which the finished garment – bones and front busk inserted – was heavily starched then placed in a steam mould to set its shape to the desired figure. The mould was of copper and steam was introduced into it, via pipes (**298**). The corsets of the 1880s became yet more rigid and agonizing. They restricted the waist excessively and were very long. They were made in longitudinal sections with whalebone inserted into the seams. Such long corsets tended to ride up and wrinkle and, after a while, the whalebones tended to break as the wearer sat down so, more and more, steel was used to replace the whalebone. By 1878 suspenders were introduced. As yet not attached to the corset, they were fastened to a belt worn on top round the waist.

It was in these years that a storm of protest arose from the medical profession. Doctors tried to inform families of the damage being done, particularly to teenage girls whose pliant bodies were being forced into such restriction but the criticism made little difference. Most ladies, young and old, followed, or attempted to follow, the fashion silhouette, accepting as a natural unpleasantness of life, fainting fits and the 'vapours'.

Gowns

In the 1870s gowns echoed the drawing rooms of the date: overdecorated and extravagantly cluttered. The square or high neckline was edged with ruffles and lace, the sleeves ended in cuffs with bows and more ruffles. The fitting waistline was most often sleek in princess style. Below this the quantity of fabric was swept up and back to a riot of gargantuan ribbon bows, ruffles and flounces to fall by stages to a train. The skirt front was often cut in apron fashion (*en tablier* in French) and had ruffled edges. Frequently two or three different fabrics and colours were to be seen in one gown. The overskirt was in one of these; as it was turned back and draped upwards it displayed a different lining then below this the visible underskirt was contrasted yet again. Knife edge pleats were fashionable for this, also decoration by fringe, lace and tassels. Stiff, rustling fabrics were in favour: taffeta, heavy silk or satin. Colours were strong and rich, patterned fabrics contrasting in one garment with plain ones (**289C, E, F, 304, 305, 306, plate 35, plate 36**).

By 1877–8 the bustle was diminishing and the draped skirt was swept up to a lower level, giving a sleekly fitted hip-line. Ladies had to walk with dainty, small steps as the fabric was pulled tightly round the knees – a precursor of the hobble skirt of the years just before the First World War. Internal tapes directed the fullness of the skirt towards the rear. By 1880 the skirt, though still long and elaborately decorated, was slim fitting. By 1884 the bustle had fully returned and complex, draped-up skirts were fashionable once more but were less wide than in the 1870s (**289A, D, H, 290, 291B, C, D, E, 304, 306, 308, 309**).

By 1880 there was a marked increase in the number of different types of dress available.

307 Maternity dress. Jacket with adjustable buttoning and ribbon ties. Manufacturer's advertisement, 1870s.

308 Tweed costume. Dark velvet hat and fur muff. German actual costume, Historisches Museum, Frankfurt-am-Main, 1885–7.

310 Pale green taffeta Worth evening gown. Skirt in three fabrics: train in green taffeta, overskirt in gold-patterned green velvet, centre panel of gold-fringed green silk. Cream net ruching at sleeves and train hem. Museum of Fine Arts, Boston, USA, 1885.

309 Blue-grey coat with shoulder capes. Dark blue velvet hat with plumes. Gloves to match. Black umbrella. English fashion journal, 1880.

The rules of etiquette governing which type of costume was correct for different times of day, function and season were strict and definitive. Afternoon gowns were elaborate, heavily decorated and made from a great quantity of rich materials. Evening gowns were yet more elaborate, with very long trains, but had décolleté necklines and short sleeves. In contrast, simpler, more practical clothes were becoming available for morning wear or for the office, where more ladies were now employed. Pleated or gored skirts without trains could be worn, accompanied by a blouse and jacket, the latter tightly waisted with a flared peplum below. Suits could be of tweed or check and plaid wool and these were popular for travelling. Despite these concessions, a bustle was still worn when in fashion and the material at the front of the skirt swept up and back (304).

Ladies too were taking up sports, albeit in a demure manner. For walking in mountains or rough country a belted tweed jacket with peaked cap was correct wear but the matching skirts still swept the ground, though the outer one might be pulled up a few inches by cords attached underneath at the waist (311). Skating, tennis and hockey attire still followed the fashion trend though with lighter fabrics and less ornamentation. In summer, ladies often adopted masculine-style straw boaters (312, 314).

Outdoor Wear

There was great variety available in coats, jackets, wraps and cloaks. Coats and jackets were, in general, fitted at the waist, the former shaped to accommodate the bustle shape, the latter finishing at waist level with a peplum. Silk, decorated with lace and fringe, was fashionable in the summer months, wool and tweed at other seasons and fur trimming and linings in winter (289A, D, 290, 291D, 309).

311 Tweed walking suit
with skirt drawn up by cords.
Cap to match. Masculine
shirt and tie style, 1886.
Newspaper advertisement.

312 and 313 Sea-side dress
in 1885. White flannel suits
with striped decoration.
Straw boaters. Canvas and
leather short boots. Gloves.
English fashion journal.

314 Striped cotton tennis
dress, straw boater. English
fashion magazine, 1884.

Footwear

High boots were general wear rather than
shoes. They were buttoned or laced and had
heels. Materials included fabric, kid and
leather often with heels and toe-caps of patent
leather. Evening slippers were of brocade,
velvet or silk, usually embroidered (315, 316,
318). Stockings generally matched the gown
or petticoat.

Hair, Bonnets, Hats

With the demise of the crinoline and rise
of the slenderer bustle styles of gown, the
coiffure became more elaborate. The hair was
swept up at the sides and dressed here and
on top with curls and ringlets, a chignon or
coiled plait at the nape. Hats and bonnets
were small, perched on top of the coiffure,
often at an angle. Decoration was by ribbons,

plumes and flowers (289A, C, D, E, F, H, 290,
291B, C, D, E, 304, 308, 309, 311, 312, 314,
325, 329).

Dress Reform and the Aesthetes

The crinoline styles had been criticized and
made fun of by reformers such as Amelia
Bloomer and her colleagues and in the cari-
catures depicted in journals such as *Punch*.
Criticism was, however, much more vocal
in these years as restrictive corsetry and
elaboration of the costume became more
extensive. Medical reaction has been referred
to (p. 100); alternative, more comfortable
forms of dress were being worn by minority
groups who felt strongly about the mode.

Aesthetic dress evolved in the later 1870s.
This was a distinctive style which allowed

a natural, uncorseted figure and garments which were loose-fitting and simple. Characteristic were the puff sleeves and plain skirts without trains. Liberty's fabrics in muted shades and eastern designs on silks and wools were popular. The aesthetes objected to fashionable dress on artistic grounds; the dress reform group objected for medical reasons, for the physical damage and ill-health which stemmed from wearing high fashion clothes. They too rejected corsetry, bustles and the weight of so many layers of garments; they also wore simpler, looser (though less elegant) clothes, made from soft wools, cottons and silk.

Children's Dress

During these years fashionable dress for children was at its most restrictive and unsuitable though some styles, such as the boys' sailor suits, continued to provide a more comfortable outfit. They were generally of dark blue serge in the summer and white drill for summer wear (**321**). In the later years of this period, the sailor suit with skirt instead of trousers became popular for girls.

Of quite different design for boys was the rather effeminate attire based upon Little Lord Fauntleroy, a character in the book of that name written by Frances Hodgson-Burnett, an English-American novelist, and published in 1886. The Fauntleroy costume was a 'best suit' favoured especially by mothers (though not by their sons) in the 1880s and 1890s. It was an elegant, somewhat elaborate costume, based upon the Cavalier style of the 1640s (p. 35) and most unsuitable for the later nineteenth century. The style became fashionable through the influence of the Aesthetic Movement of the time and had been evolving even before the publication of the immensely popular book but the illustrations in this, by Reginald Birch, of Cavalier dress, set the seal on the fashion and it was enthusiastically adopted for the rest of the century. It consisted of a black or coloured velvet jacket and matching knee-breeches and was tied at the waist with a

315 Green leather and black patent leather ladies' boot, English actual footwear, 1865.

316 Yellow satin shoe with bow, English actual footwear, 1865.

317 Circular folding fan in green silk, wooden handle. Gallery of English Costume, Platt Hall, Manchester, 1870–80.

318 Crimson satin boot. Actual footwear, Rocamora Costume Museum, Barcelona, Spain, 1880–90.

broad sash and decorated at the neck by a lace falling band. Hair was grown long and curled. White shirt, stockings and black, buckled shoes completed the ensemble (**322**).

Girls' clothes were patterned closely upon those of their mothers. They wore tightly-laced, boned corsets despite increasingly strident warnings from doctors of the dangers of so constricting the bodies of growing children. The damage which could be caused by impeding the circulation and breathing by restricting the development of the muscles of the chest and abdomen and even the displacement of vital organs was described and publicized but most fashionable mothers continued to dress their daughters in the mode of the day: the wasp waist, emerging from its swathes of bustle draperies, remained supreme (**319, 320, 323, 324**).

In contrast, and as a parallel to the Fauntleroy theme, was the Kate Greenaway costume. Catherine (Kate) Greenaway was an English artist and illustrator who produced self-illustrated original children's books.

117

319 Costume for little boy aged 2–4 years. Red and black pleated poplin skirt. Black cloth jacket with tabbed basque. Black silk braid trimming. Kid boots. From *Englishwoman's Domestic Magazine*, 1867. Costume Galleries, Castle Howard.

320 Costume for little girl aged 4–6 years. Grey bretonne dress edged with black cashmere. Underskirt of pleated violet cashmere. From *Englishwoman's Domestic Magazine*, 1867. Costume Galleries, Castle Howard.

321 Navy and white sailor suit. Grey socks and black boots. French fashion plate, 1880.

322 Little Lord Fauntleroy style velvet suit with sash and lace collar. Ribbon bow decoration, English fashion journal.

Typical was the annual almanack published from 1883–95 and the Kate Greenaway Birthday Books. The children there depicted were, like Little Lord Fauntleroy, dressed in more natural fashions from an earlier, presumed more romantic, age, in this case that of *c.* 1790–1810. They wore high-waisted sashed dresses, puff sleeves, shoulder capes and ankle-length skirts edged with lace; these were accompanied by dainty bonnets worn over frilly caps. In the late 1880s Kate Greenaway introduced the smocked yoke style of dress which was based upon the countryman's smock in which the material fell loosely from stitched smocking on the chest. Soon, blouses and pinafores were made in this style too, with gaily-coloured stitching carried out on light shades of washable

323 White piqué dress with white lace ornamentation, pink belt. Dark blue bows. White boots and gloves. Straw hat with cherries and ribbons. Swiss actual costume, Schweizerisches Landesmuseum, Zürich, *c.* 1876.

324 Dark wool dress with silk sash and accordion pleating. Black boots. French/American fashion plate, 1878.

fabrics. This fashion was especially popular for young girls and lasted well into the early twentieth century.

Laundering and Care of Fabrics

By the nineteenth century in large towns the heavier washing could be sent out to be laundered* professionally by the new laundry companies which were then being established. This custom, though, was usually only adopted in cases where inadequate space in a town house was available for the facilities of washing, drying and ironing because the mechanized and chemical processes used were thought to injure the fabrics. In country and suburban areas all washing was done at home and in towns all the finer, decorative materials were handled there also. Washday had become more frequent as cotton and linen were less costly than before and the numerous layers of be-frilled underwear and nightwear worn by everyone produced quantities of garments to be laundered.

Middle and upper class households employed a large staff of servants and these included a full-time laundry staff. Mrs Beeton[†], in her section on 'Duties of a Laundry Maid', gives us a vivid, complete account of the laundering process which took place weekly and lasted almost a whole week before it recommenced in the following one.

Mrs Beeton gives recommendations regarding the ideal accommodation and equipment needed. There should be two rooms – a washing room and a drying one (as may be seen at the National Trust house at Erddig, near Wrexham). The floor should be of York stone, sloping to a drain. A shaft or vent in the roof should carry off the steam. By the midcentury running water and hot and cold taps were more common and these, with drains, were recommended to all sinks, tubs and coppers. Adjacent to the washing and bleaching room should be a room for drying, mangl-

---

* A word contracted from the original 'lavendering'.
† Isabella Beeton, author of *Beeton's Book of Household Management* published by her husband S.O. Beeton in 1861 and regularly revised and enlarged.

325   Purple silk bonnet, ribbons and plumes. French fashion plate, *Le Saison*, 1872.

326   White collar and Ascot tie, top hat, English fashion plate, 1875.

327   Soft felt grey hat, knotted tie. French fashion plate, 1874.

328   Coiffure 1874–5 with ribbon bow and jewelled comb. English fashion plate.

329   Cream straw hat, black velvet ribbons, white birds' wings. English fashion plate, 1875.

330   Man's deerstalker cap of check tweed. English fashion plate, 1885.

331   Silk neckscarf, top hat. English fashion plate, 1885.

ing and ironing. This should be equipped with tables, drawers, creels and airers and facilities for starching.

The washing process began on a Monday with the sorting of garments of different fabrics and their initial treatment by soaking in vats containing lye liquids of soda, unslaked lime, chemical fluids etc. as suited to each fabric and the stains requiring to be expunged. On Tuesday fires were lit and garments washed in warm soapy water. After washing, and boiling where necessary, clothes were rinsed and whites were treated with blue (from indigo) to maintain their colour. Woollens and silks were treated separately and more delicately. Washing processes continued on Wednesday and during Thursday and Friday clothes were mangled, starched where necessary, and ironed.

In the second half of the century, although washdays still involved excessive physical labour, several aids and appliances had become available to make the processes easier. More houses possessed piped water. The idea of the wash boiler was developed. Housed in an out-house, these began as cast iron cauldrons set upon brick plinths with space beneath for a fire. Gradually a special fireplace was incorporated into the cast iron body and, as gas was piped into more houses, gas boilers became available. In later examples taps were fitted to empty the boiler but it still had to be filled by hand.

The dolly stick and posser were aids to alleviate washday drudgery. The dolly stick – known also as a peggy stick, dolly pin or clump dolly – varied in design from region to region but the most common type resembled an upside-down milking stool to which a long handle and cross-bar had been fitted. The three-legged dolly was then used to pound the washing in the tub and so loosen the dirt. The posser had a cone-shaped metal head with holes in the base. It too had a long handle attachment and was similarly operated. The metal-covered corrugated-surfaced washboard, upon which clothes were rubbed, was another typical nineteenth century washing aid.

For centuries soap for domestic laundering had been made at home by using rendered-down animal fat boiled together with homemade lye, that is, an alkaline solution which had been produced by water drained through wood ashes. During the nineteenth century large-scale manufacture of soap was developed, following upon the work of two French chemists who, in the late eighteenth century, had discovered a means of making soda – the necessary alkali – from salt. Soap then became more plentiful and cheaper and, in England, William Hesketh Lever – later Lord Leverhulme – contributed greatly to the widescale purchase of soap by his extensive and imaginative advertising and packaging.

There was also an attempt to provide the housewife with a convenient soap powder or flakes for domestic washing needs. She was accustomed to catering for her own needs by mixing shredded soap with soda. In the 1860s a product on these lines was made from ground soap and alkalis. Lux soap flakes became available in 1900.

An account of the nineteenth century development of irons and washing machines is given in Chapter Ten, pp. 121–2.

1890—1914

End of an Era

Laundering and Care of Clothes

The Washing Machine

As the Industrial Revolution gained momentum during the nineteenth century and mechanization speeded up the factory production of textiles, their decoration and the making of these into garments, a parallel mechanization for home needs lagged behind. A patent for a machine to 'wash, press out water and to press linen and wearing apparel' had been taken out as early as 1780 by a Mr Rogerson of Warrington but it was not until the 1850s that serious attempts were made to produce a washing machine for the home. After this many different machines were designed, manufactured and put on the market. They were purchased and, by the end of the century, were becoming popular in America but in Europe, due to a more than adequate servant supply, it was not until after the First World War that they were possessed by more than five per cent of the population.

The machines were not in any way comparable to a modern washing machine because the motive power still depended upon human energy. Also, the filling and emptying was still largely carried out by human hands and, for most models, the water had to be heated first, poured into the machine and chopped-up soap added. The machines all followed the traditional method of washing clothes but presented a marginal improvement in that the housewife had only to turn a handle or a wheel or push a lever backwards and forwards instead of pounding a dolly stick up and down. The aim of the washing machine was

to agitate the soapy water in which the clothes were soaking, pushing it through the fabric and so easing out the dirt.

Most machines, usually called dolly washers, were made of wood in the form of a round or squarish tub. Only the wheels, handles, taps and fittings were of metal. Some had a dolly stick attached inside to the lid or base, others had corrugated walls and base in order to increase water resistance and so act as a rubbing washboard on the clothes. Some designs were fitted with fins or paddles to move the washing or had a wooden roller with pegs projecting from it. In all types a wheel, a lever or a handle had to be operated to provide the motive power (332).

An ingenious design was the 'Faithfull' washing machine which harnessed the motive power of the rocker, traditionally employed from earliest times to send a baby to sleep in its cradle or, later, adopted for churning butter. The housewife could rock the machine with one foot while seated in a chair carrying out another household task. Most later machines had a wringer attached to squeeze out surplus water from garments before they were hung up to dry.

Irons

Until the emergence of the self-heating iron in the mid-nineteenth century, there had been two chief types of iron to smooth and finish laundered clothes: the box and the sad iron. The former contained either a red-hot slug of cast iron, previously heated on the kitchen stove or burning charcoal, the latter was of solid cast iron and was itself heated on the

332 *Right*: Hand-operated washing machine. Wooden tub, the inner walls and base corrugated to increase resistance. The handle is pushed backwards and forwards to make the central posser rotate. *c.* 1900–10, Carlisle Museum.

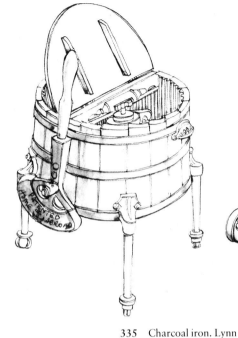

334 Gas iron. Steel with wood handle. Elizabethan House Museum, Great Yarmouth.

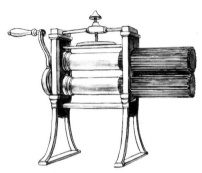

333 Iron and brass crimping machine. Gustav Holst's Birthplace Museum, Cheltenham.

335 Charcoal iron. Lynn Museum, King's Lynn.

hob. In both cases the heating agent had to be carefully handled and re-heated at frequent intervals (**335**).

There were many shapes and forms of special irons – the ball iron, the egg iron, the mushroom and the sleeve iron. These were fashioned in cast iron to smooth different parts of a garment which were difficult of access, for example, sleeves, bustles, bonnets. There were also varied items of equipment for frilling, goffering and pleating such as the crimping machine which resembled a miniature mangle with corrugated brass rollers or the goffering stack in which damped, starched material was held in pleats until dry (**333**).

From the 1850s various forms of self-heating were devised for irons, a number of which were hazardous to operate. Box irons fuelled by coal gas were in use in the USA from this time as, for example, the one patented by David Lithgow of Philadelphia in 1858. English gas irons followed, designed with a flexible tube to connect to the supply (**334**). Colza oil-burning irons were developed from lamps using the same fuel but these were somewhat unsafe to use. Paraffin heated

irons, only slightly more reassuring, appeared in the 1890s. In America, experiments were carried out in the use of naphtha for this purpose but these were deemed even more dangerous.

A great deal more satisfactory was the spirit iron, made in considerable numbers from the 1850s onwards. Heated by methylated spirits, these were much safer and many models survive. A small version of these, fuelled by solidified cubes impregnated with the spirit, was developed as a model for travelling. The petrol-filled iron was widely used from the early twentieth century onwards.

The electric iron, which was eventually to replace all other types, was slow to be developed due to tardiness in introducing the electric supply into houses, but from 1890 such irons were available, fitted with a flexible cord to be connected to the supply where it was provided.

Fashion Designers

By 1990 Paris fashion had become big business and a number of fashion houses had been established. There was Jacques Doucet (336), Callot Soeurs – founded by three sisters in 1895 and known especially in the years before 1914 for their elegant creations in tulle and chiffon – and the millinery house of Caroline Reboux. Mme Paquin, who opened her house in 1891, was the first woman to become a leading designer; she was advised in business by her husband who was a banker. She was a supremely elegant woman, highly professional and with superb taste. Her creations were famed for their beautiful fabrics and their rich fur and gold trimmings (339).

There were designers of other nationalities also: the English House of Redfern, for instance, and, in London, another woman who became a leading couturière, Lucile, Lady Duff Gordon. Canadian born and of Irish/Scottish stock, she was the first British woman to achieve an international reputation in this field; she was also noted for her insistence that such elegant gowns should only be worn over equally glamorous underwear and introduced extravagantly luxurious petticoats and camisoles of silk and satin elaborately trimmed with ribbons and lace.

The years from 1905 were dominated by two colourful personalities who pioneered a new, flamboyant approach: Paul Poiret and Mariano Fortuny. Poiret especially was more than an innovator; he was a rebel whose ideas were original and revolutionary. Abandoning the restrictions of the whaleboned corsetry and frou-frou petticoats, he dressed his models in simply draped gowns which were at the same time feminine, luxurious and exotic. Many of his designs were based upon Oriental themes – kimonos, harem skirts, sultana trousers made of costly fabrics, richly embroidered and fur trimmed. Though completely different from what had gone before, Poiret's themes were not divorced from the movements of his day. They had an affinity with Art Nouveau design and shades as well as the colours and themes of the Diaghilev Ballet which visited Paris in 1909. This could be seen in Poiret's brilliant shades of cerise, flame, emerald and royal blue. Though he freed the feminine figure from acutely rigid

336 Evening gown in silk and lace. Jacques Doucet, 1908.

337 Pale blue brocade evening gown with plain sash. Long gloves. Charles Frederick Worth, 1904. Hermitage Museum, Leningrad.

338 Chiffon and fur tiered dress. Paul Poiret, 1913.

339 Promenade costume. Plumed hat, muff and umbrella. Madame Paquin, 1905.

340 Grey wolfskin motoring coat, wool cap with vizor and tinted goggles. Photograph, 1905.

341 Fawn silk and alpaca motoring dust coat. Adjustable veil tied over straw hat with ostrich plumes. Photograph, 1905.

342 Bathing costume of cream-coloured cotton checked in green and red. Black braid edging and girdle. White stockings and shoes. Green bathing cap with white bow. Fashion plate, 1909, English.

343 Cycling costume in grey tweed. Coat and rationals to match. Fawn gaiters, black boots. Straw hat with ribbons and plume. Gloves. Advertisement, English, 1898.

corsetry and overlong be-frilled skirts, his gowns were not unrestrictive as could be seen in his wired lampshade skirts and later designs of hobbled ankles (**338**).

Clothes for Special Functions and Occasions

The variety of garments designed for both sexes for different pursuits proliferated in these years. Wear suited to holiday, travel and leisure use became more informal and comfortable. Specific garments then appeared – for motoring, for walking in the country and mountains, for the sea-side (beaches and sea-bathing), for golf, shooting, for bicycling and for a range of sporting activities.

Most popular leisure wear for men was the Norfolk jacket, matching knickerbockers and cap or hat; the material was usually tweed. The jacket was a belted style, buttoned down the centre front and was characterized by longitudinal box pleats. The knickerbockers, which were a loose form of knee breeches fastened by a strap and buckle or tie at the knee, were so-called after Washington Irving's *nom-de-plume* adopted for his *History of New York* published in 1809; this referred to his fictitious character Diedrich Knickerbocker. The Knickerbockers were a family of original Dutch settlers of New Amsterdam (later re-named New York). Cruikshank's illustrations of these Dutchmen in Irving's book showed a style of knee breeches with ribbon ties (**344**).

For summer wear the blazer and light trousers replaced the Norfolk jacket and knickerbockers. Originally a scarlet university jacket, the name blazer was applied from the 1880s to any jacket of bright colour, generally vertically striped, and this became popular informal holiday wear.

Bicycling was taken up by both sexes with enthusiasm in the 1890s. Ladies could either wear a jacket and blouse with a calf-length skirt, long gaiters, boots and a cap or, very daringly, a knee-length coat over rationals. These were the equivalent of the men's knickerbockers (**343**).

The idea of designing clothes particularly for use in motoring was an important, though short-lived, fashion. In the late nineteenth century, particularly, before the lifting of the 'red-flag' restriction, the speed of progress in an open car was so slow that cold was a severe problem. In the early years of the twentieth century the motor car travelled much faster but offered little protection from cold, wet, wind and dust so, between 1900 and 1910, protective clothing was developed for both sexes.

Men generally wore a cloth, peaked cap and goggles and covered their normal sporting wear with, according to season, long full fur or fur-lined overcoats, storm coats or dust coats. On top of these rugs were wrapped round the knees and foot muffs were added for extra warmth. The dust coats, worn in hot summer weather, were of cotton, silk or alpaca and were recommended to be grey or fawn in order not to show the dust. Woman were similarly attired and, on their heads, tied voluminous veils round their elaborate fashionable hats or wore hoods. These coverings left no portion of the head exposed, the lady peering out through a grey veil and a layer of fine dust rather like a Moslem or Hindu woman in her purdah dress (**340, 341**).

The increasing popularity of sea-bathing brought dramatic changes in the costume considered acceptable for this activity. Men had continued to bathe naked until after the middle of the nineteenth century but contemporary propriety put pressure upon them and, one by one, the town councils of fashionable resorts began to insist that men should wear a costume. A design resembling shorts was produced but, as the garment was made from a non-elasticated serge or worsted, it descended to the ankles as soon as it became saturated so not only failed in its purpose of maintaining modesty but became a hazard in struggling out of the sea and up the beach. The problem was solved by 1880 with the all-in-one costume which completely covered the body from shoulders to mid-thigh. Such costumes, often striped, were still made from serge or worsted. By 1900 a knitted jersey

344 Check tweed Norfolk jacket and knickerbockers with cap to match. Woollen socks. Suede and leather laced boots. Gloves. Newspaper photograph, English, 1891.

345 Grey worsted three-piece lounge suit. Light grey trilby felt hat with black band. Grey spats over black shoes. Leather gloves. Cane. English newspaper photograph, 1914.

346 Black cutaway tail coat for formal wear. Grey and black striped trousers. Grey top hat. Spats, boots, gloves, umbrella. Fashion plate, English, 1899.

347 Evening dress of black tail coat and trousers. Black silk lapels and braid trouser seams. White shirt, collar, tie, waistcoat and gloves. Black socks, slippers, top hat. English tailor's brochure, 1910.

fabric was adopted – a great improvement – and, with introduction of elasticated fabrics, the top part of the costume was abandoned.

Women's bathing costumes were much more elaborate. From about 1880 the usual design resembled normal day wear. Made of flannel, serge or worsted, it consisted of pantalettes to the knee or ankle and, on top, a dress with a collar, short sleeves and skirt nearly to the knee. Colours were sombre and decoration excessive, ranging from lace-edging to braid and embroidery. The costume was completed by dark stockings, tie-on shoes and a cap. As time passed the costume became more and more elaborate. By the years 1900–10 elegant hats accompanied the ensemble and ladies even wore corsets under their bathing costumes to preserve their slim waistlines. Decoration included ruching, ribbon bows and sashes. Colours had become lighter and brighter and, slowly, fabrics became less heavy. Just before the First World War the one-piece suit was introduced. Though it reached down to the knees and had a skirt and sleeves, it was a vast improvement for practical use (342). Earlier, the famous Australian swimmer Annette Kellerman had worn a sleeveless one-piece suit ending above her knees but in 1907 she was arrested on a beach in Boston for wearing such a swimsuit in defiance of accepted conventions regarding bathing wear.

Men's Dress

Fashions changed only imperceptibly in these years. There was an immeasurably slow trend towards informality. Formal day dress comprised the single-breasted cutaway morning coat or the double-breasted frock coat, in grey or black, worn with striped grey trousers (plate 38, 346). For evening, gentlemen were dressed in black 'tails' or dinner jacket – white tie for the former, black tie for the latter (347). Greater informality was displayed in the pre-eminence of the three-piece suit for everyday town wear. City suits had black or dark jackets and grey striped trousers. Other suits were made all of one material, often

tweed. In 1895 the vertical crease was introduced into trouser legs and it became fashionable to turn up the hems into cuffs. In general, colours were conservative but style turned gradually towards a looser fit (345).

Men's hairstyles were fairly short in these years; moustaches, with or without neat beards, were commonly worn but side-whiskers were now out of fashion. The top hat remained the formal style (346), otherwise, the bowler (344), straw boater and various types of cap continued to be worn (340). Soft felt hats had been introduced; the aristocrat of these was the Homburg. Appearing as early as the late 1870s, this was called after the German town of that name and, in England, was popularized by the Prince of Wales. Its crown was dented lengthwise from front to back and the brim edges were braid trimmed and slightly upturned. Another similar style – the trilby – was named in 1895 from a dramatized version of George du Maurier's novel *Trilby*. Plainer than the Homburg, the brim edges were unbound. It continued to be worn until after the Second World War (345).

Underwear

In the 1880s new principles of health and hygiene were being advocated in the design of underwear. A notable proponent of this was Dr Jaeger, Professor of Physiology at the University of Stuttgart. Dr Jaeger believed in the efficacy of wearing wool next to the skin because it was porous and would permit the body to breathe. From 1884 woollen underwear was being manufactured for both sexes in Britain under the Jaeger name. Soon vests, pants and drawers were being made in wool with a stockinette weave and the material was even experimented with for corsets and petticoats but these, unsurprisingly, were less successful commercially.

In 1887 the concept of an open textured cotton material was mooted by Lewis Haslam. This cellular fabric was marketed as Aertex which, like Jaeger, is still a household word. A third equally long-lived name is Viyella, a

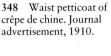

348 Waist petticoat of crêpe de chine. Journal advertisement, 1910.

349 White cotton bosom amplifier with lace and ribbon trimming. Journal advertisement, 1905.

350 Waist petticoat of silk with lace flouncing. Journal advertisement, 1905.

351 Princess style petticoat trimmed with ribbon and lace. Photograph, 1913.

352 Blue silk combinations with lace and ribbon trimming. Photograph, 1903.

353 White wool men's combinations. Journal advertisement, 1910.

fabric produced by William Hollins and Co. in the 1890s; it was made from a blend of wool and cotton. It was soon adopted for a wide range of underwear and nightwear.

From the late nineteenth century it became customary to combine two garments in one and 'combinations' (union suit in the USA) had arrived. Popular with both sexes, for men the undervest and long pants became one garment and, for women, the chemise and drawers were similarly combined (353).

By 1900 feminine underwear had become elegant and expensive (see Lady Duff Gordon p. 123). Now generally referred to as lingerie, fashionable garments were tailored to the figure in silk, taffeta and satin. Combinations, often of wool or cotton, still had legs extending down to below the knees but were less voluminous and heavy than previously. Drawers, now known as knickers, were elaborately trimmed with lace frilling and inserts (352). The fashionable figure was maintained with (apart from the corset) the flounced and lace-trimmed bosom amplifier – the current version of the earlier camisole (349). A bust bodice, made of white cotton or calico, was boned at the sides to give extra support. Lingerie could be made in sets. A 'set' comprised knickers, bust bodice, chemise and petticoat, all in one colour, material and decoration (348, 350, 351).

The corsets of the years 1890–1905 were the most restrictive of all nineteenth century versions (355, 356). A straight-busked corset had evolved from the 'health corset' suggested by Dr Jaeger and the design of Madame Gaches-Sarraute, a corsetière who had pioneered the straight front in order to give support to the abdomen but to avoid restriction of the thorax and consequent inward pressure on the diaphragm. The new straight-busked corset front was strongly re-

355 Department store advertisement, 1898.

354 Long corset. Manufacturer's advertisement, 1909.

357 S-bend front busk corset. Department store advertisement, 1903.

356 Boned corset with suspenders. Manufacturer's advertisement, 1893.

bust and hips as well as waist. To achieve this effect a very long corset was worn. This was less waisted and had fewer bones inserted in the seams than previously. Between 1908 and 1914 it was, however, so long that it was difficult to sit down comfortably, particularly as it was laced up the back and still had a front busk. Suspenders were long, attaching to the stockings at about knee-level (354).

Women's Dress

From 1890 onwards fashion changes accelerated. In the years 1890–1914 there were three distinct styles: those of 1890–1900, 1900–10 and 1910–14. In the first two of these periods the silhouette continued to be an artificial one (see corset p. 127) and femininity, gracious manners and decorum marked the lady. These years represented the swan song of the lady of leisure, displaying her feminine charms and graceful mien and with knowledge of her 'correct' place in the world of men. By 1910 a few women had begun to challenge this accepted view of their status; suffragettism was under way and more women were working for a living and earning independence; some professions were challenged and successfully entered. Dress designs reflected all of this.

The fashionable silhouette of the last decade of the nineteenth century was elegant and simpler than before – the bustle had disappeared. These were the years of the leg-of-mutton sleeve, a very high neckline, a full bosom, a wasp waist and a bell-shaped, often gored, skirt. Under this was worn a silk or taffeta petticoat which was fitting down to the knee then, below this, flared, flounced and lace-trimmed. Together with a taffeta skirt lining, this produced the coveted frou-frou sound with movement. The hour-glass silhouette needed only one petticoat and this, together with the skirt and underskirt were held up daintily at one side whilst walking in the street, an art of feminine coquetry and comparable to the earlier use of the fan (plate 39, 358).

commended by the medical authorities which had been campaigning for years to abolish the harmful concave front but the advice of these gentlemen was still unheeded in the feminine search for a tiny waist. Ladies laced up the new corset so tightly that it created a new, and worse, figure distortion. Due to the intractability of the long straight-front busk, the bosom above was pushed forward and the hips below, backwards. The new fashionable ideal was therefore achieved: a full, forward bosom, a tiny waist and generous backward-slanting hips (357).

After 1908 the desired figure was a more natural one though still very slim – now at

30 Wool coat with leather belt and white linen collar. Hat to match. Cotton trousers, soft shoes with laces. English Fashion Plate.

31 Cutaway coat with velvet collar and cuffs. Worsted trousers with braid side seams. Top hat, gloves, cane. German Fashion Plate, *Berliner Modenspiegel*.

32   Summer fashions for 1839 by Benjamin Read,
Guildhall Art Gallery, London.

33   Painting by Edouard Manet 'Music in the
Tuileries Gardens', 1862, National Gallery, London.

34   Business suit. Tail coat with trousers, waistcoat, shirt and tie. Hat and boots. German Fashion Plate, *Deutschen Herrenmoden*, Dresden, 1874.

35   Faille dress in two colours. Fringe and passementerie ornamentation. Hat decorated with flowers and ribbons. Gloves, parasol. French actual costume, Musée du Costume de la Ville de Paris, 1875.

ELABORATE BALL DRESSES IN 1873
36   Bustle dresses with full draperies edged with
multi-flouncing and ruching, long trains. Décolleté
necklines at front and back, short sleeves. Ribbons at
neck and gloves. Chignon type coiffures with curls on
top and on the forehead, decorated by flowers and
ribbons. Fans held in the hand. The gentleman wears
traditional black evening dress with white tie and
gloves. Painting entitled 'Too Early' by James Tissot.
Guildhall Art Gallery, London.

37 Transparent muslin dress painted with design in roses and with black lace superimposed on bodice. Cream lace at neck and sleeve. Black velvet waist bands. Biscuit-coloured straw hat decorated with flowers and black velvet ribbons. Long white kid gloves. Parasol, the inside covered by layers of white lace, the exterior decorated by black lace. Actual costume, Museum of Costume, Bath, 1904.

38 Fashion plate of 1906. Black cloth frock coat, with black satin revers. White piqué waistcoat. Grey and black striped trousers. Spats, black shoes. Stiff white collar, neckcloth. Top hat. Gloves. Cane.

39   Silk rep dress ornamented with deep blue velvet.
Long gloves. Straw hat decorated with flowers and
lace. Umbrella. Actual costume, Kostuum Museum,
The Hague, Holland, 1896.

40   Tunic dress with hobble skirt. Hat with bow and
plumes. Gloves and umbrella. White collar. Shoes.
Austrian fashion plate, *Wiener Chic,* 1914.

41   Loose dresses with white collars and cuffs.
Cloche hats. Silk scarf. Strap shoes, 'The Botanists' by
Joseph Southall, 1928, Hereford City Museum.

42   Fabric bias cut. Gilt leather handbag with bead embroidery. Silk chiffon evening dress designed by Madeleine Vionnet, 1931.

43   Striped wool blazer. Flannel trousers in 'Oxford bags' style. Co-respondent style of shoe in white buckskin and dark leather. Straw hat with striped ribbon. Informal summer wear, 1928. Magazine illustration.

358 Promenade dress of tiny black and white check patterned wool. White lace blouse. Black velvet hat with ribbon bows. Black gloves, parasol. Actual costume, Nordiska Museet, Stockholm, 1906.

359 Cream satin evening gown with tinted floral design. Deep crimson velvet banded trimming at sleeves, neck, waist and hem. White gloves and fan. Actual costume Victoria and Albert Museum, London, 1894–6.

360 White silk formal gown with white silk muslin undersleeves and skirt decoration. Actual costume, Musée du Costume de la Ville de Paris, c. 1900.

The early years of the new century were those of the characteristic S-bend line, an unnatural gait produced by the corset of the day (p. 128). The bosom line was worn low to overhang the tight waistbelt. The fashionable woman sailed into a room carrying all before her. The style was immortalized in the drawings of the American artist Charles Dana Gibson and became known as the 'Gibson Girl'. The full skirt was very long – trains were worn with evening and formal gowns – and dresses were elaborately decorated with lace, embroidery, fringing and fur. Except for evening wear, necklines were very high, boned at the sides up to the ears, and often encircled by dog-collar necklaces (plate 37, 358).

A particular fashion of these two periods was that of the tea gown, so-called because it was worn by ladies when being entertained to tea in their hostess's boudoir – later, gentlemen were also admitted. The gown was loose and long. It fell in graceful folds from a high waistline or yoke. Sleeves were long and, like the rest of the gown, were over-decorated with lace and ruffles; a matching cap accompanied the outfit.

The 1890s coiffure was simple and neat with curls on the forehead and the rest of the hair swept up at the sides, and back to a chignon or bun (plate 39, 358). From the turn of the century the pompadour style replaced this, backcombed and piled up on top of the head over pads; large combs of tortoiseshell or amber held the coiffeur in place (plate 37, 360).

The 1890s hats were often small toques decorated with plumes and flowers but, gradually, the large-brimmed hat took over, becoming excessively wide by 1909. Such hats were ornamented lavishly with flowers and fruit, ribbons and plumes. Both hat and face were draped by a spotted net veil. Large hat pins (useful in self-defence) were essential for these modes to hold them in place.

Between 1908–10 and the outbreak of war in 1914 new fashions followed one another quickly. Eastern influences were strong – the Russo–Japanese war was in the news – and Oriental features such as the kimono

361 Purple georgette evening dress with silver embroidered hem panel. Velvet cape richly embroidered with pearls and gold thread. Black fur collar and edging. Actual costume, Museum of Costume, Bath, 1912.

362 Royal blue silk tunic dress with peg-top skirt. Pink lace blouse, cerise belt. Pink felt hat, navy pompom. Black velvet laced boots. Fashion plate, 1913.

363 Crushed strawberry satin evening gown. Silver and mauve embroidered bands. Actual costume, Gallery of English Costume, Platt Hall, Manchester, 1911.

364 Dark brown figured velvet dress. Overdress of brown crêpe with self-coloured ribbon embroidery. Black fur edging and muff. Brown felt hat, white plume. French actual costume, Victoria and Albert Museum, London, 1912–13.

sleeve were introduced; Poiret's designs were dominant in this field (p. 123). A new figure silhouette was established (p. 128) and a whole range of skirt designs appeared. Some of these were patently absurd, the hobble skirt of 1911, for instance, in which a wide band of material was fastened round the legs in the lower part between knee and ankle, making walking difficult. Others included a variety of tunic skirts, the wired lampshade design and a more practical and elegantly feminine style, that draped and tapered towards the ankle. The most outré fashions were reserved for evening gowns (plate 40, **361, 362, 363, 364**).

Apart from the more extreme modes of skirt, clothes had become more natural and comfortable. The high neckline had given way to a square or V. Trains had largely disappeared and the hemline reached the ankles. Waists were slender but not unnaturally so. Hats had become smaller and plainer, hairstyles also. Suits and blouses and skirts were popular for everyday wear. Clothes were chic but no longer excessively and fussily elaborate. The scene was set for the development of a twentieth century attire which would be practical and suited to the working woman.

CHAPTER ELEVEN

1914–1950

Fashion for All in the Modern World

It is a truism that the First World War completely altered all aspects of life in the western world: nothing was ever the same again. Nowhere was this change more evident than in the realm of fashion where the new approach affected feminine dress more than masculine. This was because it was the woman's way of life which was more greatly altered. From 1914 to 1918 many women went out to work for the first time and a large proportion of these were doing men's jobs and mixing with masculine colleagues. When the war was over most of these women did not return to domestic service, where they had been employed before, or to solely running a home and bringing up a large family. As time passed, younger women especially entered the professions and fields of work hitherto open only to men. Many of them learned successfully to combine a career with homemaking.

This revolutionary change of attitude stimulated far-reaching alterations in the designing, working and marketing of clothes. No longer were able women willing to spend a great deal of time being fitted for new designs: they were too busy. No longer was the latest fashion available only to the wealthy and aristocratic classes. No longer was the status of high fashion so all important. There was a blurring of the social divisions and the fashionable line became available to a much wider clientèle.

Fashion was gradually established as an important industry catering for a broad stratum of society. Manufacturers began to mass-produce ready-to-wear garments in the fashionable mode in a wide range of colours, materials and sizes. The quality of such garments improved greatly and prices were modest. Department stores and dress shops stocked an increasing variety of clothes for all seasons and functions. Simultaneously a number of technical developments led to a more easy-care approach to the wardrobe of both sexes. This was evidenced in washing and cleaning of fabrics as well as in the introduction of new ones.

Home Laundering

The appearance of the washing machine was noted in Chapter Ten (p. 121), but it was the emergence of the electrically powered machine which led to its wider use. As long as it had to be operated by hand, sales were very limited. In the USA as early as the first decade of the twentieth century, electric motors were being added to existing hand-operated models. Since these machines were rarely earthed and as the motor was usually sited beneath the tub (which often leaked) the machine was at best short circuited and at worst most unsafe.

By the late 1920s American machines were being completely re-designed to take advantage of electric power so became suited to a mass market. The wooden tub was replaced by a non-leaky metal one and the familiar washing action was perfected. Such machines were soon being imported into Europe but they were costly so few were sold (366). Even as late as 1939 a washing machine was still considered to be a luxury here and it was after

365 Gas iron. Steel with wood handle. Christchurch Mansion Museum, Ipswich, *c*. 1910–15.

367 Tilley iron. Enamelled and polished steel, plastic handle. North of England Open Air Museum, Beamish, 1940–50.

366 Ewbank washing machine. Metal and wood tub. Handle is turned to operate a metal beater which swirls the washing round. Wringer with rubber covered rollers. Paisley Museum, *c*. 1930.

were not achieved, the drawback being the extreme slowness with which electric supply was being introduced into homes. Even into the late 1930s electric irons still had to be large and heavy because, due to the fluctuation of the power supply, the iron had to be able to store heat in order to allow for periods when it was forced to cut out. There was no thermostatic control until just before the outbreak of war so the temperature of the iron still had to be judged as it had been for centuries and switched on or off as it became too hot or too cool (**365, 367**).

Synthetic Fabrics

The greatest textile event in modern times has been the emergence and meteoric growth in the synthetic fibres industry. These man-made textiles are, like natural ones, derived from living organisms but, unlike those which came from still-living plants, insects or animals, they are produced from those which millions of years ago died and were slowly transformed into minerals. Synthetic fibres are made by the chemical treatment of materials such as wood pulp or, now more commonly, derive from extracts of petroleum and coal. The substances are transformed to a viscous liquid which can be extruded through a series of fine holes to form filaments which may be twisted, woven or knitted into fabrics. They may also be cut into short staples, then combed, drawn and spun as in the natural fibre processes; they may also be blended with such natural fibres before spinning.

It was the English scientist Robert Hooke who in his *Micrographia* of 1664 put forward the idea that such a fibre could be made and extruded in a similar manner to that demonstrated by the silkworm. During the following 200 years others theorized and experimented with the idea: the scientist Réamur in France in 1734, the silk weaver Schwabe in England in 1842, the Swiss Audemars in 1855 and even Sir Joseph Swan in his research for carbon filament lamps in 1883.

It was known that cellulose is the chief component of such substances as cotton,

the Second World War before marketing campaigns began to show notable results. Using centrifugal action, the domestic spin drier was likewise developed in the USA in the 1920s but, again, in Europe sales did not pick up greatly until after 1945.

The adaptation of electric power to ironing was experimented with rather earlier. The first patent was issued in the USA in 1883 but this model was not connected to the electric supply so had to be re-heated frequently on a special stand. By 1890 a design which was connected by a flexible cord to the power supply was being produced in Europe, at least in France and England. Early designs were cumbersome and not very safe but by 1910 were greatly improved though wider sales

368 Formal evening dress. Black tail coat and trousers. Corded silk lapels, braid trouser side seams. Semi-stiff white shirt. White stiff wing collar and white piqué tie and waistcoat. Black socks. Black patent leather shoes. English actual costume (author), 1941.

369 Dark fawn waterproof trench coat with leather buttons. Brown striped worsted trousers. Brown shirt. Coloured tie. Brown leather shoes and gloves. Brown felt hat. English actual costume (author), 1933.

370 Brown check tweed sports coat – hacking jacket style. Corduroy trousers. Leather sandals. Polo-necked pullover. English actual costume (author), 1950.

371 Brown tweed overcoat, herringbone pattern, raglan sleeve. Fawn worsted trousers. Suede shoes with crêpe soles. Striped shirt, tie. Felt trilby hat. Gloves, cane. English actual costume (author), 1950.

wood and paper and, after years of experimentation, the Frenchman Comte Hilaire de Chardonnet (1839–1924) produced his first fabric from a nitrocellulose solution which was extruded through fine holes to give spinnable filaments. Often, termed 'the father of the rayon industry', Chardonnet exhibited articles made from the fabric in the Paris Exposition of 1889 and, two years later, began commercial production of his 'artificial silk' at Besançon.

However, nitrocellulose made from cotton and nitric acid had a tendency to explosive qualities, so safe alternative ways of making this artificial silk were sought. The cuprammonium process was developed in Germany and commercial manufacture began there in 1899. More successful was the viscose process resulting from the researches of a group of chemists in the 1890s. The British rights for this process were bought in 1904 by Courtaulds, who have since carried out much of the research and development. The fourth method, the acetate process, was undertaken just before the First World War and its commercialization achieved by the Dreyfus brothers who marketed the product under the trade name of 'Celanese' in 1921. It was during the inter-war years that artificial or 'art' silk enjoyed its boom period. America adopted the name 'rayon' in 1924 to designate the fabric which was used especially for underwear.

With the advent of nylon a new synthetic fibre industry was created. This was the first completely synthetic fibre, produced entirely from mineral sources. A polyamide fibre, it is composed of nitrogen and oxygen (derived from air) and hydrocarbons (derived at first from coal but now from oil and natural gas). Nylon was developed in the Du Pont laboratories between 1927 and 1938 at a cost of 27

372   English Street Dress 1914–1921
A   Silk dress with double tiered skirt over peg-top design. Fur muff. Felt hat with plumes. Fashion plate, 1914.
B   Beige woollen winter coat with collar, cuffs and hem of skunk fur. Black fur and beige felt hat. Umbrella. Department store catalogue, 1917.
C   Pale blue wool coat and hat with white fur collar, cuffs and muff. White gaiters. Department store catalogue, 1920.
D   Twill oatmeal coat with self-coloured pattern and embroidery. Black silk umbrella and black velvet hat. Actual costume, Museum of Costume, Bath, 1918.
E   Grey worsted suit. Light grey trilby hat with black band. Grey spats over black shoes. Newspaper photograph, 1914.
F   Brown satin suit with darker brown embroidery. Peg-top skirt. White lace blouse. Purple straw hat with white plumes. Actual costume, Museum of Costume, Bath, 1914.
G   Brown serge suit with black fur trimming. Brown gaiters over black shoes. Cream felt hat. Brown umbrella. Fashion plate, 1916.
H   Grey satin dress with brown fur edging. Pink lining to scarf. Straw hat with plume. Fur muff. Actual costume, Museum of Costume, Bath, 1921.
I   Fawn wool overcoat. Brown worsted trousers. Spats over brown shoes. Black bowler hat, gloves, cane. Fashion plate, 1920.

million dollars. It was made into stockings in 1939 and soon into other articles. It describes a family of synthetic fibres which were later made in many countries under different trade names: Enkalon, Perlon, Nomex, Banlon etc. The British manufacturing rights were bought by ICI in 1940 and British Nylon Spinners (a joint ICI-Courtaulds Co.) were established to make Bri-Nylon in Britain.

Men's Dress

While fashions for women underwent drastic changes in the years 1914–1950 those for men advanced with slow, hesitant steps towards informality and a greater variety in the choice of colours and materials. The three-piece lounge suit, made of one material, became accepted town wear (**372E**) and the

373   Black bowler hat, white stiff collar, black tie. Newspaper photograph, 1915.

374   White wing collar, black bow tie. Newspaper photograph, 1915.

375   Straw boater with ribbon band. Manufacturer's advertisement, 1914.

376   Black bowler hat. Men's outfitter's advertisement, 1933.

sports jacket with flannels casual attire. In style, the slim-line trousers gave way in the 1920s to 'Oxford bags', a very wide trouser some 24 inches at the turn-ups (plate 43). This width was reduced from 1929 but, until after 1945, men's trousers remained considerably wider and were cut higher at the waist than is common today. Lounge suit trousers were upheld by shoulder braces. The mechanical slide fastener with interlocking teeth – the zip fastener or zipper – was first manufactured in the 1920s but only slowly replaced button fastening for men's trousers, becoming the norm after the Second World War. Since then the zip has become slimmer and neater and plastic has replaced the original metal manufacture. A more formal version of the lounge suit was characterized by a black or dark jacket and grey striped trousers.

By 1925 grey flannel trousers worn with a coloured sports jacket were in general use for holiday and informal wear. The jacket might be made from worsted or tweed (370). Alternatively a tweed jacket might accompany plus fours which had succeeded the earlier knickerbockers. Plus fours were so called because they were fuller and longer than their predecessors; they had an overhang below the band at the knee, the length being increased for this purpose by four inches. Patterned knitted pullovers were generally worn with informal attire instead of a waistcoat (431).

Formal dress was now reserved for very special occasions. The frock coat had gone,

377   Fawn felt hat, brown ribbon. Men's outfitter's advertisement, 1934.

official morning dress being provided by the single-breasted cutaway tail coat in light grey worsted accompanied by grey striped trousers. In the evening a black dinner jacket and trousers were worn by men of all ages for all functions such as dinners, dances and parties while 'tails' were reserved for special occasions (368).

Hats were less often worn by the 1930s though the bowler and felt trilby or homburg remained fashionable for men who preferred to wear a hat (369, 371, 373–77). The top hat was retained to accompany the formal tail coats. Hairstyles were short – this was the age of the 'short back and sides' mode and most men were cleanshaven or sported a neat moustache.

Shirts now more often had soft turned-down attached collars. For informal wear coloured shirts made from aertex or rayon were popular. Ties became brighter and gayer in colour and design.

Water-repellant fabrics had now been perfected and were of good quality so most men possessed a raincoat, available in a variety of styles. Both raincoats and overcoats were very long and full, much longer and looser than modern designs (369, 371, 372I).

378   Navy silk dress with white dot pattern and neckline of light blue velvet. Black hat with black net veil and white ostrich plumes. Shoes with gaiters. English actual costume, Museum of Costume, Bath, *c*. 1919.

379   Brown serge suit with black velvet and stitched trimming. Brown and red felt hat with feather. Gloves, fur muff. Black shoes with gaiters. Newspaper advertisement, 1916.

380   White satin evening dress with overdress embroidered in silver and crystal. Silk shoes. Lanvin design, 1919.

381   Plain suit with dark velvet collar. Hat and umbrella. Gaiters and shoes. English design in *The Lady*, 1918.

Women's Dress

Fashion Design and *Haute Couture* 1914–1920

With the outbreak of war the feverishly changing modes of the previous four to five years sobered. Designs were simpler. After all, although it was only a minority of women who wore uniform, many did war work of some kind. The absurdity of wearing hobble or lampshade skirts in a munitions factory or office was patent (**372A, F**, plate 40). Women's growing emancipation was expressed in a hem-line eight inches above the ground, displaying the ankle for the first time as well as light-coloured stockings and high laced or buttoned shoes of kid or suede with high, slim heels and pointed toes. New materials, such as art silk and jersey fabrics, were introduced and became popular for dresses and suits. They lent themselves to garments which fell in simple, soft folds. The chemise gown, first worn in 1914, became fashionable. It was a straight dress with long fitting sleeves and a tunic on top. Evening versions were made of gold or silver cloth, georgette or crêpe lamé. The skirt began to be designed with an uneven hem-line by 1917; at the back it was finished in a neat fishtail train while front and sides varied in length from six to twelve inches above the ground. Such dresses were often sleeveless, had low V necklines and full bodices draped over waist sashes. (**378, 379, 380, 381**).

With the end of the war *haute couture* was re-established, and the pre-war designers became active once more. But, for a few years, they did not move with the times and were out of touch with the momentous social upheaval which was creating a feminine viewpoint rebellious of returning to pre-war

382 Black patterned silk evening dress. Black feather fan. Black silk shoes. Worth design, 1922.

383 Cloth coat with fur collar and trimming. Shoes with gaiters. Felt hat with silk ribbon. French design, *Vogue*, 1923.

384 Evening gown in grey-mauve satin with overdress in pearled orange tulle. Orange satin sash. Kid shoes. French actual costume. Musée du Costume de la Ville de Paris, *c.* 1925.

385 Grey and white silk suit with black tie. Grey felt hat. Grey suede shoes. Lelong design, 1925.

restriction. Paul Poiret, now an ageing *enfant terrible*, returned to designing clothes in garish colours, Oriental in theme, richly embroidered and furred. But simplicity and the liberated woman were 'in' and Poiret was 'out'. He died penniless in 1943 on the French Riviera. Other pre-war designers – Jeanne Lanvin, Jean Patou and, later, Lucien Lelong, adapted and became renowned for their classic, elegant clothes in beautiful fabrics and simple clean-cut lines (**380**).

1920–1930

In these years feminine emancipation took off and reaction against the restrictive domesticity of pre-war life was acute. Women demanded functional comfortable clothes, a freedom to do as men did – smoking, free love, equality of opportunity and, therefore, freedom of attire. Many women mistakenly felt that to work successfully at a job as a man, they must appear to be masculine or, at least, unfeminine. For ten years women hid the attributes given to them by nature: breasts, sloping shoulders, small waist, ample hips, flowing hair. To assert their new-found freedom they emulated masculinity with flattened breasts, tubular unwaisted dresses and shingled hair; they exposed their legs instead. A specific carriage was adopted – the pelvis was thrust forward to accentuate the flatness of the bosom and hips, while arms were thrust akimbo low on the hips – a most unladylike gesture by nineteenth century standards – and eyes peered out mysteriously under a hat pulled down well over the eyebrows.

The boyish look was 'in'. Pyjamas were worn in bed as well as nightdresses, lido pyjamas appeared on the beach. The fashionable figure was thin rather than slim. One must have a slender neck, no bosom, no hips and twiggy legs. It was the age of the flapper.

386 Fur-trimmed wool dress. Velvet and fur hat. Suede shoes. Schiaparelli design, 1933.

387 Evening gown of pale green lace decorated with bands of silver lamé. Jewelled shoulder straps. Chanel design, *c*. 1932. Actual costume, Museum of Costume, Bath.

388 Chanel's jersey suit, 1929.

389 Woollen winter coat with fur trimming. Leather shoes. Vionnet design, 1929.

If one's figure did not conform, one must diet. Skirts rose almost to the knee and the waistline – or rather its suggestion – was low on the hips. Trimming and decoration were at a minimum.

This revolution in feminine dress was not immediately accepted by Parisian *haute couture*. The rank and file of ladies had run away from their leaders and were dictating terms. The couturiers attempted to win them back with eclectic designs, recreating past styles. They had to accept eventually, as designers have had to several times later in the twentieth century, that a fashion which is not in tune with public demand will not 'go', no matter how good the product or the marketing.

All efforts to put the clock back having failed, the couturiers followed the tide and designed for it. They produced clothes for all occasions, informal and holiday as well as evening and dress attire and the quality of dress improved. The negative ugliness of the line of 1920s fashion could not be obscured but it could be given a little elegance and quality. Unless its wearer had chic and was slim and beautiful, the results were likely to be unfortunate at best and hideous at worst but a good designer with a feeling for colour, cut and fabric can work wonders (**382, 384**).

The famous names of pre-1920 years were joined by new ones and the years 1920–1930 became great ones for *haute couture*. The return to a vestige of femininity was helped immensely by the bias cutting of Vionnet and the easy-to-wear suits and dresses in jersey materials by Chanel. The classic cut continued to be provided by couturiers such as Lanvin, Molyneux and Alix.

Madeleine Vionnet believed that the feminine figure was all important to successful couture and that the natural form should not be disguised or distorted. She was an artist in handling materials, in cutting and constructing. She introduced a new technique of bias cutting – cutting on the cross of the fabric – so that it would follow the lines of the body. Many of her designs were draped classical styles. Typical were her day gowns

390   Printed georgette dress in brown, orange and yellow with brown sash. Pale grey gloves and fur. Brown hat and veil. Brown suede handbag and leather shoes. English actual costume (author), 1936.

391   White evening dress with a design of musical notation in blue, black and red. Schiaparelli design, 1939.

392   The Utility suit. Prototype designed by Hardy Amies in check tweed. Black felt hat with brooch. Black patent leather handbag and shoes. English, 1941. Actual costume, Victoria and Albert Museum, London.

393   Evening dress in patterned taffeta. Mainbocher design, 1939.

of heavy crêpe while, for evening wear, she used sheer fabrics which would float and drape. Her creations were famous and successful until her retirement in 1939 (plate 42, 389).

Gabrielle (Coco) Chanel is a legend in the world of couture. Her famous trademark was her easy-to-wear suit which became a wardrobe classic. Such suits were made of soft tweeds or jersey wool and comprised a plain or pleated straight, short skirt, a jersey top or crêpe de chine blouse and an often collarless jacket. Her carefully designed, apparently simple dresses and skirts were equally famous. Decoration was sparing, her chunky costume jewellery became a hallmark. She introduced her famous perfume in the late twenties (387, 388).

Although the clothes during the 1920s were straight and tubular and similar for everyone, fashions changed quickly and each year differed a little from the previous one. The cult of simplicity was supreme for the whole decade. The most notable variation was the hem-line which was the same for all garments whether day dress or evening, suit or coat. In 1920–1 the skirt was ankle-length but from 1922 the hem-line steadily rose, reaching its shortest level, just covering the knee, in 1927. As it shortened the skirt was cut straighter and narrower so that, in the mid-1920s, it was like a tube. In 1927 designers tried to lower the line in order to give variety by introducing longer panels of draped fabric at the sides and back. This was especially characteristic of evening gowns of 1928 and 1929 but the actual hem-line did not begin its descent until 1929–30.

The natural waistline was unmarked and ignored between 1921/2 and 1930. The bodice was tubular and loose with belt or sash worn low on the hips. This was decorated by a cockade or jewel. Sleeves were long and fitting or very short but most commonly dresses were sleeveless with perhaps a floating panel of material hanging behind the arm. Necklines were very plain and either in a low V, bateau or square shape. Some evening gowns had low V backs also.

1930–1939

The fashionable figure of the 1930s was still slim but was no longer boyish; femininity had returned. The waistline quickly reverted to its natural level and was accentuated by shaping and a belt. Breasts were no longer flattened but defined by a brassière which, by 1937, was beginning to become an uplift bra (see p. 147). The skirt hem-line dropped sharply to be about eight inches from the ground and the skirts were pleated or gored. The material was often bias cut to ensure a clinging fit, especially over the hips, and a draped effect. In contrast to the fashions of the 1920s, there were now two lengths, one for evening wear and one for day. For the former the dress was ground-length and many designs were backless, sometimes with halter necklines; by 1938/9 strapless, boned bodices were ultra fashionable; these were off-the-shoulder with a straight across, turned-down cuff décolletage reminiscent of styles of the 1680s (387).

The most colourful personality of the couture world at this time was Elsa Schiaparelli, an Italian who worked for some time in America then set up business in Paris. Throughout the 1930s and early 1940s her designs were highly successful, her work being exported in quantity to England and America. Schiaparelli based these designs on very varied and unusual sources: peasant motifs and fabrics from simple communities in eastern and alpine Europe, north African garments such as the burnous and djellaba, Russian and Peruvian embroideries. She sought inspiration in negro art forms and employed artists such as Salvador Dali and Picasso to design textiles for her (386).

Schiaparelli was a volatile personality, rarely subtle, sometimes crude, always full of vitality. Her clothes were fashionable with those who wished to attract attention in the 1930s. She used strident colours – the term 'shocking pink' derived from her use of this bright colour. She designed knitwear, skirts and dresses; she promoted the padded shoulder line and the slim hips so characteristic of the 1930s design. Her evening gowns were especially elegant and eye-catching (391).

During the inter-war years there were also a number of talented couturiers who were designing for the wealthy woman who wished to be elegant and smartly dressed but not to draw undue attention to herself. Such leading designers included the Irishman Edward Molyneux and the American Mainbocher (born in Chicago Main Rousseau Bocher) (393). Both men designed clothes which were elegantly simple with, for day and evening wear, slim waists and flared skirts.

1939–1950

War-time styles were influenced by the large number of women in uniform. Civilian dress too acquired a shorter skirt, to just below the knee, and padded shoulders, especially in tailored suits and coats. This gave the square box silhouette characteristic of the years up to 1946. There was no particular accentuation of breast or hips but a belt generally confined the waist at the natural level. Most outfits had an efficient and practical appearance. In summer though dresses tended to the 'little girl' effect with their fairly full short skirts and draped bodices. Suits, jumpers and skirts were especially fashionable (394, 395).

These were the years of austerity and privation in Europe. Unrestricted *haute couture* in Paris had ceased with the German occupation of the city and did not re-emerge until France was liberated in 1944. Most couturiers left France, for instance, Schiaparelli and Mainbocher to America and Molyneux to London, In Britain the Utility scheme was introduced in May 1941 and, a month later, clothes were rationed and the supply of

394   Fashion designs, Croquis de Mode, Madrid. Cloth coat with hat to match. Sling handbag. Sling-back, platform-soled shoes. Spanish dress, 1945.

395   Pale blue rayon dress with white spot pattern. Navy suede handbag, gloves and shoes. Navy hat of velvet leaves with veil. English actual costume (author), 1943.

396   Black hat and skirt. Cream linen jacket. Black shoes. Christian Dior's 'New Look', 1947. Actual costume, Victoria and Albert Museum, London.

397   Ice blue satin evening gown with black satin cuffed décolletage. Black suede gloves. Silver sandals. Fashion drawing in *Vogue*, 1946.

coupons was very limited. Under the Utility scheme there was effective control of the quality and cost of cloth manufactured. In design control was also firm, governing the quality of material used in making a garment with curtailment of trimmings, pockets, pleating and skirt length. All of this resulted in a standstill on fashion design for the duration but this did not mean that clothes were badly designed and made. A number of the leading couturiers, such as Hardy Amies and Edward Molyneux, were among those lending their ingenuity to the problems of the day (**392**).

The best-known of immediately post-war couturiers is Christian Dior who erupted into fame with his first collection in 1947 which presented his New Look. Dior was not the only couturier to have sensed that femininity was in the air again at this time. Women were tired to death of austerity, uniforms, practical clothes and a shortage of beautiful fabrics. A number of designers had tentatively introduced tighter waists, fuller and longer skirts and sloping shoulders – Mainbocher, for instance, in the USA and Marcel Rochas who presented his guêpière*, a new corset, in 1947 to produce a tiny waist (**446**) – but it was Dior who launched his new collection entirely in the new feminine form. He staked his whole career on making women elegant and beautiful once more. In February 1947 he presented his first collection which he called Corolle (corolla, a botanical term meaning the delicate ring of petals opening in the centre of a flower); the American press aptly called it the New Look.

---

* Designed in France, in England it was translated as a 'waspie' (from the French guêpe meaning wasp) and called in America a waist-cincher. It was only five inches deep. It was made of firm material with elastic inserts and was boned and had back lacing.

398   Wool coat over black skirt. Velvet beret. Black shoes and belt. Dior design, model photograph, *Daily Mail*, 1950.

399   Dull red and black herringbone tweed coat. Black velvet collar and cuffs. Red hat with black feathers. Red gloves. Black suede ankle-strap shoes. Fashion drawing, *Vogue*, 1948.

400   Black hat, skirt and gloves. Striped bodice with sequins and pearls. Fath design, 1949.

401   Heavy silk dress. Silk and net hat. Long gloves. Christian Dior 1948.

The basis of Dior's New Look was a figure which, ideally, had a small waist, sloping shoulders and a full bosom and would display a long, swinging skirt; it was the essence of femininity. The silhouette was applied to all garments: coats, dresses, suits, skirts. Shoes were high-heeled, hats elegant, large and feminine. It was a revolution in dress because it was impossible to adapt war-time clothes to this line; there just was not enough material. So, by 1948/9 everyone had capitulated and established a new wardrobe (**396, 401**).

The New Look provided a psychological 'lift' to women at a time when it was sorely needed. All the politicians had to offer after six years of war and austerity was yet more austerity. Dior gave to women femininity and a new hope. The exact style did not last because such feminine clothes were no longer practical for women who were now com-

bining two jobs, at home and at work, but, for many years, the feminine line prevailed, at least for party wear, even with the skirt shortened and the waist less constricted (**398, 399, 400**).

Footwear

From 1920 onwards, with shorter skirts, stockings became more important. Flesh tones were worn in silk, wool or lisle. During the war the supplies of the new nylon stockings provided by American army personnel were highly prized presents.

Shoes and slippers of the 1920s tended to have high curved heels and low, pointed fronts; many had buttoned instep straps. A greater variety of footwear became available from 1930 from walking brogues to elegant town styles and types of sandal. Wedge and platform soles were fashionable in the 1940s as were the cuban heels of pre-war days (**402–411**).

402 Actual shoe, Platt Hall, Manchester, 1924.

403 Black patent leather and lizard-skin shoe, 1927.

404 Brown leather and suede shoe, 1931.

405 Blue leather shoe with natural leather heel. Magazine advertisement, English, 1935.

406 Gold kid evening shoe. Fashion drawing, French, 1925.

407 Brown leather, wedge sole. Actual shoe (author), 1945.

408 Blue leather and white buckskin. Magazine advertisement, English, 1944.

409 Tan leather and white buckskin. Wedge sole. Actual shoe (author), 1946.

410 Brown leather shoe. Magazine advertisement, English, 1948.

411 Fawn suede laced boot with black leather toe and heel. Actual boot, Platt Hall, Manchester, 1916.

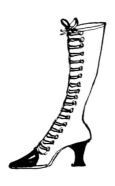

Hairstyles and Hats

Not the least revolutionary change for women after the First World War (**412**, **413**) was in the styles of coiffure. Soon after 1920 many women, for the first time, had their hair cut short to a bob then, in the mid-twenties, to a shingle (**417**). The marcel wave gave easier control and slightly longer styles re-appeared by 1928 but few women ever returned to long hair. The marcel wave had been introduced in the late nineteenth century. This enabled deep waves to be made in the hair by the use of heated scissor irons, such waves lasting a day or two. The method was named after Marcel, the Parisian coiffeur who initiated it. Much more important was the introduction of permanent waving in 1906. Few people took advantage of it at that time because the process took twelve hours and cost over £200 but, by the 1920s, mechanical systems using either dry electrical heat or steam became

available and by 1930 these were very popular when tightly waved or curled styles were fashionable. Such processes took three to four hours and cost about £3 (**419**).

Hats were worn at all times before 1939 except with informal holiday or sports dress. These were small and fitting to the head until, in 1923, the cloche hat appeared. This encased the head like a helmet extending from eye level in front to the nape at the rear (**414**, **418**). It was never an attractive style and the wide variety of designs appearing after 1930 were greeted with relief by most women. One needed to be a Greta Garbo to look attractive in a cloche. The 1930s' choice included Tyrolean (**422**), halo (**421**), sailor, cartwheel and pillbox hats as well as turbans and berets. Many of these were worn at an extreme angle, held in place by a back strap and decorated by small veils. Gaily patterned and coloured scarves were typical of the war years.

Accessories

Gloves were worn less often by 1940. Parasols had gone and umbrellas were functionally short. Handbags were large and capacious except for evenings when the dainty envelope was made of brocade, silk or gilded leather.

Jewellery and Cosmetics

From the 1920s very inexpensive but finely designed and made costume jewellery was

HAIRSTYLES AND HATS FOR WOMEN, 1914–1950

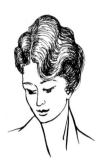

412 Waved coiffure. Newspaper photograph, 1916.

413 Coiffure. Photograph, 1922.

414 Felt cloche hat. Film magazine, 1926.

415 Felt and fur cloche hat. Actual hat, 1927.

416 Navy velour hat, red feather. Fashion advertisement, 1928.

417 The Eton crop. Fashion drawing, 1928.

418 Grey felt cloche hat. Actual hat, 1929.

419 Coiffure. Hairdresser's advertisement, 1931.

420 White woven fibre hat with navy ribbons. Newspaper photograph, 1935.

421 Turquoise felt halo style. Actual hat, 1936.

422 Tyrolean style with cord and feather. Actual hat (author), 1936.

423 Brown felt hat. Magazine photograph, 1937.

424 White felt hat and ribbon. Magazine illustration, 1942.

425 Grey felt hat with pink ribbon. Fashion drawing, 1948.

426 Powder-blue felt hat and ribbons. Fashion drawing, French magazine, 1949.

427 Page-boy bob. Magazine illustration, 1944.

428 Coiffure. Photograph, 1949.

429 White tennis dress, socks and shoes. Cap with shade. Newspaper photograph, 1938.

430 Green plastic mackintosh with hood. Furlined boots. Fashion magazine, 1946.

431 Herringbone tweed jacket and plus fours. Cap to match. Woollen pullover and socks. Fashion journal, 1930.

432 Burberry, 1915, news cuttings. Fashion Research Centre, Bath.

worn by nearly all women. Very long necklaces and earrings were typical of the 1920s. By the 1930s the hallmark of the well brought up middle class woman was the woollen twin set set off by a pearl necklace.

Cosmetics returned to fashion in reaction to nineteenth century disapproval. Ladies carried supplies for running repairs such as a powder compact, known then as a flapjack, and a lipstick. The American cosmetics industry was already big business; famous leading brand name firms set up by charismatic figures included Helena Rubinstein, Elizabeth Arden, Yardley, Max Factor and Pond.

Holiday and Leisure Wear

By 1930 there was, for both sexes, a greater choice of clothes for differing needs and occasions. Beachwear, swimwear, holiday wear, clothes for walking, cycling, sports of all kinds, parties and dances: all were available (**429, 430, 431**). The Americans were, by this time, exerting a stronger influence

upon fashion, not yet in the design of clothes which, until 1939, came primarily from Paris, but in mass-production methods, marketing and publicity and, above all, in technological advance, which was bringing great changes to fabrics, fastenings and types of clothes worn. The American way of life in the 1930s and 1940s, orientated towards centrally-heated, air-conditioned buildings and transport by private car was far in advance of the European one. From America came informality of dress and more easy-care clothing.

It was in the 1920s that the cult of sun-bathing began and by the early 1930s beaches in the south of France were strewn with sun-worshippers. Sun costumes of all kinds were designed; skirts with backless tops and with jackets or capes and floppy hats to match and, especially, beach pyjamas. These were slimly cut over the hips then flared out or were gored at the bottoms (**433, 434**).

In 1920 in America Jantzen introduced a one-piece elasticized rib-knit woollen bathing

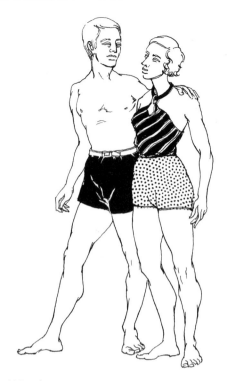

433 Beachwear. Printed cotton sun-suit. Straw hat, sandals. Fashion journal, 1938.

434 Beach pyjamas in dark green and patterned yellow cotton, linen hat. Fashion drawing, 1931.

435 and 436 Bathing suits. Fashion journal, early 1930s.

suit which became popular. Then, slowly, costumes became more daring. During the 1920s these were sleeveless then pieces began to be cut from the sides which led in the 1930s to the backless costume and the two-piece with halter-neck top and panties. Colours became bright and fabrics were often patterned (435, 436). In 1947 the French introduced the famous bikini which consisted only of bra and briefs, a design fashionable on French Mediterranean beaches but for a long time banned by such strongly Roman Catholic countries as Spain and Italy.

Underwear

From the early 1920s the weight, length and quantity of underwear was noticeably reduced for both sexes. Younger men especially adopted short, mid-thigh, elastic-topped pants and sleeveless vests or combinations made from interlock cotton and rayon (440). The boyish look for women completely abolished voluminous underwear. Slips, chemises and knickers were simple and fitting

in style. Combination garments were fashionable, cami-knickers still but also the combined bust bodice, hip belt, knickers and slip. Materials included lawn, crêpe de chine, satin, cotton and silk tricot. The garments were all comfortable and sparingly trimmed (438, 439). Names too were simplified. Lingerie became undies, petticoats first petties then slips, knickers turned into panties and combinations combs. In the 1930s and 1940s new materials revolutionized the making of underwear. Locknit (knitted rayon) was the most popular in these years. The bias cut was widely used especially for French knickers, cami-knickers and slips (437, 441). Colours were pretty pastel shades, plain or patterned. With the New Look all underwear became more feminine and decorative with added flouncing, ruching and lace (442, 443).

In the 1920s the brassière was a flattening garment designed to hide the natural lines of the breast (445). The term had been introduced in America as early as 1912 though the origin of the word is obscure. In French

437   Silk cami-knickers, bias cut. Manufacturer's advertisement, 1930.

438   Silk vest and directoire knickers. Manufacturer's advertisement, 1920.

439   Crêpe-de-chine cami-knickers, embroidered decoration. Fashion magazine, late 1920s.

440   Men's white cotton combinations. Manufacturer's advertisement, 1926.

441   Embroidered satin slip. Fashion journal, 1933.

442   Taffeta waist petticoat with flounced hem. Fashion journal, 1948.

443   Fashioned slip trimmed with ribbon and lace. Fashion journal, 1940.

it means a baby's vest, a shoulder strap or leading strings for a young child. The French term for brassière is the descriptive *soutien-gorge*. The 1920s version of the garment was made of strong white cotton which covered the body from shoulder straps to waist. As the fashionable figure line changed after 1930, the 'bra' as it came to be called, was designed to delineate the breasts. Typical versions were of rayon or cotton, elastic straps being crossed over at the back to fasten on buttons at the front. The elastic hook and eye rear fastener came later (**447**). In the late 1930s moulded rubber pads became available to be inserted into the bra as required; these were called 'falsies'.

In the 1920s ladies with a slim boyish figure did not require corsets. Those with a less fashionable shape wore a belt from the waist with suspenders attached to the lower edge. This was made of a strong cotton and was boned as required. Not-so-slim ladies then found that a spare tyre protruded between brassière and corset so the corselette – a one-piece garment comprising brassière and corset – was designed to encase the torso from shoulder to hip (**444**).

Corsetry was revolutionized from the early 1930s by the production of suitable elastic thread. The new material of natural elastic had been known to man for centuries. Natural rubber came from several different trees

447 Cross-over brassière. Manufacturer's advertisement, 1929.

444 Corselette. Satin and net elastic. Zip fastener. Manufacturer's advertisement, 1950.

445 Flattener brassière. Fashion magazine, 1924.

446 Marcel Rochas' 'waspie' (French guêpière, American waist-cincher). Fashion journal, 1947.

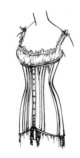

448 Short corset with criss-cross front panel for support. Manufacturer's advertisement, 1914.

449 Long-boned corset. Fashion journal, 1916.

tankers which completely changed the possibilities of its use in underwear. In the 1930s Lastex (the Dunlop trade name for the material) was produced in as great a variety of lengths and finenesses of thread as textile materials so making possible its introduction into the manufacture of corsetry and underwear of all kinds. Together with the use of the zip fastener, the resulting two-way stretch roll-on and pantie girdle made boned corsets a thing of the past for the great majority of women.

Children's Dress

As with adult dress the dramatic social changes in these years effected an acceleration of the trends in children's fashions and changes towards clothes designed especially for the young were hastened. Even so the real revolution of this kind did not come until after the Second World War, in the 1950s.

In general, children's clothes were more sensible than those designed before 1914. There was a much greater variety of garments available for different functions and climates and full advantage was taken of the development of new fabrics and means of making up and marketing. Boys generally wore a suit of short trousers, jacket and waistcoat or pullover, woollen socks to the knees, laced-up shoes and a cap. School uniform was generally adopted and blazers were the usual form of jackets – especially in summer. Girls' attire followed adult styles very closely but with short dresses for the younger children.

and plants and it was finally developed as a commercial proposition from the rubber tree grown in plantations chiefly in Malaya. During the nineteenth century research by such men as the Englishman Thomas Hancock and the American Charles Goodyear showed how solid rubber could be made into an elastic material which was then utilized in dress particularly for footwear. Elastic thread was gradually developed but its usefulness in corsetry was restricted because in the transportation of the latex (the rubber tree sap fluid), the material hardened in the air. When these sheets of latex arrived in Europe and America they were softened and cut into strips but these were too short for convenient manufacture of foundation garments.

It was the development of the method of shipping the latex emulsion in tankers direct to the factory and the process evolved by the Dunlop Rubber Company to extrude long lengths of fine elastic thread from these

CHAPTER TWELVE

1950 onwards

The Dress of Today

The fashion scene today is different from that of any time in the past. Since the Second World War there has been no obvious leading group of people who set the fashion, one which was then followed, at differing speeds, by other sections of the population. This is not to say that there have been no wealthy people or those with influence, taste and knowledge but, simply, that the upheavals in the pattern of society have brought about an overriding social change. No longer are certain garments or ensembles considered *de rigueur* for specific functions, activities or times of day. No longer need the young automatically follow the dictates of their elders or the plump or elderly try to adapt uncomfortably to the mode set by those of elegant and slimmer figure. Doing 'one's own thing' has become the norm, giving everyone the freedom to express their own taste within the wide range of fashions available, as never before.

At the same time it has become easier and easier, as the decades have passed since 1950, to buy ready-made garments in an extensive range of sizes, cuts, colours and materials at prices suited to all pockets; one of the most notable revolutions here has been in a similar availability for men. Bespoke tailoring, increasingly costly, has now become a rarity, available for the few who still require and can pay for it. Whether classic suits or casual wear, all masculine garments may be purchased in an increasingly wide range of sizes and representing a high quality of cut and fabric. Marks and Spencer have led the way in this field making possible, especially since

1970, on-the-spot purchase for all masculine needs from underwear, nightwear and shirts to fashionably cut jackets and trousers to fit any male whatever his bodily proportions and form. Though concentrating upon British manufacturers as a matter of policy, this firm, like many others, has increasingly presented a wider range supplied by manufacturers from overseas, from Europe and beyond.

Purchasing outlets have continued to be, as they have been since their foundation in the nineteenth century (p. 93–4), the department stores but these now exist in a more variable form. The large stores in the centre of big cities have continued to display a great variety of goods, not only clothes, but smaller, more specific stores have also sprung up. This trend widened in the 1960s with the advent of the boutique, which had first made its appearance in the 1930s, and now fully established itself. This type of sales outlet was tailor-made for the new market which had evolved, aimed especially at young people from teenagers to those in their early twenties. Boutiques were less formal, and so less intimidating, than department stores. Here one could browse and select for oneself from open rails. There was a comforting noise background of music especially popular with the young; there was probably also a coffee bar and the sales staff were young too. Many of these features were also later taken up by the department stores but at that time these were more formal places where an assistant would serve the customer on request.

Also in the 1960s large manufacturers of

clothing were setting up their own outlets in chains of stores throughout the country. Some of these outlets were in the form of a shop within a shop, that is, garments under the brand name of a certain manufacturer were sold by his staff within a part of a large department store. There would be several such brand names being sold in any one store. Undoubtedly successful, this practice has continued.

As time passed there were extensive business takeovers and firms grew larger. This trend was also to be seen in the field of textile manufacture and specific organizations were set up to take overall responsibility country-wide for the quality, dissemination and marketing of these textiles, whether natural or synthetic fibres. The International Wool Secretariat and the Cotton Board had been founded before and during the last war; with the growth in synthetic fibres, they were joined by the new giant, ICI.

As populations continued to increase and standards of living rose, greater quantities of clothing had to be produced. In order to achieve such increased output yet keep costs as low as possible, modern technological methods were increasingly employed. Mechanization spread to every process in production, new attachments and features to existing machines and completely new methods were introduced such as laser cutting. Sewing machines were fitted with photo electric cells, welding might replace some sewing processes and computerization was extended to all parts of the production process from primary planning to detailed sizing and grading.

Such investment of billions of pounds in the clothing industry could only be justified if the end product was acceptably attractive to a broad range of clientèle, whether for the young or for women of the 25-year-plus age range. The quality and, therefore, the price of such merchandise varies greatly but each type must satisfy its large market. It is in this field that museums of costume, in displaying modern dress, are less representative and, therefore, less satisfactory than in their display of dress of earlier ages. The current trend is to display model dresses or outré designs characteristic of a small section of the community or even specific individuals. This does not apply to all costume museums but it is particularly so where there remains a bias against accepting the 'social history' context in dress.

Synthetic Textile Fibres and Processes

The sophisticated technology which, in the last fifty years, has brought to fashion a complex range of synthetic textiles with safety and easy-care properties has, for the major part, been the result of research and development in the USA. European countries, notably Britain, have contributed important ideas and laboratory research but only America possessed the financial resources to bring the results to market. The emerging textiles have revolutionized the clothing industry, making possible for both sexes a varied and easy-care wardrobe not dreamed of before the last war. It has not, however, as was forecast in the 1950s, meant the abandonment of natural fibres – wool, cotton, linen, silk – often mixtures are used, especially in western Europe. Indeed, cotton and wool especially, now treated for crease resistance and easy washing, have increased their production greatly since 1945.

Like nylon (p. 133), the polyester fibres also sprang from work carried out in the 1930s in the Du Pont laboratories in the USA. Then, during the Second World War in England, Whinfield and Dickinson made a new fibre from a polyester derived from a by-product of the cracking of petroleum. Du Pont developed this fibre, marketing it in 1951 when they displayed to the press a man's suit made from the material. To illustrate its remarkable crease-resistant and lightweight qualities the suit had been worn for 67 days without being pressed, had been subjected to a dip in a swimming pool and had been machine-washed. The fabric, called Dacron, stood up to all this extremely well.

In 1955 in Britain ICI produced their equivalent fabric which they called Terylene; the

450 White silk evening gown with black polka dot pattern. Black gloves. Jewelled white satin bag. French dress designed by Balmain, Kostuum Museum, The Hague, Holland, 1952.

451 Spanish coat designed by Balenciaga, 1951.

452 Trapeze line dress in navy organza, House of Dior (St Laurent), 1958.

bulked form of this was known as Crimplene. Other countries of western Europe marketed their own polyester fabrics all known under different trade names, for example, the German Diolen and Trevira, the Dutch Terlenka, the French Tergal, the Italian Terital and the Scandinavian Spinlene.

Acrylic fibres are derived from an oil-refining and coal-carbonizing process; they are ideal for manufacturing fibres which are warm yet very lightweight and are utilized especially for fur-type pile materials and for knitwear. First commercially produced by Du Pont in 1952 – then called Orlon – other countries marketed their versions such as Britain's Courtelle, Germany's Dralon and France's Crylor. Metallic yarns have also been developed, notably the American Lamé, Lurex and Metlon and the French Rexor.

A revolution in elasticized materials took place in 1959–60 with the production of artificial elastic. These Spandex fibres contained no natural rubber and were called elastomerics: later under EEC terminology this has been replaced by elastane. The chief of these fibres, developed by Du Pont in the USA, is Lycra. It is much lighter in weight than rubber and is also stronger, By 1970 Lycra was being manufactured in printed tricot fabrics which, with stretch and non-stretch areas in one garment, could be made into pantie-girdles, bras, briefs and other items of underwear.

At first traditional textile machinery was adapted to process man-made fibres but soon it was realized that, in order to take effective advantage of their remarkable properties, new machinery would be needed. Various ways of spinning were developed: melt-spinning for nylon and polyester, dry-spinning for cellulose fibres and wet-spinning for acrylics. Processes were developed for bulking yarns to give to synthetic ones the qualities possessed by staple yarns. Others were found to take advantage of the high elastic quality of the materials by developing them as drip-dry fabrics as well as permanently pleating them by heat and stretch processes. Flame and mildew resistance, water repellance and moth-proofing could also be incorporated.

453 Black and white fleck wool coat with silver fox collar. Black velvet jacket and hat. White jabot blouse. Black stockings and shoes. Town outfit by House of Dior, 1974–5.

454 Khaki cotton poplin material, plaited leather belt. Socks and canvas laced shoes. Shirt dress by Kenzo Takada, 1977. Museum of Costume, Bath.

455 Bubble silhouette dress with black bodice and skirt patterned in large roses, Pierre Cardin, 1959.

Fashion Designers

From 1950 Christian Dior branched out into different designs – always feminine but a little more practical especially for working girls: the H-line, the A-line, the chemise dress. Suddenly, in 1957, Dior died. The House of Dior, then employing 1600 workers, continued first under the young Yves St Laurent then Marc Bohan (452, 453).

From then until the early 1970s there continued the traditional pattern of *haute couture* with its talented and original designers leading the fashion fields. Paris was still the chief centre of *la mode* and a wide variety of differing yet always elegant designs was disseminated. These top couturiers were individualists producing personal ensembles. Characteristic was the Spaniard Cristobal Balenciaga, a contemporary of Dior who had learnt tailoring and sewing in his home village from where he set up a small dressmaking shop in nearby San Sebastian. At the age of 42 he came to Paris to open his salon on the

Avenue Georges v. Balenciaga's designs were starkly simple and elegant. He was a perfectionist and a superb tailor particularly known for his coats and suits in quality fabrics (451).

Of other leading couturiers of the time must be mentioned Jacques Fath who, before his early death at the age of 42, established a reputation for high quality informal wear, presenting designs such as roll-necked sweaters and blazers for men before these were generally fashionable. Pierre Balmain, born in 1914, was a contemporary of Fath, who had worked for some time for Molyneux before opening his own house after the Second World War (450). Another perfectionist was Hubert Taffin de Givenchy born in 1927; he too worked for other fashion houses before establishing his own original and dramatic line. It was 1949 before Pierre Cardin opened his fashion house (455). He designed for both men and women, introducing a number of ideas which were not popular at the time but which were later taken up with

456 Aquascutum check worsted suit in brown. White shirt, patterned silk cravat. Brown suede boots. Fashion journal, 1968.

457 Brown check tweed sports jacket. Dark brown wool trousers. Light green linen sports shirt. Leather crêpe-soled shoes. Advertisement, 1951.

458 Grey worsted suit, single-breasted, cutaway pattern. Black leather shoes. Men's outfitter's advertisement, 1967.

459 Car coat of tweed with fleece lining. Striped worsted trousers. Black leather shoes, felt hat, suede gloves. English actual costume (author), 1960.

enthusiasm, for example, thigh-length boots, coloured, patterned stockings and the wearing of a maxi-length coat over a mini-dress.

By the later 1960s couture had become less exclusive as the ready-to-wear market had become important. Another generation of designers entered the field using new materials and presenting revolutionary ideas many of which were aimed at the young (p. 149). Elegant, feminine creations, up-to-date but not necessarily way-out were still being produced by a number of couture houses – Nina Ricci, Jacques Heim, Guy Laroche, Jacques Griffe, for example. Yves St Laurent left the House of Dior and set up on his own developing a novel, unconventional approach, deriving inspiration from a variety of sources such as peasant dress. His work was popular with the young, the unconventional and the wealthy.

The modern look to the fashion scene, and one which was especially an appeal to youth, was initiated by such designers as Courrèges and Ungaro in France and Quant in England.

André Courrèges had begun his career working for Balenciaga. The two men had much in common. Both were Basques – Courrèges French, Balenciaga Spanish – and both were superb tailors, perfectionists and uncompromisingly severe in design. Courrèges began on his own in 1961 and, at first, continued in his master's style. Then, in 1964, he introduced a completely new approach, what became known as the Space-Age Collection. The ensembles were still beautifully tailored, starkly plain and with sparing use of colours but were novel in form. Typical were high-waisted, short-skirted tent dresses, fitting trousers finishing at the hips leaving a bare mid-riff, sleeveless bodices and jackets and calf-length leather boots. By 1970 Cardin and Ungaro had joined the modern Courrèges line, then designing very short skirts, using a variety of materials including plastics and in a range of bright colours.

Also in 1971 was introduced a new influence which was to become important and

460 Jeans, waistcoat, woollen pullover, shirt, canvas laced shoes. Casual wear, 1983, Lee Cooper Italia.

461 Plum-coloured velvet jacket. Cherry red satin tie and cummerbund. Pink shirt with frilled front and wrist ruffles. Black trousers and shoes. Party evening wear, 1973, advertisement.

462 Batik printed cotton pull-on pants and shirt. Indian design in deep red, yellow, white and grey. Casual summer wear, 1990, American journal.

463 Light tweed jacket, dark brown trousers and polo-necked sweater, suede shoes. Elegant informality, 1978, advertisement.

long-lasting, this time from Japan. Kenzo Takada in Paris introduced Oriental features into the fashion scene: fuller, though still short skirts, kimono sleeves, shawls and draped clothing (**454**). The trend continued during the 1980s with designers in London and Japan – Yuki, Miyake and Mori – all of whom created some attractive designs in silk jersey and knitwear, beautifully cut and softly draped. The results were elegant and flattering.

A completely different but equally traditional and characteristic source of inspiration was the very English contribution of Laura Ashley who took her ideas from printed textiles of a homely, country theme. During the 1970s and 1980s the Laura Ashley imprint on both furnishing and dress textiles became widely known and fashionable, selling extensively in Europe and America though, by 1990, this popular phase is beginning to fade away.

Men's Dress

Though less subject to the rapid changes in fashion seen in feminine dress, men's clothes since 1950 have altered dramatically. The trend has been towards more variety of wear for different temperatures and occasions, less formality and greater casualness. Extensive use has been made of synthetic textile fibres for underwear, swimwear, shirts and, even, suits. No longer do most men swelter in heavy tweed on a hot summer's day. They wear lightweight suits of drip-dry, easy-care material. This has particularly revolutionized the travel needs of the business man. Similarly, the widescale use of the motor car for daily travel has led to the virtual disappearance of the felt hat and heavy winter overcoat (**459**). Adjustment of the car heater has made possible shirt sleeves as the travel norm.

For business and town wear worsted and tweed are still in use for men's suiting but

465 Evening dress of silver grey nylon net. Gold kid sandals and bag. Fashion drawing in *Vogue*, 1958–9.

464 Red, white and black jacket in wool lined with red wool. Black worsted suit. Red felt hat and fabric gloves. Black suede handbag and shoes. Design in *Vogue*, 1950.

466 Brown and white check worsted suit. Beige silk hat. Brown suede shoes and embroidered bag. Umbrella. Newspaper advertisement, 1952.

more commonly the fabric is a mixture, part natural, part synthetic textile, giving the quality appearance of wool but with the advantages of lightweight creaselessness. Weaves, patterns and colours all show wide variety (**456, 458, 467G**).

Men's clothes have also changed greatly in cut and line, fashions following upon each other more quickly than before. Various styles of trouser have been seen: narrow and cuff-less, wide flares, return to slenderness and cuffs. The hipster cut has generally replaced the higher waistband level (with the virtual disappearance of braces). Jackets have been waisted and slim, chunky and full. Separates, the personal choice in blending tops and trousers of different colours and materials, have become as popular as in feminine attire (**463**).

Evening and formal wear is most varied. It ranges from the extreme, though elegant, casualness of a silk high-necked top worn with or without jacket and with plain trousers to richly-coloured velvet jackets, cummerbunds and decoratively patterned shirts. A tie is no longer regarded as *de rigueur* for such attire (**461**).

Hats are now only rarely part of the masculine wardrobe and hairstyles are a personal choice. Since the fashion for long hair from the late 1960s, men have given much more attention to care and styling of their hair: the short-back-and-sides is 'out'. As the age of extremely long locks passed, hair care still continued, perms and blow-dry no longer an exclusively feminine preserve (**495, 496, 497**).

Women's Dress

In this book space does not allow a detailed description of the myriad and revolutionary changes in feminine wear which have taken place in the last forty years: the illustrations, presented in chronological order, give testi-

467   Airport Scene in Winter 1966–1967
A   Nylon fur coat in light brown over dark brown skirt. White fur hat. Black patent leather shoes. Patterned mauve tights.
B   Light grey raincoat over grey lounge suit. Brown gloves. Light brown boots.
C   Dark brown nylon fur coat. Black and white check wool trousers. Light coloured boots.
D   Three-quarter coat over skirt of red wool. Flesh-coloured stockings. Brown shoes and handbag.
E   Nylon fur coat dyed cerise with white fur lining. Black lace-patterned tights. Black plastic shoes.
F   Green cloth coat with grey fur trimming. Hat to match. Dark brown stockings. Green plastic shoes.
G   Light grey worsted suit.
H   Dark red tweed coat with black fur collar and hem. Brown check trousers. Brown slip-on shoes. Red felt hat.
I   Cobalt blue wool suit. White tights. Black suede boots.
J   Primrose wool suit with hat to match.
K   Grey tweed overcoat. Light grey gabardine trousers.
All costumes originally photographed by the author.

mony to the major characteristics. The paramount features have been the establishment
of the importance of the teenage market for
clothes (p. 153), effect of these designs
on the dress of adult women, the abandonment of the 'rules' which had insisted on
certain types of garments being worn on
particular occasions with consequent blurring
of previously accepted *mores* and the acce-
lerating pace of change in style and resulting
regurgitation of past themes; two current
examples are the reintroduction of the square
silhouette, masculine-type padded shoulders
characteristic of the uniform-dominated
1940s and the attempt to reintroduce the
1930s hem-line, first as a midi-skirt in the
late 1960s and again in recent years (**464–6**,
476–8).

In addition to the general acceptance of this 'do-your-own-thing' attitude of women toward buying and making their clothes – a situation which has been facilitated by the wide availability of 'separates', so making possible considerable variation in one outfit, both in warmth and for occasion – there have been introduced since the last war several new concepts never seen before: the mini-skirt, tights, trouser suits and unisex clothes. Of these, the introduction of the mini-skirt was the most fundamental and it was the one which established a specific market of clothes for the young for, although women of all ages were later to adopt a version of the style, its original introduction was aimed at the young, as it was particularly suited to the slim, youthful figure (p. 153). The mini-skirt fashion spelt the death knell (or almost) of stockings and the take-over by tights. These had been available since 1960 but had been intended at that time for somewhat sporty, gaily-coloured warm winter wear. They were, however, speedily adapted to sheer denier versions suited for use in all seasons.

The concept of the trouser suit had its origins in war-time needs. Trousers had been widely and gratefully adopted by women doing various forms of war work, in factories, in the services, driving ambulances, in ARP duties. After the war, clothes rationing continued for some time and trousers were durable and warm so were useful. Gradually they became fashionable articles of wear. Jackets, waistcoats and 'tops' were designed to combine as ensembles so that in the late 1950s and the 1960s everyone possessed at least one such smart suit and trouser fashions became acceptable wear for all possible occasions. Trouser styles changed over the years from the very slim lines to flares. The popularity of trouser suits gradually waned and the fashion began to wane in the 1970s (**467H, 468, 470, 471**).

The Culture of Youth

The tendency to cash-in on the teenage market had been growing since 1945. The trend

468 White wool trouser suit with black line check design. Designed by Courrèges, 1965.

469 Party outfit of hot pants and maxi coat in red and black flowered cotton. Black suede boots. Design in *Vogue*, 1971.

470 Trouser suit in red, black and fawn patterned wool over red wool tunic with black belt. Manufacturer's advertisement, 1972.

471 Golden-coloured polyester/wool French cut trousers with rayon blouse in dark brown and gold. Brown buttons and shoes. Throat band to match blouse. C & A advertisement, 1974.

472   White suit and boots with tartan hat. Designed by Courrèges, 1965.

473   Golden brown and white dress, mini-length. Designed by Mary Quant, 1967.

474   Striped nylon summer dress in black, white and cerise. White lacy tights. Cerise hat, bag and shoes. Design in *Vogue*, 1967.

475   Top striped in cerise and navy with white leather belt. White pleated skirt. White plastic shoes and handbag. Light-coloured tights. Butterick design, 1967.

could – and still can, for it shows no sign of abating – be seen in many forms: gramophone discs and, later, cassettes and videos, transistor radios, soft drinks packaging. Advertising has been directed increasingly towards this potentially profitable market. Teenage fashions in clothes were probably the most notable example and by 1960 a complete wardrobe for teenage boys and girls had been evolved, unsuitable and almost unwearable for adults and in this lay much of its attraction. Clothes were tight-fitting and informal.

America is usually credited with the 'discovery' of the teenager but certainly before long the trend was fully developed in Europe as well. The leaders and creators of clothes especially designed for the young were themselves also young. These trend-setters, many of them British, came from fashion schools and, before long, they had become knowledgeable also in market research and business know-how so that they could present and

publicize their ideas. For almost a decade in the 1960s Carnaby Street in London became the Mecca for the young of the western world.

The leader in this field in Britain was Mary Quant who, after studying at Goldsmiths College, went on to establish her Chelsea shop (Bazaar) where she learnt to design clothes specifically for people as young as herself. Mary Quant's name is particularly associated with the launch of the mini-skirt in 1965, produced almost simultaneously by her in London and by André Courrèges in Paris (472, 473). A symbol of youth, here was a mid-thigh length skirt, certainly the first such fashion since the masculine tunics of the antique classical world and the Middle Ages but not one which would ever have been countenanced for daily wear by girls. The mini-skirt stayed in fashion. It created a revolution in clothes for the young and skirts became shorter still, to micro-length. The style influenced fashion generally to the extent that even the middle-aged took to

476　Black wool skirt and black leather boots. Turquoise top with suede jacket in squares of fawn, rust and brown with blue edging. Black felt hat. Brown leather belt with metal buckle. Design in *Woman magazine*, 1970.

477　Printed cotton overdress in browns and yellows. White blouse. Brown shoes. Dress for the young, 1978. Magazine advertisement.

478　Charcoal grey tailored suit. Pale green blouse. Black pill-box hat, shoes and envelope bag. White gloves. Actual costume, 1979.

479　Cream silk shift dress with matching cardigan jacket. Hair band to match. Donna Kavan outfit, 1990.

wearing knee-length dresses. Despite strong efforts by high fashion to alter skirt lengths, even in the 1970s girls clung to it being less enthusiastic about the attractions of the midi- and maxi- lengths. It was the story of the crinoline all over again (p. 102). The fundamental popularity of the mini-skirt, especially for summer wear, was such that, in the late 1980s, it has been enjoying a boom once again (**467A, D, 472–75, 479**).

By 1970 hot pants provided a variant but as these were merely short shorts (often worn with matching braces and high boots) they were impracticable for office wear and suited to a minority of female bottoms (**469**).

Unisex clothes, first popular in the 1960s and 1970s, were more generally popular with the young. Garments were designed to produce almost identical versions for both sexes. This had been so in earlier times when small boys were dressed in skirts (p. 14) but, in this instance, it was usually the girls who were attired in clothes like those of their boyfriends.

It is difficult to think of a reason (or reasons) which might explain the inordinate and continued popularity of blue jeans. This is comprehensible when considering their introduction as close-fitting everyday wear for young people, wear which was suited to slim youthful figures of both girls and boys. It is understandable that the garments, often accompanied by T-shirts, should be welcomed almost as the uniform of a club for youth but what is very difficult to understand is the continued popularity of these garments over decades and their spread to a broad range of age and social groups to be worn for a variety of occasions. Jeans are not necessarily cheap nor are they always comfortable. They are drab and, often, intentionally made ragged and shabby, also dirty. This is a social phenomenon, but why has it gone on so long? (**460**).

Often known as Levi's (especially in America) and sold under this as a brand name, they derive their name from Levi Strauss

480   Stretch polyester patterned bikini and trunks.

who went to California in 1850. The work pants which he made were so practical and supplied such a basic need that he found he acquired greater wealth from selling them than by panning for gold. His pants were called Levi's and were made of blue denim reinforced at stress points with copper rivets. The word denim derives from serge-de-Nîmes, a fabric which was originally made in that area of southern France. The name jeans comes from the fabric jean, a similar strong twilled cotton cloth which originated in Genoa and had been in common use since the eighteenth century for work and leisure clothes for men, women and children. It was made in various colours but most often blue.

Apart from the overall picture of fashions for the young, from the 1950s onwards various cults began to appear, groups of young people of specific views or social background who drew attention to themselves by unusual, often outlandish attire and personal displays of demeanour, way-out hairstyles or footwear. There were teddy boys, mods and rockers and, in more recent

times, a punk pop phenomenon based on the rock groups of the day. Features of the dress of such groups were tattered, fringed garments overdecorated in heavy metal ornaments (**501**). In the later 1980s such extremes of fashion seemed to be abating somewhat.

Babies and Children

In the first half of the twentieth century, reflecting the more natural lines of adult dress, designs for children also became comfortable and suitable for active youngsters. Styles followed closely upon adult fashions as did materials, colours and decoration. The real revolution in children's dress and, especially, in that for babies and infants, came in the 1950s. This was made possible by the development of man-made fibres, easy-care fabrics and a variety of efficient and simple fasteners.

For babies and young children layers of clothes became fewer than before from the 1920s. Garments were shorter, making movement easier and, after the 1950s, fabrics were hard-wearing and suited to care in the washing machine. The all-in-one romper suit had been fashionable for some time as was also the little girls' dress with matching knickers, but the introduction in the 1950s of a one-piece coverall suit for babies made from a stretch fabric began a new trend when it was marketed in the United States as Babygro. Before long this type of adjustable stretchwear for babies had become available all over western Europe. In the 1960s Mothercare was established in Britain to cater for the needs of the expectant mother and the young child, a coverage which was later extended to ten-year olds. Both firms constantly update their ranges which have become varied and extensive. Modern fastenings essential to such wear include zippers, poppers and simple hooking straps such as Velcro (**481–3**).

Clothes for older children very much reflect those of the teenager. Denim features widely as do jeans, and stretch pants. Easy-care fabrics are used in a wide range of colours

481 Baby's all-in-one romper suit with smocking, 1950. Actual garment.

482 Brushed synthetic fibre one-piece playsuit with fur collar for toddler. Manufacturer's advertisement, 1970.

483 Padded, patterned nylon carry bag. Modern design.

484 Pinafore dress over a blouse. Actual dress for little girl, 1976.

485 Boy's wool coat with fur collar, worsted trousers. Shop advertisement, 1976.

486 Fur-trimmed wool winter coat and hat. Tights and shoes. Actual outfit, 1966.

487 Teenage girl in red blouse and patterned cotton maxi-skirt. Manufacturer's advertisement, 1977.

and decorative designs. Informality and comfort are the keys to design and there is great variation in types of garments from rainwear, duffle coats and ponchos for winter to swimwear, beachwear and light summer outfits. Trousers are universally popular. For boys, short trousers disappeared in 1945; with American influence long trousers had been adopted from an early age, similar in design to those worn by the girls (484–7).

Underwear

The advent of synthetic fibres was also a vital factor in changing the design and form of underwear. Natural, easy-support foundation garments revolutionized design. The boned corset vanished to be replaced by elastic stretch belts and girdles, suspender belts, pantie girdles and corselettes, all in Lycra-type elastic net and nylon. Varied lengths of

488 Uplift bra with circular stitched cups. Actual garment, 1958.

489 Nylon and Lycra bra and pantie girdle. Magazine advertisement, 1970.

491 Man's cotton vest and briefs. Actual garments, 1955.

490 Nylon slip with lace top and pleated hem. Magazine advertisement, 1957.

a foundation garment, a pantie girdle or pantie-corselette is suitable to accompany tights.

The 1950s were the years of the uplift bra and 'sweater girl' image. A circular stitching was used to make the high pointed breastline. A strapless bra would be worn with backless evening gowns and beachwear. By the 1960s the young had begun to abandon the wearing of a bra, a trend which has continued and increased as time has passed but the older woman has, in general, retained the habit which she finds more comfortable for support of her figure though the uplift bra has disappeared.

By the mid-1970s the preference of all women was for comfort and an attractive femininity in underwear. The young, particularly if of slender figure, wore a minimum — very short briefs under jeans and a slip or waist petticoat under a skirt. For adults and for less slender women foundation wear was still needed but it had to be comfortable and not visible from the exterior. Moulded bras and body garments were the answer. These were thermoplastic fabrics which required high temperature treatment. A variety of synthetic thermoplastic yarns was gradually produced, nylon, polyester and elastane, in a variety of weaves and blends. Panties and bras were the most widely popular of such garments (**488–91**).

Hairstyles

In the years immediately after 1945 women dressed their hair in softer, more natural ways than hitherto. Permanent waving was general but the advent of the home perm and heated rollers made it more of a do-it-yourself operation for many, especially younger women. In the early 1950s hair was softly curled and worn in a variety of styles and lengths. Towards 1959 a high bouffant beehive look became fashionable with excessive backcombing to produce the height (**493**). From the mid-1960s softer, more natural styles returned. Many young girls wore their hair loose and very long. Towards 1970 these

foundation garment, from the long-length corselette to a diminutive suspender belt could be purchased though, with the natural 'young' lines of the 1960s and 1970s, fewer women wore foundation garments at all. The availability of tights made a suspender belt unnecessary though stockings have survived for minority wear. Some of these are self-supporting, alternatively, a narrow waist suspender belt or elastic belt are still available. For women who still prefer to wear

492 Hair shampoo advertisement, English magazine, 1965.

493 Beehive coiffure. Drawn from life, 1959.

494 American crew cut. Photograph, 1945.

495 Tweed pork pie style. Actual hat, 1955.

498 Beauty competition, English magazine, 1965.

499 Blue felt hat. Wolsey advertisement, 1965.

496 Man's hairstyle. Advertisement, 1968.

497 Man's hairstyle. Wide silk patterned tie. Drawn from life, 1975.

502 Magazine model. Loose long crimped style, 1990.

503 Return to short-back-and-sides. Advertisement, 1990.

500 Typical masculine long hair style, late 1960s.

501 Punk hair style, 1984.

504　Black patent leather shoe. Platform sole. Newspaper advertisement, 1973.

505　Man's shoe of black and red plastic. Actual shoe, 1976.

506　Black suede shoe in ankle-strap design with heavy sole. Actual shoe (author), 1950.

507　White leather, 'cossack' style. Actual boot, 1960.

508　Suede boot with crêpe sole and sheepskin lining. Newspaper advertisement, Jay's Ltd. for Huskees boots, 1950.

509　Sling-back design. Actual shoe, 1972.

510　Apple green suede shoe. Magazine drawing, 1958.

511　Stiletto heel, Italian. Actual shoe, 1960.

512　Crimson suede sling-back style. Actual shoe, 1950.

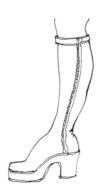

513　'Wet look' green fashion boot, zip fastener. Actual boot, 1973.

flowing tresses were often draped curtain-wise over the face, leaving the eyes to peer through like those of an old English sheepdog. Women followed their own bent, wearing their hair as suited them. Many wore it straight, others took advantage of the softer perms to give their coiffure a bouffant or carelessly windswept appearance (**492, 498, 499**). More typical of the later 1980s is a permed head which is left unset or blow-dried after shampoo, so that it hangs uncontrolled in a frizzy, rat-tail curtain (**502**).

A particular characteristic of the masculine coiffure since 1945 has been the abandonment of the short-back-and-sides barber's cut and a return to the centuries-old tradition of a studied care of the coiffure as great as or greater than that paid by women to their hair. In the years immediately after the war, the American crew cut was popular where the hair was worn very short all over and standing up on top about an inch long, rather like a bristly brush (**494**). In contrast, by the 1960s, men began to adopt longer styles. It was the young men, especially students, who led the field at first and, by the late 1960s, were wearing shoulder-length hair (**500**). This 'Cavalier' type of flowing locks lasted for many years and the fashion spread to older men though, in the case of those with a tendency to baldness, the effect was less than attractive. Many men had their hair permed and most had it professionally tended. During the 1980s shorter styles have prevailed though rarely as short as in pre-war days and men have, without exception, elected, as have women, to do-their-own-thing and wear their hair as they believe suits them (**496, 497, 503**).

A notable feature of the punk styles of the 1980s was, for both sexes, a way-out hairstyle. This meant dyeing the hair a totally unnatural colour – pink or red or green – and cutting it in various ways so that it stood up in a spiky manner with, often, part of the head shaven. Typical and popular was the Mohican plume where the hair stood up in a centre coxscomb while the rest of the head was shaved (**501**).

Glossary

The figures in brackets refer to page or illustration numbers; the latter are in **bold** *type.*

Aigrette Feathery plume used in hair or headdress decoration (**17**).

Baldric A sash or leather band slung over one shoulder and round the opposite hip. In medieval times it was decorated with gold or silver bells. Later it was fastened on the left hip and carried the sword holder (plate 10).

Band The name given to the sixteenth century ruff. (**33**). Applied in the seventeenth century to the decorative lace-edged collars worn outside the jacket or doublet (**68**).

Bandbox Round boxes made to store laundered bands.

Berthe A garment especially fashionable in the 1830s. Made of white fabric with lace or pleated edging, it covered the shoulders and ended in lappets tucked into the waistbelt in front.

Bicorne A black, flat man's hat with point at front and rear. Fashionable in the late eighteenth century and early nineteenth.

Biliment Metal, jewelled bands framing the front edges of the sixteenth-century gable or French hood worn by ladies (**40**).

Boa A long narrow stole made of fur or ostrich feathers worn especially by ladies in the very early and the late nineteenth century.

Boater A man's hard straw hat with flat brim and shallow crown (**313**).

Bolero jacket Very short, worn open and with rounded front lower edges.

Bombast Padding made of cotton and rags used to stuff the seams and linings of sixteenth century garments.

Broadcloth Fine quality woollen cloth woven in widths of thirty inches and over.

Broderie anglaise Cutwork embroidery, often in cotton, with oversewn small holes in the design.

Busk A long piece of metal or whalebone inserted in the front seam of a corset to maintain a rigidly firm shape (**258**).

Bustle A framework worn under the skirt in the 1870s and 1880s to support the heavy draperies swept up and back. At first a whalebone or metal and canvas half-cage with fullness at the rear, later a pad or wire basket tied on round the waist and resting on the buttocks at the back. The French terms *tournure* or *jupon* were also used.

Cadogan A wig style of the 1770s and 1780s worn by both sexes in which the back hair was dressed up in a loop and tied, generally with black ribbon (**194**).

Calash (Calèche, Cabriolet) A silk cage covering for the immense wigs worn by ladies in the later eighteenth century. The framework could be raised and lowered like a carriage hood.

GLOSSARY

Canezou A shoulder covering, resembling a berthe, worn chiefly between 1820 and 1850.

Carmagnole A short jacket worn by French revolutionaries in the 1790s. Originally worn by workers who came to France from Carmagnola in Italy.

Carrick (Garrick) A gentleman's overcoat worn from the later eighteenth century. It was a heavy, double-breasted style with one or more shoulder capes and derived from an earlier mode worn by coachmen for warmth when riding outside the coach.

Chamarre A rich, fur-lined and trimmed fabric gown worn by men. Fashionable in the late fifteenth and early sixteenth centuries, it was full and usually worn open; it had a wide collar and full sleeves. It originated in the Middle East but its immediate predecessor was the traditional sheepskin garment from Spain, the *chamarra* or *zamarra* (plate 2).

Chesterfield A masculine overcoat named after the Earl of Chesterfield. It was generally single-breasted, fitting and waisted with set-in sleeves.

Chopine Pattens or clogs to slip on over hose or shoes for ladies to walk in the streets. Especially fashionable in sixteenth century Spain and Italy; in Venice they were called *zóccoli* and might be two feet high.

Cloisonné Enamel inlay in metal jewellery.

Collet monté The later sixteenth century high standing collar worn by ladies. It was edged with lace and wired to stand up behind the head (**25**).

Corset A tight-fitting rigid undergarment which moulded the figure, especially the waist according to the prevailing fashion (*see* p. 112). It derived from the fifteenth century term *body* or, more commonly, *pair of bodies*. The medieval term corset referred to a quite different outer garment.

Cravat Decorative neckwear for men made from white silk, linen and lace. The name is thought to derive from linen neckwear worn by a Croatian regiment in the 1660s. Differing forms evolved during the seventeenth and eighteenth centuries (**111**).

Criarde Petticoat of gummed linen worn during the eighteenth century before the advent of paniers. The name comes from the noise made when the wearer moved: *criard* meaning clamorous (French).

Crinoline Nineteenth-century boned petticoat. The name comes from the horsehair fabric from which it was made. *Crinis*: Latin for hair (also the French *crin*) and *linum*: Latin for thread (**259**).

Culottes French term for breeches, seventeenth to early nineteenth century.

Damask A rich silk or linen fabric with a pattern of flowers and animals. The design has a satiny finish in contrast to the duller, rougher ground. Originated in Damascus.

Dolman An Oriental garment of Turkish origin. Worn in Hungary for centuries in the form of a coat also, in the late nineteenth century, a loose, long coat for ladies. Made from rich, ornamental fabric.

Doublet Masculine tunic worn from the fifteenth to seventeenth century. Originally of quilted manufacture (**19**).

GLOSSARY

Duffle (duffel) coat
A hooded, warm, short style coat fastened by wood toggles. The fashion derived from the coat worn by the Navy during the Second World War and popular, especially with the young, after this. The name derives from the material originally manufactured in the Flemish town of Duffel.

Dundreary whiskers
Nineteenth century facial hair in which long side-whiskers are separated by a shaven chin (**242**).

Dungarees
Workmen's overalls, later a feminine fashion. Made formerly of a fabric called *dungaree* (from the Hindi word *dungrì*) which was a coarse, poor quality Indian calico. Now usually made from denim.

Échelle
A fashion in which the front of a lady's bodice or stomacher was decorated by graduated ribbon bows, a name which derives from the French word for ladder (**128**).

Falling band
A deep lace or linen collar worn by both sexes. See band (plate 10).

Falling ruff
An unstarched ruff, a fashion which followed the ruff and preceded the falling band (**62**).

Farthingale
The canvas or linen underskirt containing whalebone hoops worn during the sixteenth century to provide the fashionable skirt form (*see* p. 13 and **22**).

Fichu
A white silk or cotton neckcloth draped around a lady's throat and shoulders especially in the late eighteenth century (plate 23).

Fontange
A tall headdress made of lace arranged and wired in tiers and decorated with ribbons fashionable in the late seventeenth century (**110**).

Gamurra
A lady's gown of sixteenth-century Italy.

Goffering
The process of setting ruffs (*see* **20–1**).

Golilla
A card or stiffened fabric support for the Spanish white collar of the 1620s; popularized by Philip IV.

Habit à la française
Term used to describe the gentleman's suit of coat, waistcoat and breeches in the early eighteenth century. Later the term was applied to the coat only (plate 20).

Hedgehog wig
A late eighteenth-century style worn by both sexes where the hair was cut raggedly short.

Jabot
A frill or ruffle of lace or silk worn at the neck and falling in folds on the chest.

Jerkin
A body garment, worn on top of and similar in style to the doublet but usually sleeveless.

Justaucorps
Of military origin, this garment developed in the masculine coat which replaced the jacket in the later seventeenth century (**95**). It later evolved into the habit à la française.

Knickerbockers
A loose type of masculine breeches worn in the nineteenth century (*see* p. 124).

Lamé
A rich fabric with gold or silver threads.

Love-lock
As in masculine hairstyles of the 1630s and 1640s when a lock of hair was grown longer than the rest and the end tied in a ribbon bow.

Merino
Wool woven from the Spanish sheep of that name.

Mohair
Wool woven from the Angora goat from Asia Minor.

Norfolk jacket
A man's jacket of the 1890s (*see* p. 124).

Pagoda sleeve	A lady's gown style where a fitting sleeve flared out at the elbow.	**Piccadilly weepers**	Alternative name for Dundreary whiskers.
Panier	A French term, meaning basket, applied to several varieties of whalebone structures worn under eighteenth century gown skirts to give the desired shape (135).	**Pigeons' wings**	The fluffed-out side parts of a man's wig in the 1730s and 1740s (plate 20).
		Platform sole	Footwear with a deep sole and heel (504).
Pantalette, pantaloon	The term pantaloons has been widely used over a long period to describe a fitting masculine trouser. In the early nineteenth century it was applied to feminine underwear. Pantalettes were an abbreviated form of such underwear, being lace-trimmed leglets or drawers. When worn by children they were visible beneath the dress (206, 218).	**Pluderhosen**	German word for the loose knee-breeches of the early seventeenth century and usually termed Venetians in England (63).
		Plus fours	A type of knickerbocker fashionable in the 1920s (*see* p. 135 and 431).
		Pomander	A gold or silver hollow, hinged sphere containing ambergris or other perfume. In the sixteenth century this depended from a lady's girdle or necklace.
Pantoffle	In the sixteenth century an overshoe to be slipped over the shoe or hose; it had no back. Later the word was applied to a slipper.		
		Pumps	Flat or low-heeled shoes with soft, low-cut uppers.
Passementerie	A form of appliqué decoration, embroidered or woven, in silk or cotton and incorporating metal threads, beads and fringe.	**Raglan sleeve**	A wide sleeve, not set-in but tapering to a narrow width at the neckband.
		Rebato	A support of cardboard or metal framework worn at the back of the neck under the large ruffs of the late sixteenth century.
Peasecod-belly	The later sixteenth century masculine body shape obtained by padding the doublet front to create an artificial paunch (31).		
		Redingote	A winter overcoat worn by both sexes in the eighteenth and nineteenth centuries, the style changing considerably as time passed (*see* p. 85 and 209).
Pelisse	A loose cloak, often of velvet, fur-edged and having a large collar and slits for arms. Some designs had attached hoods. A fashion of the later eighteenth and early nineteenth centuries (182).		
		Reticule	A dainty handbag fashionable in the years 1790–1820 with the thin dresses of the time (plate 26).
Periwig	The correct English term for wig, derived from the French term *perruque* via English peruke and perwyke. Most often applied to the full-bottomed wig (111).	**Rhinegrave breeches**	Also known as petticoat breeches, a masculine fashion of the years 1650–75 for full, skirt-like beribboned breeches (*see* p. 45 and plate 15).
Picadil	A scalloped or tabbed finish to the neck or shoulder of a sixteenth century doublet or jerkin (*see* p. 19, and plate 5).	**Sans-culottes**	The name given to French revolutionaries who wore trousers instead of knee-breeches

to distinguish themselves from the aristocracy: literally without breeches (*see* p. 73).

Shawl collar — A deep roll coat collar without revers.

Spatterdash — Leather or cloth leggings to protect men's stockings or trousers from being mud-splashed. Later, in the nineteenth century, spats – a shortened form – were fashionable.

Spencer — A waist-length long-sleeved jacket worn by ladies in the years 1790–1830 (**212**).

Stock — Eighteenth-century neckwear for men which replaced the earlier cravat. Made of folded white fabric (**223**).

Stocks — Sixteenth-century leg coverings. The word later developed into stockings.

Stole — A long scarf worn round the shoulders (**187**).

Stomacher — A separate front panel of richly decorative fabric worn on top of the gown bodice. Of Spanish origin, fashionable in the sixteenth and early seventeenth centuries. Laced to the figure, the stomacher was often boned and ornamented with jewelled embroidery. In the later seventeenth century it reappeared ornamented with ribbon bows; see Échelle (**128**).

Supportasse — Alternative name for rebato.

Surpied — A quatrefoil-shaped piece of leather worn on the instep of the seventeenth century boot (plate 10).

Sweeper — The pleated or ruffled edges to the hem of late nineteenth-century petticoats which 'swept' the floor so keeping the gown skirt clean (**350**).

Tablier — Gowns designed with an apron front as in the 1870s (**306**). From French *tablier* meaning apron.

Taglioni — A knee-length overcoat for men worn in the first half of the nineteenth century and named after the family of ballet dancers (**248**).

Tassets — Tabs at the waistline of the seventeenth-century doublet and jerkin (**68**).

Tricorne — Three-cornered hat worn by men in the eighteenth century (**153**).

Trunk hose — Full short breeches fashionable in sixteenth-century masculine dress (plate 5).

Valona — White collar worn by Spanish men in the 1620s. See also Golilla.

Verdugado — Spanish farthingale worn in Spain.

Verdugo — The pliant wood bands used in the farthingale petticoat construction.

Wedge shoe — Where sole and heel are made in one wedge form (**409**).

Whisk — English term for the stiffened lace or lace-edged white linen collar supported on a rear framework fashionable in the early seventeenth century. The French term was col rotonde.

Bibliography

Selected list of books recommended for further study.

ADBURGHAM, A., *Shops and Shopping 1810–1914*, Allen & Unwin; *A Punch History of Modes and Manners*, Hutchinson, 1961; *Liberty's: a Biography of a Shop*, Allen & Unwin, 1975

AMIES, H., *Just so Far*, Collins, 1954

AMPHLETT, H., *Hats: A History of Fashion in Headwear*, Sadler, 1974

BALMAIN, P., *My Years and Seasons*, Cassell, 1964

BATTERSBY, M., *Art Deco Fashion (Couturier's Creations 1908–25)*, Academy Editions, 1974

BENTIVEGNA, F.C., *Abbigliamento e Costume nella Pittura* (2 Vols) *15th–18th Century*, Bestetti, Rome, 1962 (Italian text)

BLUM, A.C., *Early Bourbon Costume 1590–1643; Last Valois Costume, 1515–1590*, Harrap, 1951

BRADFIELD, N., *Costume in Detail 1730–1930*, Harrap, 1970; *Historical Costumes of England 1066–1968*, Harrap, 1970

BRADLEY, C.G., *Western World Costume*, Peter Owen, 1954; *History of World Costume*, Peter Owen, 1955

BRAUN-RONSDORF, M., *The Wheel of Fashion; Costume since the French Revolution, 1789–1929*, Thames & Hudson, 1964

BRÜHN, W., and TILKE, M, *A Pictorial History of Costume*, Zwemmer, 1955

BYRDE, P., *The Male Image: Men's Fashions in Britain 1300–1970*, Batsford, 1979

CARTER, E., *Twentieth Century Fashion: a Scrapbook 1900 to Today*, Eyre Methuen, 1975; *The Changing World of Fashion*, Weidenfeld & Nicolson, 1977; *Magic Names of Fashion*, Weidenfeld & Nicolson, 1980

CHARLES-ROUX, E., *Chanel*, Cape, 1976

CHRISTIENSEN, S.F., *Kongedragterne, 17th and 18th Century* (2 Vols), Danish Royal Collection at Rosenborg Castle, Copenhagen 1940 (Danish text, notes in English)

COLEMAN, E.A., *The Opulent Era: fashions of Worth, Doucet, Pingat*, Thames & Hudson, 1989

CORSON, R., *Fashion in Hair*, Peter Owen, 1965; *Fashions in Make-up*, Peter Owen, 1972

CUNNINGTON, C.W. and P., *Handbook of English Costume Medieval to 19th Century* (4 Vols), Faber & Faber, 1973

CUNNINGTON, C.W. and P. and BEARD, C., *A Dictionary of English Costume*, Black, 1972

CUNNINGTON, P., and MANSFIELD, A., *A Handbook of English Costume in the 20th Century, 1900–1950*, Faber & Faber, 1976, *English Costume for Sports and Outdoor Recreations, 16th to 19th Centuries*, Black, 1969

CUNNINGTON, P. and LUCAS, C., *Occupational Costume in England, 11th Century to 1914*, Black, 1976; *Costume for Births, Marriages and Deaths*, Black, 1972

CUNNINGTON, P., *Costume of Household Servants, Middle Ages to 1900*, Black, 1974

CUNNINGTON, P. and BUCK, A., *Children's Costume in England, 1300–1900*, Black, 1965

DAVENPORT, M., *The Book of Costume*, Crown Publishers, New York, 1968

DEMORNEX, J., *Balenciaga*, Thames & Hudson, 1989

DE JONG, M.C., *Marrying in White: Two Centuries of Bridal Apparel, 1765–1976*, The Costume Museum, The Hague, 1976

DE MARLY, D., *History of Haute Couture, 1850–1950*, Batsford, 1980; *Fashion for Men: an Illustrated History*, Batsford, 1985; *Christian Dior*, Batsford, 1989

DE PIETRO, S. and L., *New Look to Now: French Haute Couture, 1947–1987*, Rizzoli, 1989

DIOR, C., *Dior: the autobiography of Christian Dior*, Weidenfeld & Nicolson, 1957

DORNER, J., *Fashion in the Twenties and Thirties*, Ian Allan, 1973; *Fashion in the Forties and Fifties*, Ian Allan, 1975

DUFF GORDON, LADY (Lucile), *Discretions and Indiscretions*, Jarrolds, 1932

DUNBAR, J.T., *History of Highland Dress*, Oliver & Boyd, 1962

EARLE, A.M., *Two Centuries of Costume in America 1620–1820* (2 Vols). Reprint of 1903, Arno, 1976

ELLIS, M., *Welsh Costume and Customs*, National Library of Wales, 1951

EWING, E., *History of Children's Costume*, Batsford, 1977; *Dress and Undress*, Batsford, 1978; *Everyday Dress, 1650–1900*, Batsford, 1984; *History of 20th Century Fashion*, Batsford, 1986

GARLAND, M., *The Changing Form of Fashion*, Dent, 1970; *The Changing Face of Childhood*, Hutchinson, 1963

GARLAND, M., and BLACK, J.A., *A History of Fashion*, Orbis, 1975

GIROTTI, E., *La Calzatura: storie e costumi* (Footwear)

(Text in English and Italian), BE-MA Editrice, 1987

GORDON, J. and HILLER, A., *The T-shirt Book*, Ebony Press, 1988

HARTNELL, N., *Silver and Gold*, Evans, 1955

HAZELIUS-BERG, G., *Women's Costume 1600–1900*, Nordiska Museet, Stockholm, 1952 (Swedish text, English summary)

HERALD, J., *Renaissance Dress in Italy 1400–1500*, Bell & Hyman, 1981

IRONSIDE, J., *A Fashion Alphabet*, Michael Joseph, 1968

JEFFERYS, J.B., *Retail Trading in Britain, 1850–1950*, Cambridge University Press, 1964

LANGBRIDGE, R.H., *Edwardian Shopping: Army and Navy Stores' Catalogues 1893–1913*, David & Charles, 1975

LATOUR, A., *Kings of Fashion*, Weidenfeld & Nicolson, 1958

LAVER, J., *A Concise History of Costume*, Thames & Hudson, 1977

LEVI-PISETSKY, R., *Storia del Costume in Italia*, (5 Vols), *Medieval to 19th Century*, Milan, 1964–9 (Italian text)

LISTER, M., *Costumes of Everyday Life, working clothes 900–1910*, Barrie & Jenkins, 1972

MCCLELLAN, E., *History of American Costume 1607–1870*, Tudor, USA, 1969

MOORE, D.L., *Fashion Through Fashion Plates 1771–1970*, Ward Lock, 1971

MORYSON, F., *An Itinerary Containing His Ten Yeeres Travell through the Twelve Dominions of Germany, Bohmerland, Sweitzerland, Netherland, Denmarke, Poland, Italy, Turky, France, England, Scotland and Ireland*, 1st printed John Beale, 1617. James Maclelose, Glasgow University Press, 1907

OAKES, A., and HAMILTON HILL, M., *Rural Costume in Western Europe and the British Isles*, Batsford, 1970

PAYNE, B., *History of Costume*, Harper & Row, New York, 1965

PAYNE, F.G., *Welsh Peasant Costume*, Welsh Folk Museum, 1969

PEACOCK, J., *Fashion Sketchbook 1920–1960*, Thames & Hudson, 1977

PENN, I., *Inventive Paris Clothes 1909–39*, Thames & Hudson, 1977

POIRET, P., *My First Fifty Years*, Gollancz, 1934

QUANT, M., *Quant by Quant*, Cassell, 1966

REES, G., *St. Michael: A History of Marks and Spencer*, Weidenfeld & Nicolson, 1969

RIBIERO, A., *Fashion in the French Revolution*, Batsford, 1988

ROCAMORA, M., *Costume Collection*, Rocamora Museum, Barcelona (Spanish text)

SAUNDERS, E., *The Age of Worth*, Longmans, 1954

SCHIAPARELLI, E., *Shocking Life*, Dent, 1954

SCHOEFFLER, O.E., and GALE, W., *Esquire's Encyclopaedia of 20th Century Men's Fashions*, McGraw-Hill, USA, 1973

THIENEN, F. VAN and DUYVETTER, F., *Traditional Dutch Costumes*, Amsterdam, 1968

THORNTON, J.H., *Textbook of Footwear Manufacture*, National Trade Press, 1964

WATKINS, J.E., *Who's Who in Fashion*, Fairchild, 1975

WAUGH, N., *The Cut of Women's Clothes, 1600–1930*, Faber & Faber, 1968; *The Cut of Men's Clothes, 1600–1900*, Faber & Faber, 1964; *Corsets and Crinolines*, Batsford, 1970

WHITE, P., *Poiret*, Studio Vista, 1973

WILCOX, R.T., *Five Centuries of American Costume*, Black, 1966

WILSON, E., *History of Shoe Fashions*, Pitman, 1969

YARWOOD, D., *European Costume*, Batsford, 1975; *Encyclopaedia of World Costume*, Batsford, 1978; *Costume of the Western World*, Lutterworth, 1980

Index